4

# ANDRUS

Idaho's Greatest Governor

*Enjoy the read!*

*[signature]*

# ANDRUS

Idaho's Greatest Governor

Chris Carlson

CAXTON PRESS
Caldwell, Idaho
2011

Printed in the United States of America.
The Caxton Printers Ltd.
Caldwell, Idaho 83605

Cover design: Jamie Sloper
Interior design and composition: Jamie Sloper
Front cover photographs: ©
Back cover painting: © Karen Piedmont
Interior photographs: pages 77-92

Library of Congress Cataloging–in–Publication Data

Carlson, Chris, 1946-
  Cecil Andrus : Idaho's greatest governor / by Chris Carlson.
     p. cm.
  Includes bibliographical references.
  ISBN 978-0-87004-505-9 (alk. paper)
  1. Andrus, Cecil D., 1931- 2. Andrus, Cecil D., 1931---Political and social views. 3. Governors--Idaho--Biography. 4. Idaho--Politics and government. 5. Cabinet officers--United States--Biography. 6. United States. Dept. of the Interior--Officials and employees--Biography. 7. Andrus, Cecil D., 1931---Friends and associates. 8. Carlson, Chris, 1946- 9. Press secretaries--Idaho--Biography. 10. Idaho--Biography. I. Title. II. Title: Andrus.
  F750.22.A63C27 2011
  979.6'033092--dc23
  [B]
                              2011036038
ISBN 978-087004-505-9

Caxton Press
312 Main St.
Caldwell, Idaho, 83605
www.caxtonpress.com

# DEDICATION

To the thousands of Idahoans who voted for Cecil Andrus over the years and who saw their faith rewarded through the accomplishments that made him the greatest governor in Idaho history.

# Table of Contents

# Acknowledgements

This book would not have been possible first and foremost without the cooperation of the good, great former four-term Governor of Idaho, Cecil D. Andrus. He sat through a series of long interviews, mostly when he would come to north Idaho. I would meet him and we would drive down to Moscow for something like the anniversary of Idaho Public Television's KUID, then drive back north to Kellogg for a speech to the Shoshone County Democrats.

I would bring along a tape recorder and just ask away. He tolerated any and all questions, no matter how inane some may have been, and always maintained his sense of humor. Only once or twice, after answering a question, would he say he would prefer not to see that mentioned in the book.

In that sense this is an authorized reminiscence and I freely concede I granted him the right to veto any part or the entire project at any time for that matter. My personal relationship with a person to whom I look up to and view as a surrogate father is far more important to me than any book project, no matter how long I worked at it.

And the book project has gone through several iterations. The governor carefully read all versions and tactfully suggested that it be cut in about half. With the help of a fine editor, Jay Shelledy, as well as my patient and devoted spouse, Marcia, we cut the original manuscript from 476 pages down to 256 pages. It reads better, flows more smoothly and makes for a more interesting story.

I also must thank Karla Morrison, from the Spokane office of Gallatin Public Affairs, who did a fine job of proofreading the final text.

A special thanks goes to the fine gentleman who publishes my weekly political rants, Dan Hammes, of the *St. Maries Gazette Record*. His agreement to help with publishing the manuscript, and his lending of the resources of his excellent weekly newspaper, especially the layout skills and talents of his daughter, Jamie Sloper, was very gratifying. Jamie's skill was incredibly valuable in putting together a fine-looking final product.

Many folks, upon learning of this project, gave me lots of encouragement, including the late Gordon Law, a former communications professor at the University of Idaho and one of the governor's earliest supporters. He passed along several suggestions while handling with grace the cancer that finally took him. Additionally, I would be remiss if I didn't mention the assistance provided by one of the governor's most loyal campaign workers over the years, Steve Lee. He loaned me three large scrap books full of pictures, clips, and memorabilia from past Andrus campaigns, all of which proved very useful, especially in helping to clarify some events which the passage of time had clouded in my mind.

Thanks goes to several other folks who kindly shared memories of the governor, especially his years as a state senator from Clearwater County and his first race for the governorship in 1966. That list includes former Lewiston State Senator (and a former Andrus chief of staff) Mike Mitchell; the late Wynne Blake, an attorney in Lewiston; A.L. "Butch" Alford, the longtime publisher of the *Lewiston Morning Tribune;* Wilbert D. "Bill" Hall, the veteran editorial page editor and columnist for the *Tribune*; Bill Berg, a Sandpoint attorney and a former public television reporter in Idaho; and, Mindy Cameron, a member of the Pend Oreille School District board and a former reporter for the *Tribune*, the *Idaho Statesman* and Idaho Public Television.

I also deeply appreciate the encouragement of a former colleague from the governor's first term, Marty Peterson. A student of Idaho history and politics who has been the special assistant to the president of the University of Idaho for many years, his enthusiastic and unqualified support for this book meant much to me.

I further want to thank attorney friends Peter J. Grabicki and Doug Siddoway, of Spokane's Randall, Danskin Law Firm, who were kind enough to lend me a spare office in which I was able to focus and write the initial chapters.

Last but by no means least, I must also thank my Gallatin Public Affairs colleague and long-time former partner, Marc Johnson, who also serves ably as the president of the Andrus Center for Public Policy at Boise State. His consenting to write the foreword meant so much to me because there is no finer Idaho political historian and astute observer of this state's political scene than Marc.

# Acknowledgements

Of course, none of this would have been possible without the patience and tolerance of my dear wife, Marcia. Not only is she a superb sounding board, her instincts when I am getting off-message and off-story are always uncanny and unerring.

Chris Carlson
Medimont, Idaho
November, 2010

# Foreword

Two of my professional associations have also become over the last twenty five years deeply personal relationships, and each is reflected in Chris Carlson's spirited memoir of a life in politics. Those two relationships – with Chris and with Cecil Andrus – literally and very positively changed my life. Many others who have had the rare privilege of knowing these two remarkable individuals could happily make the same claim.

Cece Andrus gave me a chance to be involved in his incredible political life in late 1985. His willingness to take a chance on a still wet-behind-the-ears television reporter created for me the kind of opportunities that literally opened a thousand doors. I thought I knew something about politics when I joined his comeback campaign for governor a quarter century ago, but I now realize my years as a journalist fascinated by politics and politicians served merely as undergraduate preparation for the advanced degree I earned at his side. I see the Cece Andrus I know in these pages. Chris had the privilege, as did I, of spending hours traveling with "the boss," watching him interact with a north Idaho sawmill worker and an eastern Idaho nuclear scientist, with a classroom teacher in Twin Falls and an elk hunter in Elk City.

We once caught him on film joshing with a total stranger he had just met about his granddaughter's fishing exploits. The governor pulled out his wallet to show off a photo of one of his pride and joys holding a beautiful Idaho rainbow. The obviously impressed fellow said, "Where did she catch that?" With no hesitation, but with a big smile, the governor replied, "No Tell'em Creek."

That exchange, completely spontaneous and unrehearsed, made the single best television commercial I have ever seen, because it captured the essence of the man – his love for his family, his love for Idaho and the outdoors and his unmatched sense of humor.

I have also seen him in the Roosevelt Room at the White House, testifying before a Congressional committee and charming the Basque

Lehendakari (the president) with expansive tales of fishing the South Fork or extolling the virtues of a baked Idaho russet.

I remember once walking with the governor into a room full of other governors – very prominent politicians, most everyone would recognize – and remarking to him in a whisper, "There sure is a lot of political talent in this room."

Andrus gave me that mischievous smile, eyes twinkling, and said, "Johnson, every one of these guys puts his pants on just like you and me. We'll have no trouble holding our own." Of course, he was right.

Cece Andrus, as Chris documents so well in this book, is a superb leader. He can hold his own in any company and, in the process, be acknowledged as the most thoughtful guy in the room. I've often reflected that this former lumberjack, whose military service prevented him from finishing his plans to pursue an engineering degree in college, could lead any organization. His native intelligence, capacity for hard work, profound common sense and remarkable ability to judge character combine with a whip-smart mind for numbers and details, a great memory and a crackling sense of humor. Those qualities, and an ability to listen to and process vast amounts of information, while coming up with the best answer, have placed him at the head of the table with CEO's, presidents, senators, congressmen, legislators, world class fly fishermen and college presidents. At the same time, he has always been just as comfortable with the hardworking folks who maintain the landscaping at the Idaho Statehouse, drive a logging truck or bag groceries at Albertsons.

Cece Andrus has never met a stranger, rarely had a bad day and always had a "glass half-full" view of life. I was driving a big motor home festooned with Andrus campaign signs when we pulled into tiny Eden, Idaho, late one afternoon in 1990. The governor jumped out, campaign brochures in hand, and headed into a little tavern, always a dangerous place to seek political support.

"I'll be right back after nailing down a few votes," he allowed as I stayed in the rig. Minutes later he bounded back to the motor home and happily declared, "I got four of seven. The rest are undecided."

I am profoundly grateful that he took me along for some of his remarkable ride and grateful that Chris has devoted the time and effort to put so much of both of them in this book.

# Foreword

Like Chris, I respect and admire Cece Andrus as much as anyone I've ever known, and I owe my longtime friend and former business partner a lifetime of thanks for his friendship, mentoring, his profound kindness, and for helping connect me with Cece.

Chris and I met in 1975, when I was a freshly minted television reporter trying to understand Idaho and its politics. Even though Chris isn't that much older than me, he had cultivated what I'll call a "command authority" that made him the ideal gatekeeper, foil, confidant, and advisor to the governor. We kept in touch during the years Andrus and Carlson spent in Washington, and my admiration grew for both of them. At about this time, I acknowledged to myself that maybe, just maybe, someday, I'd like to work with these guys.

Chris has a remarkable ability to make connections, and he has taught me the value of developing and maintaining connections with good people in every walk of life. I've seen him many times at a baseball game – and believe me, we have been to a lot of baseball games together – strike up a conversation with the fan in the next seat. Before long they'd find a link, a shared interest, or a common friend. For some unfathomable reason, Chris early saw some promise in me and eventually helped pave the way for me to first become, as he had been before me, an Andrus press secretary and then a partner at Gallatin Public Affairs. Hardly a day has passed over the last twenty-five years that I haven't talked politics, business, books, baseball, fishing, family, faith and life with Chris. He is a loyal friend, complete in his devotion to those fortunate enough to be his friend.

Over the last several years, as Chris discusses in this book, he has bravely and good-naturedly battled not one, but two debilitating diseases. Those who have watched him mount his offensive against Parkinson's and cancer can only be awed at what I have taken to calling this "modern medical marvel." Faced with his adversity, Chris was determined to master the facts about his condition. I swear he knows more than his physicians. Secondly, he took charge of his treatment, organized conference calls to make sure his various doctors were adequately comparing notes and strategies, and demanded information, alternatives and, as always, a lot of attention. His faith, family and, I hope, his friends have helped sustain him, and he has truly become an inspiration to all of us.

With this book, Chris has written a deeply personal political memoir that begins with and continues his friendship and regard for "the boss." Like me, Chris loves Cece Andrus. You won't find the surrogate son dissing on the old man in these pages. This is a loving, admiring tribute and, in a way, a political handbook. The history and stories relayed on these pages provide great insight into why Cece Andrus, with Chris's help, became a great governor and a first-rank Secretary of the Interior. Political junkies should read this book and take to heart the fundamental political advice, regardless of party or philosophy, that is contained here. As a four-term governor and one of the nation's great Secretaries of the Interior, Cece Andrus lived by a set of principles that I would argue could help anyone who aspires to a life of public service and public trust.

Cecil Andrus had a passel of chiefs of staff over his long career, and I was honored to serve as one of them. He had only a handful of press secretaries. Chris and I each held that title at different times, and I know we would agree that working day-in, day-out in that position with a truly great governor and outstanding boss was simply the best job either of us has ever had.

I'm honored to know, admire, and count as friends the two Idahoans you'll get to know better in the pages ahead. I'm betting you will come away liking them just as much as I do.

Marc C. Johnson
Boise, Idaho

# Introduction

In mid-October of 2009, a Virginia based research firm, Myers Research and Strategic Services, polled 600 Idahoans on a variety of issues and political figures in the Gem State. The poll was commissioned and paid for by Idaho's Democratic Party. Far and away the most popular political figure, the person with the highest score on the firm's "warmth" scale, was a man who had not held any political office for 15 years: Cecil D. Andrus, the former four-term governor and former Secretary of the Department of the Interior during the Carter Administration.

Even after being out of office for a decade and a half, he was still recognized by three-fourths of those being polled. His "mean average" on their warmth scale was a 68, on a scale of zero to 100, zero being dead cold and 100 being red hot. By contrast Idaho's then current governor, C.L. "Butch" Otter, a former lieutenant governor under Andrus, and a former three-term member of Congress, had a mean average of 56. That was also the score for the then First District member of Congress, Democrat Walt Minnick.

The poll only confirmed what any observer of Idaho's political scene would tell anyone inquiring – Andrus is the most beloved political figure the state has ever produced. Many voters would tell any pollster that if he were to have run for a fifth term as governor in 2010, despite turning 79 in August of 2010, he would easily have vanquished his former lieutenant governor (who used to tell people that his initials, C.L., stood for Cecil's Lackey! They stand for Clement Leroy.).

Wherever he travels throughout Idaho, his bald head and distinguished visage is readily recognized. He is constantly approached by folks with stories about something he did for them or for someone they know, and thanked again for his service. Many people start off with "Governor, you may not remember me, but. . . ." almost always they are cut off by a "Sure, Bob, I remember you. . . ." His memory for names remains one of his many remarkable assets, and it is a constant source of surprise to folks which only endears him all the more.

One of the primary purposes of this reminiscence is to answer the questions: how did this man become the political phenomena he is; how did he emerge; and, then stand out so far above others who have held high public office in Idaho?

This goal is not as easy as one would think. In approaching the writing of this book, I concluded one key to understanding Andrus' unique political success is his ability to develop and maintain wonderful relationships with people from all walks of life across the political, economic and social spectrum. Andrus has the God-given ability to instill in a person he is talking with the sense that at that moment they are the most important person in the world, they have his undivided attention, he understands what they are trying to communicate, he empathizes with their plight and somehow he gives them a sense their issue or challenge is solvable.

He treats everyone the same with genuine sincerity. Walking through downtown Boise with him is a marvelous experience as he meets folks on the street, whether it is a barber stepping out of his shop, or a clerk headed out the door for lunch, or a state legislator headed for Moon's for a bowl of soup, or a state government bureaucrat on an errand, or a Basque groundskeeper working a flower bed on the grounds of the State Capitol. He likes people. They know it, and they like him in return.

Once, shortly after he completed his last term in the governorship, I flew from Spokane to Boise for a business meeting he would also attend. As he often does, Cece insisted on picking me up at the airport. As we drove out of the parking lot he stopped at the booth to pay the parking fee. The toll booth operator, recognizing Andrus, refused to take the ticket and the couple of dollars he was handing him, saying "You know, Governor, we've always comped you."

Andrus replied, "Thanks, but you know I'm no longer the governor." The attendant simply said, "You'll always be *MY* governor," and tripped open the cross bar.

In further thinking about how to try to convey to a reader the unique figure Andrus was and still is, I knew it was important to tell an interesting story, or series of stories which would hold one's interest. We write to be read, and in this case, I also wanted to entertain while capturing a man who's legacy and fingerprints are all over modern Idaho. While not readily recognized, his legacy covers the United States, especially when one gives him due credit for orchestrating the largest expansion in the National Park system, wilderness areas, wild and scenic rivers and wildlife refuges in our nation's history with his masterful handling of the Alaska Land Claims issue while Secretary of the Interior.

I'm a great believer in the phrase attributed to the English poet, William Wordsworth: "the child is the father of the man!" I knew not much was known about Andrus' early years. Instinctively, I felt his development while child and teenager could help explain the political phenomena that emerged.

Still, I came back to the importance of focusing on his skill at inspiring an incredible degree of loyalty among those who worked for him or served with him or supported his candidacies. For Andrus, his success in part has always been about his ability to establish and maintain numerous quality relationships. I was privileged to be one of the recipients and beneficiaries of one of those quality relationships.

For Andrus, the essence of being a successful governor was always about helping people and solving problems. Engaged in his 1986 comeback campaign for governor, he told the *Wall Street Journal's* Dennis Farney, "Governor sounds like a fancy title. But take the gold braid off his golf cap and what you have left is a problem-solver. That's what I am: A problem-solver."

The voters agreed, returning him to office for two more terms and enjoying his service as Idaho's leader for an unequaled 14 years. "Governors are elected to solve problems and help people," he would constantly repeat to his staff. "That's what it's all about, that's what we're here to do."

For me, it was and always will be an honor to have worked for and with him. I make no apologies for wanting to help preserve a legacy he earned by trying to convey to a reader what made him so special. Next to marrying my wife, the second smartest thing I ever did was go to work for him. I freely concede any success I may have achieved in a limited sense in this old world is attributable to what I learned from him and my good luck at being in a position to help him achieve his goals while in public office.

This book is clearly a reminiscence, not a biography or an autobiography. What's the difference, one may ask? For me the difference is easy to understand: reminiscence is based in large part on one's memory of events. A biography or even an autobiography implies a degree of research to confirm dates, a review of historical sources that exist and other literature written at the time, more an academic undertaking to be peer-reviewed. Reminiscence is a very subjective undertaking; it is one's perception of how and why events unfolded. It often reflects bias and is subject to the charge of selective recall. Still, in the end, how one recalls things, and what he or she recalls in and of itself says much and reveals much.

Psychologists contend people cannot really objectively look at themselves or their participation in various events. We all tend to look with rose-colored glasses and exaggerate our own roles. This result, relatively speaking, is a shading of the truth at best, and at worst, outright misrepresenting the past event. All I can offer is a commitment to the reader that I did my best to be objective and accurate while being conscious of the rose-colored glasses factor. The reader will be the ultimate judge. The degree to which this reminiscence resonates with history and other accounts is a measure of it as an authentic and honest recounting.

Let me add that this reminiscence makes no claim to being a complete recalling of the Andrus' remarkable career. While there are anecdotes from his years as governor, Interior Secretary and businessman, this book primarily recounts his rise to successful election to the governorship in 1970. To a limited degree, it also updates the reader with the telling of some aspects of his successful post-governor years. These are the time periods NOT well documented and thus I hope this effort will fill some gaps.

I leave to trained historians and better writers than I to pore through the extensive records and files that document his years as governor and Interior Secretary. The record is there, mostly assembled at Boise State University, and awaiting a first-rate biographer to condense and tell. It is hoped this reminiscence will provide some useful insights and help to burnish further the distinguished record of one of America's most talented politicians.

And so, the story begins...

Medimont, Idaho
July 19, 2010

*Chapter 1*

# The Early Years

Hal Andrus, father of Cecil D. Andrus, the future four-term governor of Idaho and U.S. Interior Secretary, was born on March 19, 1906, on a modest family ranch north of John Day, Oregon, near a now non-existent post office called Dale. From that place Cecil Andrus, who was born in Hood River, Oregon, on August 25, 1931, derived his middle name. The birth certificate simply said "Cecil Andrus." Later, his parents, for whatever reason, decided he needed a middle name and added "Dale." When their second son came to prominence, he made a point of emphasizing his middle initial, especially in press releases as well as official documents.

It was one of the few signs of vanity one could observe in a man who has dominated the Idaho political scene for fifty years, besides leaving an indelible mark on the national political landscape through his deft handling of the passage of one of the great landmark pieces of conservation legislation, the 1980 Alaska National Interest Lands and Conservation Act (ANILCA).

Andrus' grandfather was one of those early Oregon pioneers who had come across the plains and the prairies on the old Oregon Trail as a small child with his family in a covered wagon. They homesteaded, put down their "tap-root" as Andrus liked to say, near that Dale post office. His grandfather grew up on the family homestead, and Andrus thought life must have been pretty tough for his granddad because he didn't marry, probably couldn't afford to marry, until he was forty-three years old. When he did marry, it was to a seventeen-year-old.

He made up for lost time, however, as they had ten children, five boys and five girls, Andrus' father, Hal, being the youngest. Hal attended a one-room school a short distance away from the ranch and

1

rode a saddle horse to and from school. After the eighth grade, he dropped out to work.

Hal met Dorothy in Hood River in the mid-1920s and they were married in 1928. Hal was twenty-two and Dorothy eighteen. It appears the men in the Andrus family, over several generations, liked to marry younger women, because eighteen-year-old Cecil continued the trend when he married Carol, who was sixteen at the time -- younger than either his mother or grandmother when they married.

His mother's maiden name was Dorothy Johnson. Her father's was Elias. Andrus recalls having seen him, even though he died from a heart attack when Cecil was six. His grandparents on Dorothy's side operated a little country store with a single gas pump about two miles outside of Hood River on the Mount Hood Loop Highway near the little community of Odell. Andrus can still see that old gas pump in his mind's eye.

He recalled many years later, "It was one of those you pumped up by hand and the glass filled on top to determine how many gallons you were buying. Maximum per pump was ten gallons, but if you only wanted to buy two gallons, you pumped up two gallons and then had to squeeze the handle until it all drained out of the glass container."

There was an old lumber mill across the road from the store and there, in a little garage on the side, Hal performed his mechanic work and whatever else needed to be done. Andrus believes this is where Hal first spotted Dorothy at her parent's store. It must have been close to love at first sight because it wasn't long before they were married and then moved into a little place between Odell and neighboring Parkdale.

Hal did anything and everything he could in 1929 and 1930 to make a living. The nation was sinking into the Great Depression. Hal, however, was an excellent mechanic and had enough jobs to keep providing for his family.

Hal was not just a mechanic. He had a bit of the salesman about him, what today one would call an entrepreneur. For example, he had an old flatbed truck and would buy apples in Hood River. Usually they were lower grade apples which he had been able to buy cheaply. He would load up his truck, drive to California, set up along a highway, sell the apples, use the money to buy oranges, and drive back to Oregon to sell the oranges. He usually made money doing this.

It was in that old truck that Hal drove Dorothy to the hospital in August of 1931 for Cece's delivery. They did not have a car and almost didn't make it to the hospital in time, due to Cece's older brother, Steve, unintentionally sabotaging the truck.

Hal had what was pretty typical in those days, a barrel up on a rack which he kept filled with gas and then would fill the truck up with "farm gas" when he needed it. According to family lore, just about the time Dorothy was due to deliver Cece, two-and-a-half year old Steve had seen Hal fueling the truck, and he decided to help out when no one was looking, so he stuck a garden hose in the opening of the tank, and turned on the water thinking that he was doing his Dad a big favor by filling up his gas tank.

"So, Mom starts into labor," Andrus recounted years later, "Dad dashes for the truck, and they take off, headed for the hospital in Hood River. Of course, the water got sucked up into the carburetor and the truck quits. Dad, being a good mechanic, throws up the hood, immediately sees that the fuel pump, which in those days used to have a glass sediment bottle on the bottom, is full of water. He realized he had to drain the water out of the tank, put in new gas, and get the truck running."

Despite this delay, they still managed to get to the hospital in time for Cece to make his entrance onto the world stage. His mother stayed in the hospital five days, which made him wonder in later years whether there were some complications, a subject he never asked about.

Andrus still has the receipts from his Mom's hospital stay. The bill came to a whopping $9 plus an additional $5 from the doctor.

Steve and Cece were joined by a sister, Margaret Lucille Andrus, who was born on February 24, 1934, also in Hood River. Some one in the family started calling her "Margi," a nickname that stuck with her all her life.

When Cece was three years of age, his Dad had the opportunity to move to Junction City, Oregon, to put together a saw mill with his brother, Bud. Both were good mechanics and skilled builders. Four miles west of Junction City, they built what could only be called a "mill shack" for their family. It was constructed of basic studding with rough boards they had sawed themselves, and then nailed to the outside with no inner wall. Six foot partitions separated the rooms. Above the partitions, the rooms were open all the way to the roof. It was a glorified shed. And, of course, there was no indoor plumbing. There was a path out their back door that led to the outhouse. When Andrus took his bath, his Mom just heated the water on the stove and he bathed in a galvanized washtub on the kitchen floor.

When a customer placed an order for lumber or timbers, his dad and uncle would crank up the sawmill next door and fill the order. When they weren't doing that, they would work in the woods falling trees to supply other mills.

Like most folks who lived outside of a town or city, the Andruses had a little farm and a big garden to supplement the food on the table. To Cecil, it seemed like they raised almost everything they ate. In their barn were a couple of cows, and hogs as well as a chicken house. Cece gathered eggs in the morning and milked the cows. All the siblings had chores to do and the Andrus matriarch canned everything.

Within a couple of years Hal was able to build a better house for his family. According to Andrus, friends and neighbors found Hal to be a capable and competent, self-taught individual with a savvy intuition about how machines worked. He came to understanding the basics of engines from tearing apart Model T Fords, and, as engines became more complex, he progressed right along with the new innovations.

One night in the late 1930s, the Andrus brothers' mill burned to the ground, and Hal found himself unemployed and in debt. He owed almost a month's wages to most of the men who worked in the mill. The only asset he had was a fair amount of lumber stacked in the yard. Hal paid off the men in lumber that they could sell in turn. He paid his other bills in the same mannter.

(Cecil never forgot the example his Dad set of paying off one's debts, which is why, during his first campaign for governor in 1966, he took real umbrage when some Republicans levied the false charge that the Andrus mill in Orofino had gone through a bankruptcy.)

Once in a while, Hal could afford to buy a calf, but as the time drew near to butcher it and all the siblings began anticipating real beef on their plates, somebody in Junction City would invariably offer Hal $15 for the calf, and the family would keep eating venison. Perhaps surprisingly, given how much their larder was stocked with venison, elk meat and birds they hunted near and around their home during these lean years, Cece still loves to hunt and eat wild game.

The love of hunting was one of the great legacies Hal passed along to both his sons. At a young age, driven by necessity, he taught the boys to hunt and fish, and passed on a skill they've pursued all their lives. Hal not only taught them where and when to hunt and fish, he also taught them what signs to look for on the land or water, how to track, the importance of taking care of their gear, and to be true conservationists.

Andrus was twelve when he shot his first deer and fondly recalled the memory some sixty-six years later.

"We were back at the old ranch where Dad had been born. I had a .25/35 Winchester carbine that belonged to an uncle who had loaned it to me. It had a peep sight on it and I shot a young forked horn buck mule deer," he recalled as if it were just a week ago.

"There was a group of us out hunting that day, and I was supposed to meet the others around behind what were called 'the big rocks.' I went around the rocks like I was supposed to do, sat down by this tree, and was somewhat hidden by some brush. I was eating some raisins when all of a sudden I spotted some does. Of course, you can't shoot does most of the year so I was looking for horns and right at the end of the string of does was this little forked buck. I nailed it with one shot!"

Andrus later recalled to a friend "A man always remembers his first deer, his first big fish, his first kiss, and his first love. They are just indelibly imprinted in a man's memory."

Andrus guesses he was five when he and Steve started fishing for small trout in nearby Bear Creek. They would also go with Hal to Florence on the Oregon Coast, and fish for salt water perch. Closer to home, they fished for sun fish and crappie in the local gravel pits.

"Sometimes it was family recreation and we'd make an evening of it," Andrus recalled. "Mom would fix a picnic lunch, we would build a fire on the beach and set our cane poles with old thread for line and a cork bobber usually made by trimming the cork from some wine bottle. We would toast marshmallows and watch for the corks to start bobbing, and then we would catch plenty of small sun fish."

Andrus says his memories of his youth are mostly pleasant. That he doesn't remember ever going hungry, though they did do without a lot of things. He wore hand-me-down shoes that older brother Steve had outgrown.

"He would get a new pair of shoes when Mom had saved enough money. She would have him put his foot down on a piece of cardboard, and she would take a pencil, draw round the foot, and mail it to Montgomery Ward. Before long Steve had his new pair of shoes, and I had his," Andrus stated.

Like many families during the Depression, the Andrus family seldom wasted anything. For example, Dorothy would always use sugar and flour sacks after they were empty. She would wash them out, bleach them, iron them and turn them into pillow cases or dish towels. The family would buy twenty-five or fifty pound sacks of oatmeal, which always contained a cup or saucer or another piece of dishware inside the sack as a sales gimmick. The tableware didn't match -- some items were orange colored, some had flower prints on them -- but they served their purpose.

Dorothy earned the family extra money by doing things like separating cream or doing extra sewing. Times were tough, and while the Andrus family did not thrive, they survived the worst of the hard times.

Andrus would often joke in later years, especially when on the campaign trail, that while he wasn't exactly born in a log cabin, he did start school in a true one-room rural schoolhouse. It was a half mile from the Andrus house up a gravel road. It was typical of what one would then find in smaller rural communities throughout the west. There were blackboards with chalk and erasers and windows on one side. Eight rows of desks filled the school, with the first grade kids closest to the blackboard. The next row back was the second grade and so on, on back to the eighth graders.

There was a wood stove in the back of the room, and like every other building in the area, no electricity. And like their home, the bathroom was an outhouse -- actually two outhouses, one for the girls and one for the boys. Cece once said he "didn't know folks went to a bathroom inside a house until the family moved to Eugene when I was eleven."

With no electricity, school couldn't start until it was light and the school children always went home, as a matter of safety, before it got dark. This meant, of course, that the wintertime school day was shortened.

The first teacher Andrus can recall with any clarity was a young woman named Audrey Cole. Like most teachers in such schools, she had gone to a "normal school" for two years after high school in order to obtain her teaching certificate. Most western states had at least one "normal school" that specialized in producing elementary school teachers.

Ms. Cole was at most twenty, and since Cece was just starting the first grade, he was seated up front. He laconically said later, "She left a good impression on me."

One practical effect of sitting up front was that he heard all that the teacher was teaching to the second graders, and by osmosis, he picked up lessons for both the first and second grades. The net effect was he was able to skip the second grade altogether and moved from the lst grade to the third grade, eventually enabling him to graduate from high school at age sixteen. Cece remained at that one-room school house until midway through the sixth grade, when the family moved into Eugene.

As mentioned earlier, the Andrus family home had no electricity during those years, as FDR's rural electrification hadn't yet reached them. There was also no running water in the house and no refrigeration. They did, however, live next to Bear Creek and they kept "cooler boxes" in the creek. These boxes were built with screen sides allowing the cold water to run through, keeping the food inside fresh. In the winter time, they would scoop fine snow off of the boxes to make ice cream cones.

Cece and Steve were also the irrigation system for the garden during the summer. From a young age they started carrying buckets of water from Bear Creek up the bank and pouring it into the ditches Hal had designed to irrigate the garden. Cece used to get a little frustrated during the hot summer because he would carry a bucket of water up, pour it into the very dry ground and it would seem to just disappear. He would make trip after trip to water the garden, but it seemed like nothing was really going down the ditches.

Bear Creek also allowed the boys to fish for crawdads. Sometimes they would catch one as long as eight inches. In those days rural folks would cure their own bacon by the side and there was always bacon rind which Dorothy would save and use to flavor boiled beans.

Crawdads cannot resist bacon rind. So the Andrus boys would take a chunk of bacon rind, tie it on a string, put it in the creek and a crawdad would come up, and take hold. If one would slowly bring the string and bait to the bank the crawdad would hang on until it was too late to escape.

When the boys had a crawdad close enough, they would snatch it off. After they had gathered a bunch of them, they would go up to the house and fry the crawdad tails.

When it came time to get the garden ready in the spring, Hal would borrow a neighbor's horse. Using an old single, walk-behind plow blade, Hal would plow and disk the garden and the boys would work the soil to get it ready for planting.

Andrus had two pairs of old striped bib overalls that he wore when he was a youngster. One pair was part of his school clothes and the older pair served as his work clothes. He would come home from school and Dorothy would say, "Alright boys, get your school clothes off and your work clothes on." That meant they were to take off their good bib overalls, which weren't too badly patched yet, and put on the older, patched up pair. Then, they set about chopping wood, splitting kindling to fill the wood box, or cleaning the barn and gathering eggs - often all three.

It seemed to Andrus they had about a thousand chickens, and, of course, that meant he had to gather lots of eggs. Sometimes they had so many eggs gathered up that he and Steve would throw the eggs at trees. At that time eggs were selling at eight cents a dozen, if you could even sell them. For Cece, it was an early lesson in the law of supply and demand.

Cece also learned early the truth of the old saying, "Be careful what you wish for." He must have been eight or nine and was watching Hal milk their two cows. Hal would go out in the morning and again in the evening to milk the old cows. Like many folks tasked with milking, Hal would play games by squirting milk at the boys watching him, and squirting milk into a little pan for the barn cats to drink from.Cece thought that looked like fun, so he started clamoring for Hal to teach him how to milk. "Boy was that ever a mistake," he later recounted. "Once Dad had us boys where we could really milk the old cows and strip them out, the Old Man never went to the barn again other than to inspect after we had cleaned it out."

Like all kids, Cece and Steve would make up games to play in the barn. One time Hal caught them playing a game they thought would get them in big trouble. It was summer, and hot, and they were taking a three-tined pitch fork, slipping it under a fresh cow pie that had crusted over on the hot ground, but was still soft, tipping the fork up to loosen the pie, then picking up the cow pies and throwing them against a tree or the side of a barn. They were having a good old time chucking the pies around when they spotted Hal, leaning on the fence, watching them. "Oh God, here it comes, we're in deep trouble," Cece remembers saying to himself.

"Boys," Hal said, "you'd better learn right now, it's not how much of that stuff you can throw that counts, it's how much you can make stick!" For Cece that was the end of the game that day, but later in life he often thought about the truth of his father's statement as political opponents or critics tried to tear him down. To put it proverbially, he had a lot of cow shit tossed at him during his career, but not much ever stuck!

Like many kids in those days, especially high-spirited ones like Cece and Steve, they would sometimes get ahead of themselves to the point the parents felt some discipline was required. Also, like many families, one parent is the tough-love parent, and the other is the soft-love. Hal was the hard-handed disciplinarian; Dorothy also could be tough, only she used a switch.

Hal had big hands and he used them. The boys learned quickly not to talk back when he told them to do something, or they would get the proverbial cuff on the ears. When they were smaller it is fair to say they were probably afraid of their Dad even though Cece does not recall many spankings. But when Hal did spank, he turned them over his knee and paddled until they felt it.

Cece also could recall a few whippings administered by his mother with an old switch. He said the last whipping he received from her came when he was twelve years old. She ordered him to lie down across a bench and she started swinging the switch. "I made up my mind I wasn't going to cry, so I gritted my teeth and she just flailed away, from the back of my knees right up to my shoulders, until the old switch broke into pieces. Man did I hurt, but I didn't cry."

Today many folks would call that counter productive, but as the recipient of the punishment Cece didn't see it that way. While it physically hurt and, at times, produced welts, he knew his parents loved and cared about him. Some may frown on that kind of tough love today, but that was an era when, as a kid, you did as you were told or you suffered the consequences. It was also an era that still adhered to the old admonition "spare the rod and spoil the child." While the spankings didn't happen all that often Steve and Cece usually knew it was coming, and why.

Many times, Dorothy, instead of being the administrator of instant justice, would say, "Wait until your Dad gets home. I'm gonna have him whip you!" As one would expect, the prospect of this was almost worse than the reality, and the boys would spend the rest of the day praying, pleading, crying and saying, "Oh Mom, *please* don't tell Dad." Usually, Dorothy would relent, saying, "Okay, but don't you ever do that again." And they rarely ever did. Neither Steve nor Cece wanted any part of Hal coming home tired at the end of a long workday and face being told his boys needed discipline.

One of the major sources of amusement and information for the Andrus family was the radio. They had an old Philco radio that, owing to the lack of electricity, was battery operated. The family used kerosene lanterns and candles for light in the evenings. Like many rural folks in the northwest, the Andruses were promised in the 1930's that they would benefit from a federal program, under the Rural Electrification Act, that was supposed to get electricity to their part of Oregon by 1939 or 1940.

The Federal Government had an ambitious program to bring more water to the desert of central Washington, and electricity to many families like the Andrus family through the construction of dams like the Grand Coulee Dam on the Columbia River. World War II came along and postponed electricity coming to their part of rural Oregon.

Like many rural families struggling to get by during the Depression, the Andrus family was raised on the gospel according to Franklin Delano Roosevelt. Even though they didn't have electricity until after World War II, Hal had a way of rigging up a battery system so they could power up the radio and listen to Roosevelt's fireside chats. Hal always supported Roosevelt because he felt FDR truly cared about the common man as opposed to the rich, even though Roosevelt was rich himself.

Cranking up the radio was always an interesting task. It took two batteries, a wet cell and a dry cell. The wet cell was the standard six volt battery that Hal used in his truck and was fully charged, but the dry cell had a different voltage. When Hal knew FDR was going to give a fireside chat, he would take the battery out of the his truck, bring it in the house, and hook it up to the radio to ensure that the family could hear the President's talk.

Before the President spoke the family would sometimes listen to *The Lone Ranger* or *The Green Hornet*, which the boys always enjoyed. Sooner or later, Hal would say "Alright boys, sit down there and listen to your President." They dutifully listened, though like most young boys, they probably cared little at the time who was president and were far more interested in who the Lone Ranger or the Green Hornet was chasing or saving.

Even though Hal was a supporter of Roosevelt, and even though the Andrus family was poor by most measures, Hal refused to get into any of the Work Project Administration's programs cropping up around the country. He had several opportunities but in Hal's mind, those programs were welfare and charity. He told Cece, "I can support my family and I'm not going to *work* on welfare. I'm not going to *receive* welfare. I don't want anybody to ever say Hal Andrus had to go on welfare!" Thus, the Andrus family was never the beneficiary of any of the food commodities programs, nor did they patronize any early versions of what today are called food banks.

As far back as Cece can recall, both Hal and Dorothy were FDR Democrats. They felt Roosevelt had devised a number of programs in the early days of his first Administration that truly helped the common man and started the process of pulling the country out of the Depression. Despite this legacy in the home, Cece was never a politician who would claim to have imbibed politics from his earliest days, or that as kids they used to sit around the table and listen to the family talk politics or join in vigorous family debates.

"I cannot and will not claim such, because in our family it just didn't happen. They were too busy just trying to make a living," he said years later.

Cece also said he honestly did not recall politics ever being a keen interest of his father.

"Politics really didn't capture my interest until a personal situation involving the inadequacy of the public schools and the inferior education I saw unfolding for my first daughter arose, when I was in my late twenties. As a matter of fact, when I first became involved in politics in Orofino and ran for the state senate, one of my aunts on my dad's side said, 'Oh, the family has gone to hell! Little Cecil went into politics!'"

*Chapter 2*

# Cece's Teenage Years

W hen Cece was eleven years old (in 1942), the family moved to Eugene, the second largest city in Oregon and home to the University of Oregon. Hal and his brother, Bud, had become known region-wide as experts at rebuilding old sawmill machinery. Cece's Uncle Burt was still building filers. Since sawmills in those days burnt down with alarming regularity, there was always fire-damaged equipment to be bought for a fraction of its original cost. The brothers would restore and sell it.

During World War II there was no machinery built that wasn't dedicated to wartime activities. Hal and Bud would rebuild from scratch or repair old mill machinery, other machinery used in the woods, and just about any machine that operated in a sawmill. Needless to say, they did well financially with a machine shop.

The Andrus brothers ended up doing work for most of the mills, including the big name mills in the area. Even up into his early eighties, Hal Andrus would still get calls to come and oversee the rebuilding of old, burned planers because he had "a real touch for it," according to his son.

So the brothers built the Andrus Brothers Machine Shop at Second and Polk Streets in Eugene. Hal's family moved into a two-bedroom house at 1005 West Seventh Avenue that had only one bath. Hal built a stairway that led up to the loft and he made a little bedroom where Cece and Steve would sleep.

When the family moved to Eugene, Cece was in the middle of the sixth grade and attended Eugene's Lincoln Grade School. For the seventh, eighth and ninth grades, he attended Woodrow Wilson Junior

High and then Eugene High School for his sophomore, junior and senior years, graduating in 1948 at the age of sixteen.

Just as he had jobs to do on the farm, he worked in the city, as early as the sixth grade. The various odd jobs that would come up for a sixth grader included mowing lawns and picking up people's trash. Starting in the seventh grade, Andrus had two paper routes. He would deliver the *Eugene Register-Guard* in the afternoon and *The Oregonian* (one of Portland's papers) in the morning. That worked out fine every day of the week except Sunday, when both papers published morning editions. The paper routes were next to each other, so Cece could get the job done in a reasonable amount of time, however.

Being a newspaper carrier was a terrific learning experience. In those days, a paper carrier had to pay for the papers and then collect from his customers. Profit was derived by collecting on a regular basis from all customers because the early money he collected all went back to the newspaper. Andrus quickly learned much about human nature, especially that there were more than a few people in this world who didn't mind stiffing a newspaper boy.

"With all the skips, drops, runaways, and shysters, I ended up eating quite a bit. The financial lesson I carried away from that experience was the importance of watching one's account receivables," he said later.

As Andrus got older, he graduated to other jobs, including pumping gas after school and on weekends at an Associated Gas stationand sweeping out an old print shop. Both Steve and Cece had to take on these paid tasks because that was the only way they could get the "pocket money" every young man likes to have. The "allowance" that other young men may have received (though it was more prevalent in the next generation) was something unheard of around the Andrus household. The boys were expected to earn their keep, and they learned early in life that if they wanted something, they had to work and save for it.

On this point, years later, Andrus said "We're all better for having learned that life lesson early, and no one will ever say that either Steve, my sister, or I were born with a silver spoon in our mouths."

Despite the time it took to do these odd jobs, Andrus did have time for other things, including sports and girls, not necessarily in that order. Though he was tall and lean and enjoyed athletics, Cece felt himself to be just an average athlete. His future wife, Carol, first caught a glimpse of him while he was playing basketball in a neighborhood pickup game.

In baseball and football, Andrus considered himself to be more of a B-squad player. He could play both games but didn't consider himself to be a great jock and he never tried to pretend he was any sort of high school star. He played end on the football team and first base and centerfield in baseball, a sport in which he did have a good throwing arm. He often nailed runners at the plate with a strong throw from the outfield. He particularly enjoyed playing first base, though, because that position almost always was in on the action.

Oddly enough, in discussing baseball years later with members of his staff who loved the game, Cece confessed he did not particularly like sitting and watching the game. "While I can marvel at and appreciate the skills of an Ichiro while watching the Seattle Mariners, I just don't enjoy spending three or four hours watching other folks exercise when I could be out doing something active myself."

As Secretary of the Interior, he found his old glove and enjoyed playing slow-pitch softball when his staff organized a team to play in the department's recreational league. Not surprisingly, he played first base. It was a great morale booster throughout the department when the "Boss" would show up --he rarely missed a game-- to play first base for his team, the Buffaloes, against a team comprised, for example, of the National Park Service's D.C. maintenance workers. Many of those folks had never seen the Interior Secretary up close and it was a nice benefit. Andrus would mingle and mix with a wider cross-section of the department staff while enjoying the fun of a good softball game. The secretary's team comprised of, as he delicately put it, "mostly overweight, over-the-hill jocks" which usually made for easy pickings for the teams against whom they were competing.

In high school, Andrus also participated in a club called "The Pack Rats." Far from trying to emulate Frank Sinatra, Dean Martin, and Sammy Davis, Jr., their club was comprised of a group of like-minded students who liked to hike and camp. Another club was called "The Obsidians," also outdoor-oriented but focused on wintertime activities, especially skiing. Throughout his high school years, despite his involvement in these varied activities, Andrus maintained decent grades.

15

Early in his junior year he was elected president of his junior class -- thus beginning the process of seeking the approval of one's peers for the honor and privilege of providing leadership, and giving an outlet for his thoughts on how to solve problems. Achieving this office led him to run for student body president, a race he narrowly lost. Initially, the race was a tie, prompting a run off with one Keith Stenchill, who went on to be a dentist in Eugene, and is one of the few folks who could later say he had beaten Cece Andrus in an election.

Reminiscing years later, Andrus confessed that he was not sure why he decided to seek the student body office but he speculated that it had more to do with a young man's ego and wanting to prove that he was somehow worthy of being held in high esteem by his peers. Being young and handsome with a full head of curly hair, as well as lanky, lean, and quick with a quip, also made him more attractive to the fairer sex. He acknowledged that some youngsters pursue student office because they know it will look good on their college application, but he insists that was not a consideration in his thought process.

"In those days, I was one of those kids who just took life a day at a time."

One factor that complicated sports participation was that throughout high school Andrus was always employed, somewhat out of necessity. Summer during his high school years was the period when he could make good money while working on farms in the area. Such boring but lucrative tasks included sewing sacks together while on a combine and throwing hay bales onto a truck or feeding livestock. It was hard work which paid fairly well. It also kept the young man out of any serious trouble.

Andrus' adolescence coincided with World War II, which in later years he readily acknowledged had a profound influence on just about everything happening in his world, centered even as it was in and around Eugene. Certain dates are etched indelibly in most everyone's memory, dates in which one can always recall where they were and what they were doing when they received shocking news. For folks of Andrus' generation, the dates that stood out included Pearl Harbor, V-J day, and President Roosevelt's death.

On December 7, 1941, "the date that will live in infamy," as FDR put it in his December 8th radio address to Congress and the nation, the Andrus family was still living on the farm outside of Junction City,

16

Oregon. It was a Sunday, and the family had come into town to visit with Uncle Burt and his family. Young Andrus was outside on the porch of their house when he noticed a boy riding on a bicycle down the street hawking newspapers and shouting out loudly "Extra! Extra! Read all about it! Buy a paper! The Japs have bombed Pearl Harbor!"

Andrus quickly ran inside and told his parents, "Somebody just bombed Pearl Harbor!" Then he said he asked "Where's Pearl Harbor? What's Pearl Harbor?" The families quickly turned on Burt's radio and learned what was happening.

Andrus was only ten but he knew this was something big, that life was going to change in some sort of ill-defined way. Recalling that day years later, Andrus acknowledged he was probably too young to understand and fully appreciate all that it meant, but he said he could sense the anxiety and uncertainty in his parents and others regarding what the future held. Andrus vividly recalls, in the first few weeks after December 7, the rumors circulating about Japanese carriers off the West Coast, and a sense of panic among some that the West Coast might be invaded. The fear and panic subsided with the passage of time, but life in a war environment quickly became different with things like gasoline and rubber, as well as rationing of certain food items.

Like most Americans, Andrus kept up on the news of the war both through reading newspapers and attending movies, where they could watch the ubiquitous "Movietone" newsreels with reports (often pure propaganda) on the war's progress before the main feature was shown. Movies then cost twelve cents and Hollywood quickly cranked out war movies starring, as Andrus succinctly put it, "draft dodgers like John Wayne and Ronald Reagan."

Andrus did understand and grasp the significance of the American Navy's defeat of the Japanese in the battle of Midway. The loss of carriers and life for the Japanese was devastating and later historians of the war considered it the true turning point in the Pacific theater.

Looking back on those years, Andrus said he did not recall ever seeing or knowing any Japanese-Americans around Eugene while growing up in Oregon. He wasn't aware of the internment program the U.S. government undertook with regard to Japanese-American citizens. With hindsight, Andrus understood what an assault this was on American civil liberties.

"Only later did I come to understand what a tragic suspension of one's civil liberties had occurred, and what a black mark this was in the land of the free. And only after I came back from the Navy, having served in Korea from a base in Japan, did I begin to learn more about the internments. When I became governor of Idaho, I learned much more, including the fact that one of the major internment sites had been in Minidoka County in Southern Idaho," he told an interviewer.

Andrus also recalled V-J Day, the day the Japanese announced their unconditional surrender following the dropping of atomic bombs on Hiroshima and Nagasaki. On that day the Japanese people heard for the first time the voice of their God-Emperor, Hirohito, telling them they must bear the unbearable and endure the unendurable. Andrus remembered the day vividly, in fact, because it led to the only time he was fired from a job.

He was working for the Christiansen brothers, who grew and sold hay and raised rodeo stock on a farm outside of Eugene. With the war ending, there were massive celebrations in cities and towns across the nation, including one in downtown Eugene. After hearing of the Japanese surrender, Cece and a group of friends headed downtown to join in the marching, cheering and other festivities. It's fair to say that Cece and the other farm crew members enjoyed themselves and caroused until the wee hours of the morning.

Normally, Andrus was picked up to go to work at 6:30 a.m. by another crew member from the farm, who would drive the forty-five minutes to the ranch. He mentioned to some of his fellow workers while they were celebrating that he thought they had to be up at the usual time, but was told that was not the case, and that since it was a national holiday they were not going to have to work the next day. That made sense to Cece, so he stayed in bed the next morning. Before long ,the Andrus' telephone rang with one of the Christiansen brothers on the other end asking where he was. When he told the caller he wasn't coming to work that day because it was a day of celebration and a national holiday, the caller disagreed and fired him on the spot, saying they would mail him his final check.

This became another one of life's lessons for Andrus, who learned early and often from what he later liked to call "the school of hard knocks." In this case, the lesson was one that would recur several times in later years: "Trust but verify!"

Two days later, the phone rang again. This time it was Mrs. Christiansen, the matriarch of the family, and she wanted him to come back to work. Andrus told her he was sorry, and declined to come back to work, pointing out that her son Billy had fired him and that he had already taken another job.

## Chapter 3

# Courtship & Marriage

A ndrus dated quite a number of girls while in high school, including the daughter of Wayne Morse, a well-known Oregon politician who had also at one time been the dean of the University of Oregon's Law School. It's interesting to speculate in the "what if" sense had that date led to Cece marrying into the Morse family. There seems little doubt that Andrus would eventually have been bitten by the political bug had he stayed in Oregon. Those familiar with the drive and energy he was able to apply, along with his intelligence and phenomenal memory for names, have little doubt he would have become governor of Oregon had he not moved to Idaho where he emerged as governor of the Gem State.

At that time in his life, though, Andrus wasn't paying much attention to politics, so he did not know what a controversial figure the Oregon senator was, and how he had engendered the dislike of many people for switching parties several times, from being a Republican to being a Democrat to being an independent. All that switching though was redeemed in the eyes of some when Morse, along with Alaska's Ernest Gruening, voted against President Lyndon B. Johnson's phonied up pretext to expand America's incursion into Vietnam---the Tonkin Gulf Resolution. The career of this unique Oregon figure has never been better documented than by the independent columnist and correspondent A. Robert Smith, who wrote a terrific biography on Morse, aptly titled *The Tiger in the Senate.*

Andrus enjoyed the book years later, especially the part about the Oregon maverick being kicked in the head by a horse at the Montgomery County (Maryland) Fair. The story had some parallels to Andrus' similar incident with Ruthie, his mule, while on an annual elk-hunting foray above Lowman in 1991.

However, by the time Andrus was a senior in high school, another young cutie had pretty well captured his heart, and more than sixty years later, still has it. Carol Mae May, the future Mrs. Cecil D. Andrus, lived a block and a half from the Andrus home in Eugene. When she was a junior high student they noticed each other one day while Andrus was playing in a neighborhood pickup basketball game. A vacant lot abutted the street, where a post with a hoop and backboard had been erected. In the evening, especially during summers, kids from the neighborhood would gather to play games. According to Cece, Carol and some of her girlfriends would come over to flirt with the boys bouncing the round ball.

Years later, Andrus claimed that when he first noticed Carol, "She was much too young for me to be messing around with." He was starting high school and she was just into junior high. But when he was a senior, "Lo and behold, here was this cute sophomore, so I thought, 'Well, why not?' So, we started dating."

Carol was born on her grandparents' farm in Scranton, North Dakota on December 26, 1932. Her parents were living with her grandparents at the time because her father, Russell Hughes, was working there. So the name on her birth certificate is Carol Mae Hughes. Her mother's maiden name was Mildred Mae Downing.

When she was a toddler, Carol's parents divorced and her mother remarried Homer May, who legally adopted Carol. Thereafter, she was known as Carol Mae May, which was the source of a few jokes when she was young. Her half-sister, Sally, was born six and a half years after Carol.

Carol ended up in Oregon because her grandparents, who had homesteaded in North Dakota, found that life on the farm was too challenging. Eventually, they were able to sell the spread, pick up stakes and moved to Eugene, to be followed shortly by Carol's mother and stepfather.

Homer was a jeweler and watchmaker by trade, but he had grown up in a small town. Homer's father was the proverbial big fish in a small pond. He owned pretty much everything in the town, from the bank to the grocery store to the hardware store. When Homer arrived in Eugene, he initially worked for another jeweler.

Carol was twelve when the family moved to Eugene in the summer of 1945, just before she started the eighth grade. Unlike Cece, Carol actually had indoor plumbing in the homes she lived in, first in Scranton and then Bismarck. She attended the Scranton elementary school through the third grade. In Bismarck, she attended the fourth through seventh grades.

When they came to Eugene, her family bought a home at Eighth and Van Buren Streets, just around the corner from the Andrus home. It was a "fixer-upper," but Carol's mother was talented when it came to painting, wallpapering, and covering furniture, and she turned the place into a comfortable home, with an equally nice yard. Carol lived there until she and Cece were married, and several times thereafter when Cece was away in the Navy.

The summer before Andrus entered his senior year, he and brother Steve bought a 1937 Lincoln Zephyr for $600. It was a big, black, shiny four-door sedan with a V-12 engine. The price was a little steep, but immediately after World War II everything was expensive. They removed the V-12 and put in a 1946 Mercury engine, which was a tad smaller than the original. Andrus said he felt like he "could walk around in the new engine there was so much room."

In the beginning, the car was a partnership with Steve, with each having the car on alternating weeks. Steve was then a student at Oregon State in Corvallis and Cece was still in high school. Steve would take the car up to the campus for a week, and then come home for the weekend to drop it off for Cece. Steve would then hitch-hike back to Corvallis or catch a ride back to campus with a friend.

Then Cece would have the big car for his week. "Man, did I feel like a big wheel with that car. Of course, it also made it easier to court Carol because we had wheels and could go places."

Toward the end of his senior year Cece ended up having the car most of the time. Steve was a disciplined student. While education matters came easily for Cece, they came harder for Steve. Both received good grades, but Steve had to work harder for his than his brother. One day Steve told Cece he really wasn't using the car much around campus, that it was largely parked during the week. So he proposed that Cece drive him to Corvallis, buy the gas and shuttle him back home when he wanted to return to Eugene. When Cece had a little extra for gas money in his pocket this deal worked out well.

In December of his senior year, after Cece and Carol had been dating pretty regularly, they started going steady. Cece gave her his class ring and that was the beginning of the end of his independence.

In the fall of 1948, Cece followed Steve's footsteps and enrolled at Oregon State, declaring a major in engineering. Sixteen when he graduated from high school, Cece spent the summer working in a sawmill near Florence on the Oregon coast, driving back to Eugene on the weekends to see Carol. He tried to maintain the same routine after he enrolled at Oregon State, just after his seventeenth birthday.

As many young couples do when faced with the same situation where one is still in high school and the other is away at college, they decided they shouldn't be going steady, each could date others. They pledged to remain friends and said this new arrangement would test the strength of their commitment to each other – just what thousands of other couples have said to each other when confronting the inevitable problems of separating distance.

As Cece put it years later, "It didn't work worth a damn because, truth be told, I couldn't stand the thought of her going out with other guys. I didn't want her going out with anybody else, period. So we stumbled along with this new arrangement for a few months, and then actually broke up altogether for awhile towards the end of my freshman year at Oregon State."

Opportunity and fate intervened following Cece's freshman year. First, he landed an excellent job working for Eugene Water & Electric, the area's large public utility, constructing a substation and climbing power poles. He worked hard most of the summer, saved his money and late in August he proposed to Carol. Thinking neither set of parents would approve, they eloped to Reno and on August 27, 1949, were married. Cece had just turned eighteen and Carol was just sixteen.

They took off for Nevada on a Friday night after Cece got off work. Two acquaintances of theirs, who had been married the year before in Reno in similar circumstances, said they would drive them to Reno since they knew the routine. They sent telegrams back to their parents that simply said: "Married this morning. We'll see you soon."

In reflecting years later, Andrus observed, "We were young, in love, and obviously impetuous. Both of us can be a bit head strong. Realistically, the odds against the marriage surviving were astronomical, but young though we were, I think we both recognized the importance of making and keeping a commitment, and we both recognized that as we grew up together, we hoped to grow together. And we trusted that the Almighty would help us understand the need to work constantly at making the marriage work for each of us."

Andrus knew Carol's parents did not like the idea of his running off and marrying their oldest daughter, but there was never any animosity between them nor were there any adverse consequences. His parents were not thrilled, either, but he had basically been on his own for some time, so from his parents' perspective it mattered little. His brother, Steve, said he would give the marriage about six months.

Andrus likes to say even today that Carol still says whether the marriage makes it remains a "marginal issue." Marginal though it may be, they have managed to make it work for over sixty years. While by no means a record, it has certainly beaten the odds.

Andrus' decision to drop out of college was not taken lightly. He liked attending Oregon State, was good at mathematics, and, like Steve, wanted to be an engineer. Then and today, Oregon State has an excellent reputation for its engineering programs. Andrus was not there on any sort of scholarship. He paid for his tuition, room and board. At the end of his freshman year, though, he did have an outstanding room and board bill of $61. Andrus did not have the money to pay it off, so he borrowed it from Hal. He paid his Dad back after going to work for Eugene Water & Electric.

As a freshman, one had to live in a dorm, but Andrus pledged the Delta Upsilon fraternity and soon was caught up in "frat boy" activities. As usual, he also had a job to help make ends meet, in this case, a dry cleaning route. He would visit dorms, pick up dry cleaning and take it to the local dry cleaning establishment. Three days later he would follow the same route to return the dry cleaning and collect.

Andrus applied the hard lesson he had learned from running a newspaper route where he found so many folks willing to cheat a newspaper boy. In the case of dry cleaning, the customer had to pay cash when he delivered, or they didn't get their clothes back. The route kept him busy four evenings a week, two hours each evening. None of the dorms in those days had elevators, so Andrus charged up and down the stairs. It seemed to him he was constantly in motion but he was making good money.

The dry cleaning route also served to sharpen his communication skills and salesmanship abilities with obvious implications for his political successes years later. It was one of the building blocks and a crucial one at that.

Even though he was in a fraternity, the Delta Upsilons were not the partying types, nor was Oregon State known as a party school. Most of the kids were serious students. Sometimes, there would be little ad hoc get-togethers with a sorority, such as a hay ride, and someone would smuggle along a few bottles of beer. During that year at college Andrus said he was never one to imbibe much.

However, Andrus did develop one bad habit at Oregon State which took him years to break: he started smoking. He hadn't smoked in high school because it was verboten for even so-so jocks like him. At colleges in those days, cigarette companies already knew the truth of the marketing expression "sex sells." They would hire young, good-looking co-eds on the OSU campus who would wear short skirts and get all dolled up, put on small "reader boards", and stand around the quad passing out sample packs of cigarettes. "Well, hell, most young studs would stand around flirting with the girls, take the samples and light up," Andrus recalled.

After winning the governorship, Andrus reflected on the damage done to his lungs and the poor example he was setting for his children. He mustered the fortitude and discipline to be able to quit the habit.

He once stated "it made him more than a little angry" to recognize how unethical and unscrupulous the tobacco companies were. They lured folks and hooked them on what we all know now are truly cancer sticks. How many lives were needlessly shortened by these techniques we will never really know.

As September 1949 came around, though, Cece was "hard up against it," as the expression goes. He had a wife, and no one was subsidizing their marriage. Initially, he kept working for Eugene Water & Electric. "The bloom was still on the rose, and like most newlyweds, we were enjoying getting to know each other." Andrus figured, young as they were, that they could still set up a house. They would get it all squared away, and then he would go back to college, while Carol went to work to help put him through school.

Andrus had a good job, was making sufficient money to rent an apartment and he was putting a few bucks in the bank, saving for the return to college. Then came the Korean War.

*Chapter 4*

# Andrus Serves
# His Country

Cece and Carol had been married about eighteen months when he decided to enlist in the United States Navy. The Korean conflict had dominated much of the news during the latter half of 1950, beginning with the sudden attack in late June by the North Koreans to the successful counter-attack by American-led United Nations forces that pushed the invaders back across the 38th parallel. General Douglas MacArthur, unfortunately, failed to heed a warning from his Commander-in-Chief, President Harry Truman, as well as the Chinese and the Russians, not to approach too closely the Yalu River, the boundary between China and North Korea.

When MacArthur ignored the warnings, Chinese troops quietly infiltrated into North Korea and in November, 1950 launched a devastating counter-attack, catching by surprise the American army and Marine units who had become dangerously over-exposed and over-extended. Heavy casualties resulted.

Almost all of Andrus' buddies from high school and college were either being activated or enlisting. Reflecting later on his enlistment, Andrus said he was raised in a period "when the presidency still enjoyed a great deal of prestige. And when the president points at you like that famous poster of Uncle Sam and says, 'I need you,' well, the patriot genes in my body just told me that it was time to do something for my country."

Carol and he discussed the matter. She wasn't exactly happy at the prospect of being left alone. Andrus, nonetheless, decided he needed to do his duty.

On February 23, 1951, in Eugene, Andrus signed up for a four-year hitch in the United States Navy. Had he realized Carol was already a month into her pregnancy with their first daughter, Tana, he might have thought differently about going into the Navy. But, he was young, headstrong, and felt a patriotic urge to serve his county.

He wanted to be a pilot. The Navy recruiter who signed him was pretty shrewd. He told Andrus he could guarantee him a spot in flight school only if he had had two years of college. With just one year, he said, Andrus would have to join up, go to boot camp, and then to Officer Candidate School. From OCS, he would move to flight school. That sounded good to Andrus, and "I signed my life away."

He was sent to San Diego for thirteen weeks of boot camp. He had a twenty day leave before being sent onto a flight crewmember school in Jacksonville, Florida, for eight weeks. From there, Andrus attended the Navy's radar and communication school in Memphis for eight months. Initially, Andrus held the rank of Airman First Class, but he studied hard and took the service-wide exam to become an Aviation/Electronic Technician Petty Officer 3rd Class.

Andrus was sent to the Naval Air Station at Moffat Field, California, and finally deployment. Andrus was assigned to VP Squadron 17, stationed at Whidbey Island Naval Air Station north of Seattle. While there, he was promoted to Petty Officer 2nd Class. Following months of training, initially in the Navy's version of the B-24 and then the more modern Lockheed P2V Neptune, his unit deployed in early 1953 to Iwakuni, their base on the southern end of the main Japanese island of Honshu.

Carol had joined Cece for the last five months of the eight months they were in Memphis. When he joined his squadron, just after it had returned from a tour in Asia, they had additional months together stateside at Whidbey Island before the squadron was redeployed overseas. They lived in the base's married housing until that redeployment, at which time Carol and Tana, who had been born in Eugene on August 21, 1951, returned to Eugene to stay with her parents.

Becoming a father was a life-altering experience. Andrus recognized with stunning swiftness the responsibility of parenthood. During his parenting years he came to believe that if one is to err on one side or the other of tough love versus indulgence approach, it is better to fall on the side of pouring more love onto a child. It is fair to say that the Andrus daughters, as they grew, in turn adored their dad.

Andrus is truly a man's man – a hunter, fisherman, outdoorsman, competitive, one for whom excellence is the only standard. Andrus is also a talented, natural teacher. Over the years, besides providing much sound instruction to his daughters and grandchildren, he also "adopted" several surrogate sons; young men whom he took a liking to and saw something worth investing his time. As an extraordinary teacher, he was and still is patient in explaining things, as well as helpful in leading one to analyze what went right or wrong, whether a matter is personal and private or public and impersonal. He possessed an extraordinary ability to keep confidences.

Among the numerous surrogate sons he nurtured, one could count Roy Haney, John Hough, Larry Meierotto, Wayne Mittleider, Wally Hedrick, Marc Johnson and me. Not all the surrogates appreciated the finishing course in life skills he was offering; some fell by the wayside. Others, including me, flourished and grew under his skillful mentoring.

Andrus always felt he and Carol were fortunate with regard to Tana's arrival. First, her birth weight was low – three pounds, twelve ounces. While small, she was perfectly formed, so when they put her in the incubator for twenty-one days oxygen wasn't needed. He and Carol later learned that many children placed in incubators with oxygen later suffered eye problems, inducing blindness.

Carol also had taken a drug called DES (diethyl stilbesteriol) during the pregnancy. Later research indicated a causal relationship to the lupus Tana developed in her twenties, which, unfortunately, restricted what she could do in her life. The disease has been manageable in a medical sense, but the family has marveled at the tenacity with which she has handled her condition over the years.

There was one aspect of Tana's twenty-one days in the incubator that Andrus recalls vividly and laughs at now, but at the time it didn't seem so funny. Tana's twenty-one days cost him his 1939 Oldsmobile Coup. When Andrus got the hospital bill, he didn't have the money to pay it. Had Carol given birth to Tana in a naval hospital, everything would have been covered. Instead, Carol gave birth to Tana in a private hospital in Eugene.

When the bill came, Andrus sold the car and got just enough money to pay the hospital bill. He has never been comfortable with accumulating debt. He liked to acquire IOUs, but never wanted to feel beholden financially to any other person. He had learned early from Hal that one pays his bills when they come due, draws up a household budget and lives within one's means. "You don't spend what you don't have," Cece would tell his aides and his budget directors years later as governor.

When he had the opportunity to shape the budget of the state of Idaho when serving as its twenty-sixth governor, he made it clear, though a social liberal, he was a fiscally conservative Democrat. There would be no deficit spending on his watch. "You have to pay as you go and you don't mortgage your children's future by excessive borrowing," he would tell staff. To this day he doesn't carry balances on his credit cards. "When the bill comes, we pay in full. It's the only way to do it."

In the late winter of 1952-53, Andrus headed for his duty station in Japan and to the theater of conflict during the Korean "police action." Andrus and his unit flew what was called the Great Triangle route along the east coast of the Korean Peninsula over the Sea of Japan up the 38th parallel, then east towards Russia's Kamchatka Peninsula before turning south back to the base at Iwakuni. It was a long and arduous flight often taking up to eight hours.

They also flew a route up the west coast of the Korean Peninsula over the Yellow Sea to the 38th parallel and back. It seemed to Cece and his flight mates that they were often on the plane for 18 hours, though that was rarely the case. They usually flew four missions a week. Their duties included tracking submarines, particularly Russian, as well as performing general reconnaissance work. They also checked on various ships, mostly Greek-registered, carrying supplies and material to North Korea. Finally, they engaged in electronic counter-measures including identifying various radar sources as well as conducting electronic eaves-dropping.

Iwakuni was actually an old Japanese air base reportedly used by kamikaze pilots during the latter stages of World War II. When Andrus first arrived, personnel lived in tents until they were moved into the slightly refurbished barracks that used to be inhabited by the kamikaze pilots.

Iwakuni is still a Marine Corps Air Station, one of the few installations the United States still utilizes on any of the main Japanese Islands. The base is located in the Yamaguchi Prefecture in the Nishiki River Delta and faces the Inland Sea. As the crow flies it is only about 30 miles southwest of Hiroshima, which, of course, during the war was one of two Japanese cities destroyed by atomic bombs.

When the Korean War first started, the base was home to units of the British Royal Navy, as well as the U.S. Navy, and the U.S. Air Force. The Air Force took command of the station on April 1, 1952. Numerous sorties supporting troops on the Korean Peninsula were flown every day from Iwakuni and because it also was a processing center for many it was called the "Gateway to Korea." Several months after Andrus arrived, the U.S. Navy officially took over the air station on October 1, 1954.

Andrus had a lot of time during off hours and a lot of off hours to write letters home, (he guesses he and Carol averaged about two letters a week), read books and do some touring. In particular, he enjoyed visiting special places in Japan, some of which, like the ancient city of Kyoto, had been spared from the onslaught of American fire-bombing because of their historical and cultural significance.

Andrus could cite only one close call: a crash landing caused when a landing gear could not be lowered. The crew was able to get out safely.

"It had been a long night flight and the weather was just plain nasty, very stormy," Andrus recalled. "We were landing back at Iwakuni around 2 a.m. A subsequent inquiry into the crash did not resolve the key question of whether our landing gear collapsed upon impact, or whether, for whatever reason, the pilot or coilot failed to make sure the gear was down. The inquiry simply reported that upon inspection of the cockpit by daylight the next day, the lever for lowering the gear was in the down position. It is possible that the hydraulic system driving the landing gear failed, but we'll never know.

"What I did know was all of a sudden I saw lots of sparks flying by my window towards the rear of the plane and heard the loud grating sound of metal scraping concrete. I knew we were doing a belly landing. There were two other crewmates in the aft section with me: the tail gunner and an assistant who worked the electronic gear with me. Immediately, I popped the aft escape hatch over the wings, and we were out the hatch, off the wing, and dashing for safety in case there was fire or an explosion.

"I did remember to grab the code books and the other "top secret" material I was responsible for protecting and/or destroying if we were shot down. Only one crew member was slightly injured, cutting a finger as he dashed from the plane. We easily survived the crash landing, but I wasn't so sure we were going to survive the ambulance ride to the base hospital. In a scene that could have been right out of the *M.A.S.H.* TV series, we were stuffed into this old GI ambulance and bounced all over the place as the driver took off, charging across rice paddies and over berms in a mad but totally unnecessary dash to the hospital.

"We were all thoroughly checked out at sickbay, and then released. Of course, when daylight arrived a couple of hours later, we were back out at the site to look over our plane. It was only then that it became clear that God had truly been our co-pilot.

"To enable us to do the extra long missions, there was a 450-gallon high-octane tank installed in one half of the bomb bay. This tank hung low in the plane. It was wrapped in canvas and tar with a spigot device which had just started to be ground down by contact with the runway as the plane slid along. Had that tank ruptured, and if we had slid another twenty feet, there would have been a disastrous explosion and devastating fire which would have destroyed the plane for sure and easily incinerated many of the crew.

"It only takes one incident like that to make one realize how close to death one can be and how easily and quickly your life can be snatched away. Such incidents tend to make one somewhat of a fatalist – *que sera, sera* – what will be, will be."

Because of his extensive flying in the Navy, Andrus was always a calm air traveler in later years. He liked to turn to aides flying with him, especially on cross-country jaunts, and as the plane landed and taxied to the gate, say "Well, we cheated death again." Over the years he accumulated several million miles in all kinds of aircraft, from the small Piper Cub he flew when first in the Idaho State Senate, to the fancy jets maintained by the Executive Government Flight Service at Andrews Air Force Base outside of D.C., to the King Airs and Aero Commanders he flew out of the Boise Interagency Fire Base when traveling as Interior Secretary.

34

One other incident while in the Navy brought home how often one's future is beyond one's control. Andrus and his crewmates were flying the Great Triangle route on a mission early in his tour of duty when a radar station warned that Chinese or Russian MIG fighter jets were rapidly approaching their position. The pilot took evasive action, diving the plane towards the sea deck. That afforded some protection because the MIG pilots were skittish about getting close to the sea, where they could lose depth perception and crash. The maneuver succeeded.

Upon return to Iwakuni, Andrus and some of the other crew members took flare cans, stuffed whiskey bottles in them with padding and when they next made a run on the same route swung by the radar station that had flagged the warning. They parachuted the booze down to the site as a token of appreciation.

Chance, fate, kismet - whatever one may want to call it - intervened one other time for Andrus in the Korean theater. His squadron, designated VP-17, rotated missions with VP-21, a squadron based at Barber Point, Hawaii. For some unknown reason, the squadrons switched runs one week along the east coast of the Korean Peninsula. Andrus' squadron completed its run without incident, but the next night the plane from VP-21 was shot down by enemy fighters on what would have been his regular run. Several crew members lost their lives.

The incident was protested, but the Russians claimed the plane had violated Russian air space. Andrus thought it was saber-rattling, plain and simple, and intuitively understood that a longer "Cold War" between the United States and Russia was beginning to take shape, a supposed non-shooting war that would last thirty years more.

During his almost two-year deployment in the Korean theater, Andrus went by the nickname of "Andy." Crews tended to take one's last name and make a nickname of it, a form of a long *nom de guerre* tradition throughout history, so just as their ordinance man, one Thomas Edward Martin, was known as "Marty," Cece was "Andy."

As mentioned earlier, during his leave time, Andrus enjoyed traveling to Kyoto, the historical capital of Japan when its politics were dominated by the strong shoguns that manipulated the figurehead Emperors and ran Japan. Over the centuries, these powerful war lords constantly jockied for dominance until one family in particular, the

Tokugawa clan, won and transformed Japan into a modern power following American Admiral Perry's visit in 1854.

As some historians have pointed out, General Douglas MacArthur, the Supreme Allied Commander in the Pacific theater following the end of World War II, understood and played well the role of the new "shadow shogun," the power behind the throne of Emperor Hirohito for six years following the war. Cece, with hindsight, said he understood now that MacArthur's ego got the better of him and his arrogance in disobeying a direct order from President Truman left Truman no choice but to fire the general in April of 1951, just a few months after Andrus had enlisted, at a dramatic meeting between the President and his Pacific Theater shogun on Wake Island.

At the time, Andrus, like many of his colleagues, was angry with the President. To many in the military, the action appeared to be one of pique on the President's part, and an exercise in "who was the king of the mountain" that overlooked the best strategic interests of the country. The passage of time has vindicated Truman's judgment with historians now wondering what took him so long.

In November, 1952, he cast his first presidential ballot for General Dwight D. Eisenhower, the first and only time he ever cast a presidential vote for a Republican. He later said he voted for Ike over former Illinois Governor Adlai Stevenson because Ike promised to end the Korean War. The more Andrus saw of the military life and conflict, the more the idea of bringing the troops home seemed like a good idea to one "Andy" Andrus.

While Andrus revealed Ike to be the only Republican presidential candidate he ever voted for, he supported, sometimes publicly, other Republicans for other offices when he felt the person a superior candidate and one capable of being the better public servant. He always was a strong admirer of Washington's three-term Republican Governor, Dan Evans, who he thought was one of the nation's finest governors. In addition, Andrus greatly respected Oregon's two-term Republican Governor, Tom McCall. He considered himself privileged to have served over-lapping terms with McCall and Evans. "They were both extraordinarily capable chief executives," he told reporters on multiple occasions. Andrus was particularly honored and personally touched when both GOP governors broke party ranks and supported his successful bid for re-election to Idaho's governorship in 1974.

One of the most extraordinary and successful fundraising events ever held in Idaho occurred in March of 1974, when 1,500 people jammed themselves into the Rodeway Inn's convention center in Boise for an evening of entertainment and political speeches. Headlining the event were Hollywood stars Jack Cassidy and Shirley Jones, followed by Las Vegas entertainer Wayne Newton, who wowed the crowd with his complete show. Governor McCall led the political speakers including Idaho's senior senator Frank Church and the witty remarks of Arizona's droll congressman Morris Udall. It was an evening those who attended will never forget and the presence of the Oregon governor made it respectable for the many Republicans present to take out their checkbooks.

Andrus returned the favor by endorsing and campaigning for Dan Evans when he ran for the U.S. Senate for the five years remaining in Scoop Jackson's senate term following the legendary senator's untimely death in 1983. Governor McCall was already in his second term and Andrus did not have the opportunity to return the favor as he did not again run for public office. Had he done so, Andrus would have been in his corner.

Even in Idaho state politics, Andrus never made any secret of the fact he respected and voted for long-time Secretary of State Pete Cenarrusa, as well as successor Ben Ysursa, both Basque-Americans and lifelong Republicans. Those who know Andrus well, suspect there were a few other Republicans he voted for. The suspects would be U.S. Senators Len B. Jordan and James A. McClure, men Andrus greatly admired for their leadership qualities and bipartisanship when the best interests of Idaho were at stake. It is no coincidence that after Jordan retired from the Senate in 1972, then-Governor Andrus proposed naming a new state office building after the former governor and the ten-year senator.

It was during the Korean War that Andrus says he first began developing a political philosophy. About that time, he started referring to himself as a "Harry Truman Democrat". That meant being a plain-speaking, lunch-bucket Democrat who believed government has a constructive role within society, but also that it must live within its means. He especially liked the sign on President Truman's desk that read, "The buck stops here."

In later years, Andrus would reflect on what he learned in the Navy that was helpful to him in his political career. The most obvious influence was the simple fact of being a veteran. "Most people rightly respect those who dedicate some of their life's precious and limited time to serving their nation and their countrymen in the armed forces. Veterans stand in a long line of citizens who have chosen to bear arms in defense of the American way of life.

"It is an implicit recognition that one owes this great nation something, and that one should live for something besides his own personal aggrandizement. I deplore that there are so few veterans in high public office these days. For me, it holds little wonder that so little gets done by a Congress largely populated by folks who, usually with malice aforethought, have deliberately avoided military service, and have by such choices and actions demonstrably put their own personal ambitions first.

"Whenever anyone has other people he is responsible for and has to manage, commanding their respect is critical. Such respect only comes by having an ability to listen very carefully to what another is saying. While the regular chain of command in the military ensures obedience, it is one thing to have an order obeyed, and quite another to command the respect of those in subordinate roles."

Andrus felt that it was in the Navy where he began to hone that most critical of political skills: an ability to listen carefully, to focus his full attention on the person speaking, look them in the eye, and then respond thoughtfully.

"We've all seen political office holders or office seekers who work a room, giving one a hearty greeting, a handshake, a 'Hello, how are you doing?' and the entire time they are looking over your shoulder to see if there is someone more important in the room to whom they should be talking, someone who is a bigger contributor, who is more influential."

Andrus was different. Early on, he intuitively understood the importance of listening, and remembering names. "Nothing is more important to most people than to hear their name mentioned by someone in high office," he once noted to an aide. "For some reason, it momentarily gives them a validation of their existence and provides a source of satisfaction. Indirectly, it gives them a feeling of sharing in the elected person's accomplishments."

For whatever reason, Andrus has been blessed with an exceptional memory for names. As his press secretary, I saw this talent put to great use for years. It never ceased to amaze me how many people the Governor knew on a first-name basis, whether supporters or not. During my time working for him in Idaho, I carried what I called the "black book", a list of elected officials in the forty-four Idaho counties. The book also contained the names and numbers of the media in each county, as well as local Democratic Party officials down to precinct captains, and all the Governor's major contributors. Almost all the names had phone numbers. Cece never had to look at it. I had to study the book diligently.

Only rarely would I realize that Cece was not immediately recalling a person's name. In such rare instances I would quickly jump in with a sentence or a phrase using the person's name, which Cece then wove into his response to the person, who never had a clue. In ten years of working and traveling with Cece, this temporary blank moment occurred less than a half dozen times.

What was especially impressive was his ability to recall people's names away from their natural surroundings. I might recall Floyd Jensen while we were in Bear Lake County, but have Floyd walk into the office in Boise and I'd be dumbstruck. And just about then, the Governor would burst out the door, see Floyd, who had just dropped by and wasn't on the schedule, and he would say "Well, hello Floyd. What the heck brought you all the way to the big city?"

Andrus received an honorable discharge from the Navy on February 21, 1955, two days short of four full years, and about a month after his return from Japan. He had five campaign ribbons on his uniform, wings, and a United Nations medal. He also received a "Good Conduct" medal, of which he once said, "Let's just say there was never a 'Captain's Mast' that was officially recorded that involved me."

The comment indicates there may have been one or two instances where his conduct was not as exemplary as it should have been, but that instead of a formal hearing on misconduct (such as a brawl in a bar perhaps), his superior officers let him off the hook with just a chewing out.

Despite his solid record of service during the Korean War, many years later, his Republican opponents still questioned aspects of it. In his comeback campaign for governor in 1986, the GOP seized upon one word in a biographical sketch written by a reporter who described Andrus as an "aviator" and tried to foster the impression with the public that Cece was exaggerating his military role, misleading the public by insinuating he had been a pilot.

The fact that Cece's campaign literature made no such claim that he was a pilot, and that he always described his service as that of a naval aviator/aviation crewman, made no difference to the Republican spinmeisters seeking to denigrate his character and distort his record. It amazed Cece, though, that even an exemplary record could be misrepresented.

In retrospect, Andrus may have let this seemingly minor issue fester longer than he should have. He long ago had learned the lesson that in politics one has to rebut falsehoods and phony charges immediately, and that a charge unrebutted can often become a charge believed. This was an absolute to be followed if a charge could be seen as reflecting on one's character or personal ethics. A candidate's word and the perception that one could be trusted to tell the truth, were in his mind absolutely critical to establishing a bond of trust with his constituents.

During his long political career, nothing would arouse his ire faster than someone challenging his integrity. For him, integrity was the *sine qua non*: to provide leadership, one must be trusted by his constituents. Any form of deceit or lying, regardless of how trivial it might seem, eroded that trust. He expected people to honor their word. If they did not, he never forgot it and, if possible, would not deal with them again.

On that February day in 1955, Andrus received the standard $300 the Navy gave departing seamen along with his discharge papers. He set his sights on Eugene and reuniting with Carol and Tana. Initially, he had a sawmill job lined up. Shortly thereafter, though, his dad called with an offer to go to work for him and some other partners at a sawmill they were building in a place unfamiliar to Andrus: Orofino, Idaho, the county seat of Clearwater County and a town of about 3300 souls perched along the Clearwater River forty miles upstream from Lewiston.

In April of 1955, Cece loaded Carol and Tana in their car, and headed for their new home in what was to become his adoptive state. He never had an inkling that he would become the longest serving, and greatest governor in Idaho's history.

## Chapter 5

# The First Race

Orofino is one of many small towns dotting Idaho that owe their existence to what Andrus labels the base of society's economic pyramid: resource conversion. Though he never took an economics class, Cece always intuitively understood that what brought new dollars into an economy was the conversion of trees into lumber, minerals into metals, and wheat into bread.

Orofino was a timber town. At one time before the recession of the early 1960s, there were nine sawmills operating in the Orofino area. The town grew because the postwar nation was experiencing a housing boom as thousands of veterans, like Cece, scrimped and saved to buy their first home.

Orofino also owed its existence in part to the fact that the state of Idaho had sited one of two state mental institutions there. The town fathers, following the establishment of the hospital, renamed the high school teams the "Maniacs." Even today, the town has refused to acquiesce to political correctness and rename its sports teams though the community no longer hosts a mental institution. Today the site is a correctional facility.

Orofino has a sprinkling of churches, several for Protestants and one for the Catholics. Cece and Carol joined the Lutheran Church. The comings and goings of the town and county have long been noted and recorded in the pages of the weekly newspaper, *The Clearwater Tribune.* (A running joke in the region was that the population stayed the same because every time a baby was born a man left town.).

When the Andrus family got to Orofino, all they could find for housing was a basement apartment in the home of one of the town's bankers. As an employee of Tru-Cut Lumber, Cece was paid $600 a month, decent money in those days, but he often worked seven days a week, sometimes twelve hours a day as a foreman and a millwright. On weekends, he would work in the woods as a gypo logger, falling timber which would be taken by a skidder or a long-line jammer to a landing.

Andrus never expressed anything but pride in his hands-on, working knowledge of what he called the "slab, sliver, and knothole business," though he confessed that in his youthful ignorance, he did skid fallen logs down stream beds before he really understood the damage he was doing.

He also came face-to-face with greed and dishonesty when he opened a "passbook savings accounts" in his landlord's bank. A few months later, bank auditors discovered the banker had been dipping into the savings accounts of some of the depositors, including Cece. By the time the fraud was exposed, Andrus had lost $800 from his account, which the bank eventually made good.

Andrus waited the obligatory six months after moving to Orofino before obtaining his Idaho hunting license and shooting an elk that first fall. Every year he lived in Orofino he bagged both an elk and a deer, which provided extra meat for the family larder. On February 10, 1956, they added another young mouth, when daughter Tracy was born at St. Joseph's Hospital in Lewiston.

Andrus looks back on those Orofino years with fondness. He was making good money, new friends, and he and Carol were becoming active in their community. He joined the local chapter of the Veterans of Foreign Wars, in part because they had a hall and a nice bar where one could gather with other veterans to reminisce, and because it was a good social outlet.

The VFW gang liked to have a good time. Once, as part of the Post's annual "beauty contest" to raise money for fighting polio, he got all "dolled up" for a skit. Years later, he laughingly told an interviewer, "Thank goodness no pictures exist. My political career might have ended pretty early. And thank goodness no pictures exist of me from an occasional brawl I got into now and then."

Maybe it was part of the logger mystique. Maybe Andrus still had a bit of a temper. Whatever the reason, this was a period when Cece would take only so much from someone who made the mistake of suggesting they step outside and settle their differences. Cece recalled one morning, following a bout in the alley outside of one of Orofino's local watering holes, when he awoke, looked at himself in the mirror, and blanched. His face was all roughed up, he had a cut lip and he couldn't help saying to himself, "Lord Almighty-and you *won* the fight!"

Years later, when walking the streets of Orofino as part of his gubernatorial outreach effort called "Capitol For A Day," he bumped into the adversary from that particular fight. They exchanged pleasantries, and he turned to me and recounted the last time the two had met. Like he said, fortunately there were no pictures from those days, but the truth of the matter is that in Idaho that kind of past would only have burnished his stature further in the eyes of many independent Idahoans.

Cece served two terms as commander of Harold Kinne VFW Post 3296. The friendships he formed served him well, as his fellow VFW members formed the core of his early supporters when he ran for the state senate. Other friendships established while playing on the town baseball team also provided him with the early vital support for public office.

Bill Harris, a fellow member of the VFW post, and the Ponozzo brothers, Les and Don, with whom he played baseball, were key early political supporters. The Andruses also became good friends with Marilyn and Bill Crutcher, both of whom joined his first administration in Boise. Another wonderfully supportive individual was the then Democratic County chairman, Ray McNichols, who Cece helped become a federal district judge later in his career.

While Andrus often would tell folks he was a "political accident," (see his book *Cecil Andrus: Politics Western Style* published by Sasquatch Books, Chapter One, page 9) he later acknowledged that the line made for a good story, and helped counter the image of a young, on-the-make, and ambitious political aspirant that plagues many seeking office. His entry into the political realm was actually more focused on a single issue than it was due to ambition.

A few of his friends, parents like he and Carol with young children getting ready to start school, were not happy with the Orofino school system. Not only were there no kindergartens, but overall state support for education was badly allocated, with larger school districts in more populated areas receiving far more state dollars on a per-pupil basis than smaller, rural districts. Andrus felt the playing field needed to be levelled, regardless of locale or population.

The incumbent state senator was Republican Leonard Cardiff. He had served ten years and, in Andrus' view, had not shown proper support for public education. Cardiff was a man in his mid-sixties and set in his ways. His response to the parents' expression of concern was the schools were good enough for me when I was growing up, and they are good enough for your kids.

That didn't go over well with Andrus and his compatriots. "Being young, and full of vim and vigor, I was more mouth than brains, and pretty loudly, in several places around town, denounced the incumbent state senator's lack of support for public education," Andrus recalled.

It was fellow VFW member and World War II veteran Bill Harris who first started floating the idea he ought to run for the state senate. Cece said initially he was flattered but did not give it serious thought, in part because he had never been to Boise, let alone seen a legislature in action. However, he had started to develop an interest in politics, enough to volunteer to serve as his precinct committeeman.

When some Clearwater County Republicans heard Andrus might be a candidate, many laughed and scoffed at his pretensions. In their eyes, he was just a twenty-eight-year-old independent mill operator and gypo logger who shot off his mouth too often and had only lived in the community a few years.

After talk of his possible candidacy began to circulate, Cece bumped into the local GOP county chairman, Bob Oud, at the hardware store.

"Hey, Cece," Oud said. "Understand some of your VFW buddies want you to run for the Legislature but you told them no. Is that correct?" Andrus told Oud that was indeed the case. Then Oud threw down the gauntlet: "Well, it's a good thing you're not, because we would have beaten the hell out of you!"

"Well, we'll see about that," Andrus responded, and apocryphal as it sounds, marched straight to the wrong office in the courthouse, seeking to find out where and how to file. The county treasurer nicely directed him to the clerk's office.

Andrus recalls the filing fee being $5. He went home to tell Carol of his decision and, not surprisingly, she wasn't thrilled with the idea of Cece becoming a politician, without her consultation. Cece later conceded he understood her reluctance, though at the time he was disappointed that his first and most important supporter had not immediately jumped on the bandwagon.

"Most wives in this world understandably crave security and take seriously their nurturing role both for their spouses and for their children," he said. "By definition, politics is full of uncertainty and controversy. It takes an exceptional spouse to tolerate it, let alone like it. Because one's spouse knows one better than anyone else, she has an innate ability to keep one humble and in one's place. As an office seeker one tries to project a certain image to the electorate of competence, capability and compassion, but a spouse all too often is aware of one's 'feet of clay,' and the insecurities that confront most mere mortals."

Another factor contributing to Carol's less than enthusiastic response was that she was again pregnant with the couple's third child, daughter Kelly, who was born a little less than two weeks before the end of that first campaign on October 20, 1960, also at St. Joseph's in Lewiston.

Despite his spouse's reticence, Andrus set about putting together a campaign and working it for all it was worth. Andrus' lack of experience was offset by his seemingly unwavering energy, enthusiasm, passion, ability to listen, a great memory for names and an incredible desire to win.

Andrus hates losing at anything. Plain and simple, he is one of those intensely competitive personalities who cannot stand to lose, whether a game of checkers, cards, or friendly wagers on political races or sporting events. To him, life is all about competing. He is almost Darwinian in his belief that life really is all about the "survival of the fittest." He once kept two of his staff playing a game of hearts for hours as they flew across the broad expanse of the Pacific Ocean in 1979 because he was behind. They played and played and played until Andrus finally went ahead, at which point the exhausted staffers threw in the towel and proclaimed him the winner some twelve hours after they had begun.

He is the same when it comes to golf, though he is a duffer who is delighted to break one-hundred. But Andrus knows everyone's handicap, and usually walks away with most of the money. He even once had his press secretary put together a booklet to hand out to golfing partners. To wit:

Rule 1 – The Governor never loses! Rule 2 – The Governor can cheat to ensure victory! See Rule 1!

Shortly after the campaign began Cece found an old 1937 labor handbook on politics which he read carefully and followed scrupulously. It laid out the importance of breaking one's district or political subdivision down into blocks and methodically knocking on doors until one had covered all the precincts. In the evenings and on weekends, Andrus tracked down voters wherever they were, from residential areas of Orofino to homes up the hollows, and canyons around the county. Where two or three people were gathered you would find, Cece in the middle making his pitch. He also didn't have a campaign manager, or treasurer. He did not have to file a campaign expenditure report detailing who contributed, how much they gave, who employed them, or their occupation. Times have certainly changed.

As Andrus reminisced about that first race he marveled at how much shoe leather he put into that campaign and how little it cost. Besides the $5 filing fee, Andrus spent $6 more to get a bunch of business cards printed with his picture and the simple words "Elect Cecil D. Andrus State Senator." He didn't have a slogan and, to this day, can't recall that he had the word "Democrat" on the cards. He was sure he didn't have the union mark on the cards, something in the future he would never neglect. Unions across the state became one of the mainstays of his future statewide campaigns.

As he worked the county, if he found someone wasn't at home he would write a short note on the business card to let them know he had been there and then stick it in their door. However, he also performed a more literal "card drop" that has become somewhat of a legend.

Having obtained his pilot's license shortly after moving to Orofino, Cece rented a single engine airplane at the Orofino Airport and flew northeast to an isolated timber community called Headquarters, which was nothing more than a big logging camp maintained by the Potlatch Company. He flew low over Headquarters several times to draw attention to his presence, then swooped low again and dropped a bunch of his campaign cards out the window.

Over the some fifty-plus years of his political career, Andrus has had a mixed relationship with the Potlatch Company. Some years, the company supported him, and some years they did not. Potlatch's unions always supported him, more with money than with volunteers. The company's outside legal counsel, Wynne Blake, was an early, ardent supporter.

Potlatch is the largest private timber owner and mill operator in the region and has always wielded great influence. Over the years, the giant timber company, its leadership, and Andrus demonstrated mutual respect for each other. From time to time, they would see eye to eye on some issues, but just as often they would not. The fact that Andrus was always popular with the Potlatch unions' leadership was proof enough that those closest to the scene never viewed him as a yes-man for Potlatch's political positions.

Potlatch did make corporate contributions to some of his races, but there were years when it didn't. Andrus heard stories early in his career that Potlatch was in fact quietly supporting his candidacy, likely due to an incident in the first run he made for governor when some of his large yard signs were made with Potlatch plywood. When people saw the Potlatch logo on the back of the sign, they just drew the wrong conclusion.

The truth of the matter was that by the time Andrus was in the state senate, Potlatch had driven eight of the nine independent sawmills in Clearwater County out of business, including Hal Andrus' sawmill, Tru-Cut Lumber.

The demise of Tru-Cut Lumber, unfortunately, led to a painful, but temporary, rupture between Cece and his dad. Even with the passage of years, it is hard for Cece to look back on the rupture in the relationship and not feel some pain. The bottom line, though, is that Cece feels to this day he was correct and Hal was wrong.

The sawmill's demise later lead to completely false accusations by Republican opponents that he and his Dad had declared bankruptcy. The implication, of course, was how could one aspire to run a state's budget if he couldn't keep a business solvent. As noted with his service record, truth is often the first casualty in a campaign. Despite evidence to the contrary, operatives for the Republican Party clearly tried to besmirch Andrus' reputation during his first campaign for governor in 1966.

Echoes of it would be heard in later whispering campaigns during his other runs for governor. It reminded Cece of the lesson learned long ago when Hal told them about throwing cow pies against the barn wall – hardly any of that kind of thing ever stuck because of its nature.

Andrus, with foresight about such later political ramifications, knew the issue of the mill closure had to be handled differently than his Dad wanted to handle it. He knew folks would draw different conclusions, but not being a partner or a shareholder he had no say in the matter and his father did not listen to him. The result was a rupture in the father/son relationship that lasted several years. Hal worked diligently to repay and did repay every one of his creditors.

In mid-May 1960, Cece encountered one of those rare transformational moments where everything falls into place and he was never the same again. The galvanizing event was a Democratic political dinner at the Lewis-Clark Hotel in Lewiston, Idaho, where the featured speaker was a young, dynamic United States Senator seeking the party's presidential nomination: John F. Kennedy. The presidential aspirant had flown into Lewiston in his campaign plane, "The Caroline," named after his young daughter, to give a speech before continuing on to Portland for appearances related to the Oregon presidential primary, which he subsequently won.

Andrus later said he could not recall exactly what was said that evening, but he did know he was inspired by what he heard and conclusively thought to himself, "By God, I really am doing the right thing in seeking public office. If that young man can be elected President of the United States, I can be elected state senator."

For Cece Andrus that night, public service became less a duty and more a true calling. The young logger responded to the call made the following January by the newly elected President in his memorable inaugural speech when he challenged all Americans to "ask not what your country can do for you; ask what you can do for your country!"

"JFK helped to instill in me the notion that to serve the public is a high calling, can be a noble endeavor and it helped me to understand that people place trust in leaders who can inspire them to answer their better sides; and, most of all, people elect others to high office whom they believe can help solve problems. Those notions and *inspirations*, if you will, have stayed with me ever since that night."

In February of 2008, Andrus was to have a comparable experience, which occurred almost fifty years after hearing JFK. As the former four-term governor of Idaho and the former one-term Secretary of the Interior under Jimmy Carter, Cece was asked to introduce another young, dynamic, articulate, inspiring U.S. senator seeking the party's presidential nomination, the junior Senator from Illinois, Barack Obama. More than 14,000 Idahoans jammed into the Boise State University pavilion to hear him. Thousands more were turned away.

Andrus said it sent chills up and down his spine and gave him the kind of goose bumps he had not experienced since listening to John Kennedy almost fifty years earlier. It was the same message of hope and change, but delivered to a new generation of Americans. Barack Obama was offering new leadership which would take on the challenge of bringing people together with a promise to end the divisive partisanship that had characterized the early years of the 21st Century. He was pledging to unite the American people in a renewed pursuit of the "newer world" JFK's equally articulate brother, Robert F. Kennedy, spoke so eloquently about before he too was cut down by an assassin's bullet.

As Andrus listened to Obama, he looked into the faces of a diverse array of people assembled, and saw what he had not seen in years, "people renewing their faith in the future of the nation, realizing once again there was standing before them a leader in whom they could place faith and trust, someone worthy of that trust, a person who understood the power of words and the importance of delivering on what he was saying and the equally important need to not corrupt the language with spin phrases designed to divide rather than unite."

As Andrus' first campaign began to unfold in the summer of 1960, it began to dawn on Senator Cardiff that he was going to lose. Not wishing to be ousted and preferring to retire "undefeated," Cardiff withdrew from the race. Clearwater Republicans then named as their nominee "Buss" Durant, who owned a mercantile and grocery store in the nearby town of Pierce.

It became increasingly clear, though, as summer turned to fall that Andrus was going to win. He didn't let up, though, keeping his foot on the peddle. He knew there's only one way to run, and that is full bore, full tilt until Election Day.

As Election Day drew closer, Cece began to hear reports that "Buss" was telling folks that if he won, he was going to get drunk, and if he lost, he was going to get drunk, so he had better get started. Buss did almost all of his campaigning the final weeks sitting on a bar stool. Cece crushed him, winning with over 70% of the vote.

At the age of twenty-nine, Cece Andrus became the youngest person, at that time, ever elected to the Idaho State Senate.

*Chapter 6*

# A Newly Minted
# State Senator

In late December 1960, Carol and Cece left their children with his
mother and drove down "the goat trail," as U.S. Highway 95 was
then called, to find a place to live in Boise during the upcoming
session of the Idaho Legislature. Neither had ever set foot in Boise,
nor did they know another soul in Idaho's capital city, then a rather
small town of some 35,000 people. They found a sparsely furnished
apartment with a small kitchenette unit in what was then called Boise
Hills Village. Their primary transportation mode was a 1957 hard-top,
four-door Pontiac Chieftain. They loaded the car with Kelly's crib and
a high chair for Tracy and off they went to spend the next three months
in Boise.

Boise was not yet the dynamic and vibrant city of 200,000 it is
today. Boise State University was still a junior college. Its transforma-
tion into a modern, research-oriented university was something Cece
Andrus would help guide during his two stints covering four terms and
fourteen years as governor of Idaho. Nor did there exist a Micron or a
Hewlett-Packard, major high tech industries today, which, along with
a growing workforce of state employees, have played critical roles in
the subsequent expansion of the state's economy, again due in part to
economic policies authored by Andrus.

The Idaho Legislature then met every other year for sixty days.
While in session, legislators were paid the princely sum of $10 a day.
The theory was not to encourage legislators to spend too much time in
town enacting laws that would only complicate people's lives.

Andrus took to the work like the proverbial duck to water. He carefully read every bill so that he would know what he was talking about

if he rose to debate it. He also listened to and cultivated relationships with the legislative elders, veterans and old bulls. He wisely selected certain senators, like Shoshone County's Arthur "Pop" Murphy, who was respected on both sides of the aisle, to be his mentors.

The Legislative Class of 1960 turned out to be one of the most distinguished ever, with several of its members, besides Andrus, going on to serve in higher public office. This group included a young Republican from Payette County, James A. McClure, who later served six years in the U.S. House and 18 years in the U.S. Senate. While they crossed swords in the Legislature and later when Andrus was governor and Interior Secretary and McClure was in the Senate and chairing the Interior committee, they also could and did cooperate on issues.

Other members of the illustrious 1960 class included Idaho County's Bill Dee, Benewah County's Cy Chase, Bonner County's Don Samuelson, Bonneville County's Orval Hansen, Madison County's Dick Smith; and Ada County's Bill Roden. Dee, Samuelson and Smith ran for governor against Andrus in 1966; Orval Hansen served as the Second District's Congressman for two terms; Chase served as Democratic Senate Minority leader several times, and Roden became one of the state's most successful "super lobbyists."

Of all his new colleagues, though, Andrus most admired Shoshone County State Senator "Pops" Murphy, who taught him several invaluable lessons.

Early in the session, Andrus had his first succcess as his first bill was passed and signed into law by then Governor Robert E. Smylie. It was a bill designed to curb unscrupulous Christmas tree operators who would raid state lands and harvest vast numbers of trees, while not paying a cent to the state, and then selling the trees to the public. Everything these tree thieves reaped was essentially pure profit. Cece's bill limited any one person to no more than two Christmas trees a year off state land and effectively put the tree predators out of business.

"I was speaking, quite eloquently I thought, about the merits of the bill, when I was asked to yield the floor for a minute for a clarifying question from State Senator Tony Nagle, a rancher from southern Idaho. Nagle asked me whether this bill was like an anti-rustling bill and I responded 'Yes, Senator, but without the hide and the horns!' That brought more than a few chuckles," Andrus recalled.

"I continued to speak, when all of a sudden I felt a tap on my shoulder from Senator Murphy, who sat behind me, and he passed me a note. It read 'Sit down and shut up. You got the votes to pass it!' I was so taken aback I could think of nothing better to do than to read his note aloud and tell my colleagues I was taking his advice – and I sat down and shut up. And of course the bill passed overwhelmingly."

Andrus' committee assignments that first session were the Business Committee and the Education Committee, on which he had diligently sought to be placed. He started working almost from the first day he arrived on putting a sparcity factor into the state's education fund formula for distributions to school districts. That Andrus succeeded as a rookie legislator is a testament to how well he listened, how helpful his mentors were, and how quickly he mastered the art of legislating. Patience and adaptability to changing circumstances were also necessary ingredients, as well as the too often unappreciated "c" word, compromise. Andrus persevered though with his major concession being a willingness to break his original education bill into two separate measures. Both were approved.

The fruits of Andrus' early success became apparent when he stood for re-election in 1962. He drew no opposition. Likewise, in 1964, he ran unopposed. Andrus did, however, come out of the woods, so to speak, in 1964 -- he changed jobs. He went to work for the Worker's Comp Exchange, an entity which handled worker compensation claims for employees in northern Idaho's lumber and logging industries. It was his first exposure to the insurance world.

Ironically, the executive director of the Exchange was Roland Wilber, a person who was deeply involved in Republican politics serving as the state national committeeman and also functioning as a fundraiser for Republican candidates. Quite conservative by nature, Wilber was to gain some notoriety later when he joined forces with the national committeewoman for the state, Gwen Barnett. Both Wilber and Barnett despised the incumbent Republican Governor, Bob Smylie, and both played significant roles in backing Sandpoint state Senator Don Samuelson's successful primary challenge of the incumbent governor in 1966.

When Andrus asked for a leave of absence to mount his own gubernatorial race in 1966, Wilber left him with the impression that if not successful Cece would be welcomed back to his old job. This turned out to not be the case and Andrus always felt that Wilber had deliberately misled him.

Because Cece had no opposition in his 1964 race, the Senate Democratic Caucus and the State Democratic Party designated him to become a traveling campaigner who would stump for candidates who asked for some outside support. This assignment led to one of his favorite stories.

He was invited to campaign in Valley County for Harry Nock from Cascade, who was running against Warren Brown, the scion of a lumber and sheep-raising family in McCall. Even though there were only eight registered voters in the little burg of Yellow Pine, some 50 miles east of Highway 95 and on the western edge of an Idaho wilderness area, Andrus convinced Nock that they should load a supply of beer in an ice tub in the trunk of Cece's '57 Pontiac and drive to Yellow Pine and campaign.

On election night of 1964, the Yellow Pine election officials reported to the county elections office twelve votes for Harry Nock, and none for Warren Brown. The clerk taking the call reportedly said "but there are only eight registered voters in your precinct!"

Back came the response, "I'm telling you, we have twelve votes for Harry Nock and none for Warren Brown!" The result stood and Harry Nock won the seat by six votes.

Later, when serving as governor, Andrus appointed Nock to the State Public Utilities Commission. Warren Brown later won back the Senate seat and served several terms with distinction. One suspects, though, that a certain bitterness over his first race was never far from the front of his mind when dealing with the administration of Cecil D. Andrus.

Despite Andrus' success in the 1961 session in equalizing the sparcity factor, a larger and more divisive issue began to emerge in the 1963 and 1965 legislative sessions, one around which the 1966 and 1970 races for governor would also revolve. For Andrus and other progressives, it was clear that Idaho had to provide more funding for public education. His bills helped equalize education funding, but they equalized the distribution of an all too scarce resource. Cece and others, both Republicans and Democrats, realized the state of Idaho had to increase the size of the revenue pie.

54

The solution though was fraught with risk and controversy. Idaho, in Andrus' estimation, had to adopt the third leg of a sound tax policy stool – a sales tax, the majority of which would go to increase the state's support for public education. This solution was opposed by many, not just because it was a new tax, but also because it could adversely impact business in communities that bordered Oregon, which did not have a sales tax.

The issue came to a head in the 1965 session of the Idaho Legislature, considered by most political observers to be the most historic in all of Idaho's 120 plus years of statehood.

Opposition to the proposed sales tax, and to even putting the proposition before the voters, came not only from traditional anti-tax Republicans, but also from conservative Democrats and lobbyists for major businesses who did not want to pay more for the goods and services they purchased. Among these powerful lobbyists was Tom Boise from Lewiston, who skillfully raised funds for favored candidates in northern Idaho and exerted a tremendous amount of political influence. Boise's clients opposed any new tax and Boise expected beholden legislators from Idaho's ten northern counties to toe the line.

In an act of political courage, Andrus, alone among north Idaho Democrats, stood up for public education, and passage of the sales tax, and in the process defied the political boss of north Idaho. Andrus' vote provided the one-vote margin on the first roll call to put the sales tax measure on the ballot in 1966. For Cece, this bravery would have ramifications, both good and bad, for his gubernatorial ambitions in 1966. One thing for certain, it earned him the undying enmity of Tom Boise.

When Cece got home on the night of that historic vote, he told Carol he thought his career in politics was over, but that he had voted for better funding for education and for more opportunity for Idaho's children. His conscience was clear.

In most circumstances, Andrus never carried a grudge, recognizing that today's opponent may of necessity be tomorrow's ally. Tom Boise, though, was in a different category almost by himself. The enmity ran deep and Cece neither forgot nor forgave the animosity he felt Boise held for him.

It was Tom Boise, after all was said and done, who personally recruited anti-sales tax and conservative Democratic State Senator

Charles Herndon from Salmon to run against and ultimately to narrowly defeat Andrus in the August 1966, Democratic gubernatorial primary. Boise also helped to raise funds for Herndon's race.

In early October of 1966, Boise lay dying in a Spokane hospital. His soon to be widow reached Cece on the campaign trail and asked him to visit Tom. Cece declined the request. On October 10, at the age of eighty-one, the long-time political boss of northern Idaho died.

Andrus was one of the first to use the analogy of a three-legged stool, telling voters that for the state to continue its progress it needed three forms of tax generation in proper proportion to each other: the sales tax, a graduated income tax and a reasonable level of property tax. Even though the voters had rejected a referendum that would have established a 2% sales tax, the 1965 Legislature voted to establish a 3% tax and forward it to the voters for a hoped-for ratification. This came also in the face of a defeat just two years earlier, when, despite passage of a sales tax measure in the House, lead by then Republican Speaker Pete Cenarrusa from Carey, the Idaho Senate dropped the measure by a vote of 32 to 12. Cece was one of the twelve.

As 1965 rolled around, though, attitudes were changing as more voters recognized the need for additional revenue and a balanced tax structure. More to the point, there were a number of moderate Republicans who recognized the need and weren't about to be stampeded by conservative Republicans into taking a Grover Norquist-like "no new taxes" pledge.

Besides Cenarrusa, who went on to be Idaho's longest-serving Secretary of State (he never lost a race in forty-seven years), there were forward looking Idahoans in the legislature like future Governor Phil Batt, of Wilder; future Speaker Bill Lanting of Hollister; future gubernatorial aspirant and PUC commissioner Perry Swisher, then a state senator from Pocatello; future Supreme Court Justice Charles McDevitt, then a state representative from Boise. Others in that famous session included future Lieutenant Governor and then-State Senator Jack Murphy, from Shoshone; future gubernatorial aspirant Dick Smith, a state senator from Rexburg; the then-Senate Majority Leader, George Blick, from Castleford, a member of the "Sirloin Row" group of conservative ranchers; Senator Lloyd Barron, from Corral; then-State

Senator Bill Roden, from Boise; and, future Congressman Orval Hansen, then a state senator from Idaho Falls.

All of these Republicans recognized the need and the importance of tying down progressive Republican Governor Robert E. Smylie, who, serving his third consecutive term as Idaho's governor was increasingly becoming the personification of arrogance. Despite Smylie's allegiance to the liberal wing of the Republican party (he had supported Nelson Rockefeller for the GOP nomination in 1964, in part because of an unfounded notion he might be a possible vice presidential pick), the governor was trusted by few and was largely seen as already contemplating a fourth term.

The Republican leadership and the sales tax advocates orchestrated a meeting with Governor Smylie at State Senator Jack Murphy's home in Shoshone, overlooking the Wood River. The railroad town sits about half way between Twin Falls and Sun Valley on U.S. Highway 93, and was enough out of the way that Governor Smylie had to fly into the town's air strip in a National Guard plane in order to meet with the group. The pro-sales tax coalition managed to pin the Governor down to a solid promise to sign the sales tax legislation, after which he then flew, unnoticed, back to Boise.

A critical key to the passage of the sales tax was the need to redress the inequity in the assessment of property taxes across the state. Cece recognized this reform had to be passed in order to make the three-legged, properly balanced, stool argument and he supported the effort at reform spearheaded by Republican State Senator Bill Roden. The legislation, though ultimately overturned by the State Supreme Court, became another of the considerable achievements of the 1965 Legislature.

The assessment reform was viewed as a critical linch-pin because it was the key to swaying several conservative legislators worried about increasing voter pressure on the issue of property taxes. Proponents of the sales tax in the State Senate, led by Senator Swisher, who shepherded the bill to passage, were able to persuade several rural legislators to support the legislation by appropriating several million dollars for counties whose property taxes were rising but whose share of state funding was not.

In this manner, Swisher was able to lasso Canyon County State Senator Bill Young and Owyhee County State Senator Walter Yarbrough, both of whom had previously voted with the majority that rejected the sales tax, 24 to 20, on March 2, 1965. Finally, on March 11, after hours of renewed debate lasting late into the night, several votes switched, and along with the steadfast Andrus, the only Democratic State Senator to vote yes on the first roll call, the sales tax proposal prevailed by a final formal vote of 26 to 18.

Andrus, having been the lonely Democratic vote during the initial roll call, was viewed by many observers as the most critical vote. In the final vote, five other Democrats joined him in support of the sales tax. Andrus later cited the old saying, "Success has a thousand fathers; failure is a bastard."

One issue not resolved in the 1965 legislation continues to haunt Idaho to this day: Did the Legislature intend the revenue generated by the sales tax to be used exclusively for the betterment of education, or did it intend it just to be added to the general fund with education as the constitutional priority but not the exclusive recipient? Over the years, as more and more exemptions to the sales tax were passed by subsequent legislatures, state support for education again began to lag, so much so that by 2010 Idaho was again ranked as one of the poorest states when it came to support for public education. This has lead to calls for exemptions to be rescinded and for the sales tax to be dedicated exclusively to supporting education.

As one of the few pioneers still around from that historic session, Andrus today says he always felt that all funds generated by the sales tax should have been dedicated exclusively for the support of education, but by the time he became governor in 1970 the die was cast. It was just another source of revenue for the general fund. Likewise, he points out, even the original bill contained seventeen exemptions from the sales tax and allocated funds generated by the tax for purposes other than education.

In November of 1966 Idaho voters approved the sales tax by a decisive 61 to 39% margin. The irony is that in the August gubernatorial primary races, the partisan Republican and Democratic voters chose state senators opposed to the sales tax --Don Samuelson for the GOP and Chuck Herndon for the Democrats --to be the party standard bearers.

In addition, the 1965 session saw the following:

• Better coordination of higher education endeavors through the creation of an Office of Executive Director working with the State Board of Education;

• Legislation permitting the establishment of community colleges;

• Establishment of the Idaho Administrative Procedures Act;

• Authorization of the creation of community mental health centers; and,

• Reapportionment of the Legislature itself, and the abolishment of districts based on counties with new districts reflecting population and complying with a mandate from the US Supreme Court dictating an individual's vote as having the same power as other voters. This reapportionment signaled the beginning of the end of the dominance of "sirloin row" (rural dominance) in the Legislature with the balance of power now beginning to shift away from the numerous rural counties to the more populated urban counties.

Andrus was also integral in the establishment of Idaho's Public Employees Retirement System (or PERSI) in 1965 as he carried the perfecting legislation in 1965 creating a merit system for state employees, including teachers. PERSI is viewed by many as the model for a state merit system and state employee retirement program.

The upshot of all of this was that by the fall of 1965 Andrus had established a reputation as a thoughtful, moderate Democrat, progressive despite roots in a rural county, and someone with convictions and the courage to stand behind them. The one issue that had yet to emerge as part of his appeal to the public was the environment.

Andrus did not launch his career in politics as an environmentalist, despite his later evolution to a "common-sense conservationist" as he often described himself. His opposition to mining in the White Clouds Mountains beneath Castle Peak in 1970 played a role in earning him the governorship but Andrus was never the tree-hugging enviro his critics portrayed him to be. Truth be told, he was often at odds with the environmental community in large part because of its frequent excesses.

Andrus was consistent in calling himself a "lunch-bucket Democrat." And his philosophy over the years was always summed up by the phrase: "First you have to make a living; but then you have to have a living worthwhile." Andrus considered himself somewhat of a reformed conservationist – that is one who came to the correct position because of recognition of previous mistakes. Among his environmental transgressions was skidding logs down streambeds in his younger days as a gypo logger. He soon recognized the damage he was doing and the adverse impact on fishery habitat. As a state senator in the 1969-70 session, he sponsored and succeeded in passing Idaho's first Stream Channel Protection Act, which prohibited practices such as streambed skidding and severely restricted theretofore unrestricted sluice mining and hydro-blasting practices by individual miners seeking gold from Idaho's streams and rivers.

Andrus initially did not embrace moves to create additional wilderness areas beyond the vast tracts of Idaho's primitive and roadless areas in central Idaho. He reflected the views of his Orofino constituents, most of whom saw more wilderness designations as an unnecessary lock-up of precious timber resources.

Andrus, however, took strong exception to views expressed in a 2005 book by Boise author J. Meredith Neil, called *To The White Clouds,* which contended he actually supported legislative joint memorials to Congress calling for no more wilderness areas to be created.

"The author never talked to me. Had he talked to me, he would have learned that such joint memorials are not the subject of roll call votes, are always passed by voice votes and aren't worth the paper they are written on. To infer that I supported such a joint memorial is nonsense," Andrus said.

Another environmental issue frequently the subject of political debate during the early days of Andrus' Senate career was that of the construction of the Dworshak Dam on the North Fork of the Clearwater River near Orofino. A subset of the dam-building issue was the construction of several dams on the lower Snake River to enable Lewiston to become the furthest inland seaport in the country.

With 20/20 hindsight, Andrus has come to regret his support for these projects, though at the time he acknowledges he was caught up in the community boosterism behind them. Andrus says he never really gave any thought to whether the Dworshak Dam project was worthwhile, nor did he ask if it would extract too high a price in lost elk habitat, lost salmon and steelhead fisheries, or lost cutthroat streams.

"I've since come to recognize the high values attached to wildlife, wild fisheries, and the wild. Later in my career I became more familiar with an interesting phrase my friends in the conservation community applied to proposed dams: cost/benefit analysis."

Andrus recognized with the passage of time and the insight only experience can give that Chamber of Commerce boosterism was shortsighted and considerably undervalued what the community already had. Instead, the community of Orofino, and its state senator, succumbed to the blandishments of the Army Corps of Engineers. Community leadership fell into lockstep for what is now one of the nation's largest dams, a structure that inundated hundreds of miles of prime elk habitat, destroyed a major tributary fishery, and produces only modest megawattage for the regional grid (Approximately thirty megawatts annually; in fact, not all the pinstocks have turbines and Congress actually precluded a few years later funds for additional turbines.).

The dam's primary purpose is not power but rather "re-regulation." It is a dam used to provide water release to create "head" and generate additional peaking power in the complex system of some thirty dams the Corps and the Bureau of Reclamation built throughout the Pacific Northwest to harness the hydroelectric potential of the region.

Andrus is not anti-dam, and he has supported dams where measures are taken to mitigate damage and protect economically important fish runs. Dworshak was not one of them. Likewise, he regrets his support for the four dams on the Lower Snake.

"We all got snookered by claims of the Corps that bypass facilities and fish ladders would preserve the salmon and steelhead runs many sportsmen prize. Fifty years later, we find ourselves enmeshed in a series of lawsuits trying to enforce the promises made with regard to fisheries and an emboldened environmental community which sees the only answer for protecting and preserving the precious fish runs to be that of breaching those four useless dams on the Lower Snake."

Andrus believes that a Federal District judge somewhere may well order the dams be breached, since most other efforts to preserve the runs have fallen short. He adds, though, that he expects Congress will never appropriate the funds to carry out the dictate, thus leaving the unsatisfactory status quo in place.

During his third term as Idaho governor, Andrus came up with a plan to carry juvenile fish to the sea in a manner that replicated their natural migration before the advent of dams. He remains convinced this is the only plan that will work short of breaching -- which Congress will never fund -- but other powerful economic interests have successfully opposed the plan. Andrus believes the inevitable consequence may be the eventual breaching of the dams, and only when it looks imminent will folks revisit his proposal and recognize its benefits.

Andrus chalks up most of his thinking on these issues to the school of hard knocks. While he cannot help wishing he had been more prescient and farsighted on these issues, he recognizes that if he had been an outspoken critic of the dams he might never have had the chance to serve as governor.

Andrus also acknowledges that losing the 1966 race for Idaho's governorship - "Not once, but twice in the same year!" he points out,- ultimately was for the better.

"If there hadn't been a Don Samuelson, there would not have been a Governor Andrus," he has stated. This is a tacit acknowledgement that his later success in 1970 was due, in no small part, to Samuelson's incompetence and the many shortcomings of his administration.

However, in 1966 conventional wisdom was that Governor Smylie was expected to brush the Samuelson primary challenge aside easily. However, among Democrats it was believed that, in going for a fourth term, the incumbent was overreaching and would become a vulnerable candidate in the general election. Democrats smelled an opportunity to end twenty-four straight years of Republican control of the statehouse.

Andrus was part of a group of state senators and representatives loosely dubbed the "Young Turks" by the media. The common factor binding them was support for the sales tax and better funding for Idaho's schools. As 1966 drew near, the group cast about for a standard bearer. Not seeing anyone outside their group that immediately came to the fore, they turned inward and started to lobby one of their own -- Cece Andrus.

Already held in high esteem by most of his colleagues, the charismatic thirty-five-year-old Andrus, a mere three-term state senator from a small northern Idaho logging town, found such talk intoxicating.

"I drank the Kool-Aid," he said later. He knew he could do the job. He had already accomplished much as a state legislator and he had developed a good feel for the state and its needs, especially through his travels around the state and his campaigning for senate colleagues in 1964. He knew the top issue would be defending the adoption of a state sales tax, and, having taken the measure of the other aspirants, he felt he could do a better job. So, on July 30, 1965, he signaled his intentions publicly by telling a gathering of Ada County Democrats in Boise that he was considering a try for the Democratic gubernatorial nomination.

One of the "Young Turks" encouraging Andrus to run was Lewiston teacher and coach Eddie Williams, a member of the Idaho House of Representatives. Williams became the de facto campaign manager. Other members of the core campaign team included Lewiston attorney Wynne Blake; Clarkston, Washington banker and Hillcrest Aviation owner Jerry Wilson; Lewiston businessman and theater owner Harry Wall; Lewiston beer distributor, future state senator and Andrus chief-of-staff Mike Mitchell; Moscow motel owner Jap Inscore; and, in the primary, campaign press secretary Van Wolverton, a former United Press International reporter.

During the 1966 race, Andrus drew his base of support from three areas: educators; labor unions; and attorneys. The most critical was labor, which was personified by Bob MacFarlane, a towering presence with a perpetual scowl, who served as head of Idaho's AFL-CIO Labor Council for years. Despite his gruff appearance, he cared deeply about the welfare of union members and about improving their lives and the lives of their children. He adored Cecil Andrus and was a loyal presence in most of Cece's gubernatorial races. He always saw to it that labor unions contributed generously.

The 1966 campaign was largely "retail" oriented, with Andrus criss-crossing the state wearing out tires and shoe leather, appearing before whatever group would invite him. His other base of support, fellow state senators and whatever organizations they might have within their home counties, was diluted considerably with the entry into the race of State Senator Charles Herndon of Salmon (largely at the behest of lobbyist Tom Boise), and by another candidate, northern Idaho Democratic State Senator Bill Dee of Grangeville.

Still, Cece, tried to tie his campaign whenever possible, to those of like-minded progressive candidates and state legislators. In the process, he cemented relationships and developed friendships that he would draw on years later. A good example was teacher and state representative from Bonner County, Merle Parsley, who was running for and won the State Senate seat vacated by Don Samuelson when Samuelson ran for governor in 1966. Elfish, ebullient, constantly smiling and quick with a quip, Parsley, a native North Dakotan, epitomized the kind of loyalty Cece inspired among his peers.

Years later, when fishing on Lake Pend Oreille during a fishing derby, I listened as Cece and Merle retold campaign war stories, or listened as Cece would tell about the time he almost froze while staying overnight in Merle's cabin because the guest room in the log home had cracks large enough in the chinking to see through. By that time, Merle and his family were living in Hope on the northeast side of Lake Pend Oreille. Merle would often tell people he lived in Hope but would die in despair. He rarely failed to laugh at his own joke.

Because of fund raising challenges faced by Andrus, the 1966 campaign media strategy relied largely on billboards designed by the campaign's Boise ad agency. Cece never liked the billboards and never again made the mistake of not having his campaign media rely heavily on television and radio. His campaign slogan, "My kind of man!" left a lot to be desired. Years later he ruefully quipped, "Obviously, I wasn't!"

When the smoke had cleared from the August primary, Andrus had lost to Herndon by approximately a thousand votes. In the aftermath, he couldn't help thinking that his political career was over. He no longer held his Senate seat and shortly thereafter he found out from his boss at the Workman's Comp Exchange, Roland Wilber, that he no longer had a job waiting for his return. It was a bitter pill to swallow.

The need to put bread on the table soon focused his attention on making a living. He and Carol made plans to sell their home in Orofino, and move to Lewiston where Cece had decided to do consulting work for firms needing advice in the handling of worker's comp issues. That was the plan until, one month later, Idaho's political world was rocked by the news that Democrat nominee Herndon had been killed on Labor Day in a light airplane crash high up in central Idaho's Sawtooth Mountains.

After consulting with his core supporters and Carol, Andrus reached the decision to step back into the race and pick up the Democrat standard. Despite Herndon's absence, the race remained crowded and contentious. In the intervening month, the champions of Idaho's sales tax, recognizing that neither party's primary winner supported the tax, had prevailed upon Pocatello Republican State Senator Perry Swisher, who had guided the sales tax legislation through the Senate thicket, to enter the race as an Independent.

Swisher, believing he had the defeated Andrus' support, felt he had an excellent shot at winning what had become a four-person race, the fourth candidate being a pro-gambling advocate from Lewiston, Phil Jungert. Cece on the other hand, while publicly supporting the state sales tax and implicitly supporting Swisher behind the scenes, had never endorsed Perry publicly, in part because he doubted that any candidate outside the major political parties could win the governorship. For Cece, no party organization meant no ability to win.

It was clear that the tragic Labor Day death of Herndon had changed the political calculus in Idaho. Andrus and his supporters, however, were not the only ones doing the calculating. Conservative Democrats opposed to the sales tax, such as Tom Boise, and other lobbyists representing business interests opposed to a new tax, quickly launched a search for a worthy heir to the Charles Herndon wing of the party. They came up with Max Hanson, then serving as Federal Agricultural Services director for Idaho, courtesy of an appointment by President Lyndon Johnson.

Rather than anoint Andrus as the new standard-bearer, the state Democratic Party quickly called a meeting of the State Democratic Central Committee to select its nominee. The meeting would be held after a respectful but short period of mourning for Herndon. Those eligible to vote were identified by party rules, and then the Andrus and Hanson camps went to work lassoing enough votes for a simple majority.

Late on the afternoon of September 20, 1966, the day before the Central Committee vote, Hanson stopped by the mailbox in front of the Post Office Building across the street from the Hotel Boise and dropped his resignation from his federal position into the mailbox. He was confident that he had the votes to win the nomination, and at that point he did. Hanson, however, failed to take into consideration the skills of one of Idaho's most legendary political operators, a person who few outside the political cognoscenti even knew -- Verda Barnes, chief of staff to Idaho's senior U.S. Senator, Frank Church.

Not only did Verda like Cece personally, she thought Andrus had the best chance of winning and then helping Senator Church in his upcoming re-election bid. This sealed the deal for her.

Verda stayed up all night working the phones, calling in chits, making it clear whom she, and implicitly the Senator, thought was best choice to lead the party ticket. When the smoke cleared on September 21, Cece had eked out a win by two votes.

However, receiving the nomination was a classic Phyrric victory, coming at a high cost and rendering the victor a loser. Swisher made it clear he was not dropping out to let Andrus carry the pro-sales tax banner. And Cece, by running, had made it clear he was not backing away.

The biggest beneficiary of course was Don Samuelson, the likable Republican nominee who had exhibited the courage to take on Smylie along with the backing of the rising influence of the Goldwater wing of the Republican Party. Those opposed to the sales tax, especially conservative Democrats, had no choice other than to turn to Samuelson.

Thus, on Election Day in November of 1966, Andrus lost again, with Samuelson winning a plurality that represented 43% of the electorate and an approximately 10,000 vote margin over Cece. Swisher collected 12% of the vote, siphoning off more than enough votes to deny Cece election. In Perry's mind, Cece had siphoned off votes that, had they gone to him, would have given him the victory. It took years for Perry to get over his loss and to once again build a relationship with Cece.

Andrus came out of the election with a debt of $8,000 between the two campaigns. He had raised $231,000 but had spent $239,000. This was a time before candidates could write off such debts, or loan themselves the funds to cover campaign expenses. Cece felt it was an obligation and that he was honor bound to pay the campaign's creditors. Difficult though it was, over the next two years, he paid every creditor.

Cece, Carol and their daughters went ahead with their plans to move to Lewiston and did so on December 6, 1966, having resided in Orofino for eleven years. Cece purchased a new home in the Heights above Lewiston that just happened to be right across the street from the home of Bob Paine, an influential lobbyist for northern Idaho's dominant utility, Spokane-based Washington Water Power.

Those that know Cece well know that this was no coincidence.

Cece's knowledge of the insurance field soon caught the eye of the management of Boston-based Paul Revere Insurance Company, which offered him the position of regional manager, a post he accepted.

The political bug continued to itch deep within him, which led to a decision to seek a return to the state senate by taking on an appointed Republican incumbent, "Hud" Hulbert, from what was then the 6th Legislative District. In the Clearwater Valley, at least, the Andrus name was still magic and he easily won the November 1968 election and made plans to return to Boise.

*Chapter 7*

# Cece and Chris
# Cross Paths

In early September 1969, I found myself in Pocatello, where I had
a teaching assistantship at Idaho State University to help sustain
body and soul while pursuing a master's in English Literature. I
had but three needs: a car, a place to stay and more money than my
teaching assistant's stipend could provide.

The first two situations came to resolution through the generosity
of my uncle, Fergus Briggs, Jr., who owned and operated the National
Laundry in Pocatello. Uncle Fergus, with whom I discussed my needs,
took me down to the laundry, where, in a shed outside the garage, sat
an old 1957 fire-engine-red Plymouth with impressive tail fins. He
told me I could have the car for $75 and the cost of getting it running.
It had been owned but seldom used by an aging janitor at the laundry.

It was love at first sight. I quickly dubbed it "The Shark," and I
drove it all over town with great pride. A car like mine shortly thereafter was the subject of the horror film called *Christine*, in which the car
displayed murderous tendencies, but I found my model to be considerably more benign.

Housing was also covered. Fergus invited me to stay at his home
rent-free, which, shameless moocher that I was, I accepted. The arrangement allowed me to spend many quality hours with my favorite
cousin, Fergus' oldest boy, Paul.

The third requirement was checked off quickly. I put together a
portfolio of my writings from the late summer of 1968 for *The North
Idaho Press* and, with no idea whether the local daily, *The Idaho State
Journal,* needed reporters, sauntered into the newsroom and met with
the managing editor, Lyle Olson. It so happened the newspaper had a

vacancy in the political/education beat, and I was hired on the spot. I had some big shoes to fill as I was following Wilbert D. "Bill" Hall, who had moved on to *The Lewiston Morning Tribune,* where he continued to carve out a distinguished record as one of the state's most astute political and editorial writers. As my future boss, Cecil Andrus, later liked to tell me, "Sometimes it's better to be lucky than good."

Having bluffed my way into yet another newspaper job, I scrambled over to the ISU library, where I devoured four books on journalism. While they provided some assistance, none of them matched what I had already learned about the trade during the summer of 1968 from Jay Shelledy and R.J. "Rolly" Bruning when I had taken on a brief stint at *The North Idaho Press* in Wallace.

I now had a full-time job, around which I also had to work in the two classes of freshman English Comp I was teaching as well as classes I was taking for my M.A. It was little wonder over the next ten months I averaged about four hours of sleep a night.

Rather quickly I became disenchanted with the academic life. At times, I felt I was some sort of political football being kicked among members of the faculty, with some trying to show others no Ivy League kid (I had received my B.A. from Columbia in 1968) was going to breeze through their classes, and others competing to be my faculty advisor.

More than anything, I began to note how folks with a Ph.D after their names and supposed expertise in some narrow discipline, felt their degree made them experts on anything and everything. As I became attuned to the academic politics around me, I became more interested in the real world politics.

At the newspaper, for a cub reporter, I was given remarkable latitude to cover and write about issues beyond my beat. Two non-beat writings led to major controversy in the community and to changes in the review processes of the newspaper.

One had to do with what I thought was a well-reasoned and logical editorial published shortly after an inmate at the state mental hospital in Blackfoot had been released, and had promptly walked into a hardware store on Main Street in Pocatello, purchased a handgun, walked out and started shooting at people. My editorial said this situation could easily be remedied by having the state legislature pass a law requiring a three-day waiting period when purchasing a gun while a background check was conducted. By the reaction in the community one would have thought I had called for a law requiring women to walk around nude.

Publisher Al Ricken and newspaper owner, Nick Ifft III, were besieged by businesses threatening to pull advertising, by gun-rights citizens who saw this as the first step in a leftist plot to take away their weapons, and by sportsmen who didn't want any delays for background checks if they wanted to purchase guns. It was an awesome and intimidating display of the power of the gun lobby in a western state, and I never forgot the lesson. As for Ricken and Ifft, they directed Editor Olson henceforth to run all editorials by them, especially any written by me.

The second incident involved a movie review. One Saturday evening, I went to see a then-X-rated movie called *Midnight Cowboy*, starring Jon Voight and Dustin Hoffman. A poignant show, the story line involved a country kid named Joe Buck (Voight) coming to New York to exploit women and the city. The city quickly teaches him its harsh lessons, but in the dreariness of his life he discovers and makes friends with one Ratzo Rizzo, played to perfection by Hoffman.

I correctly predicted to readers that the movie would win the Best Picture Oscar, but my write-up was a bit too colorful for a "family newspaper." One line in particular seemed to antagonize the good Mormon citizens of Pocatello, in which I wrote that Joe Buck was coming to the big city intent not on riding horses but riding women. Tame stuff by contemporary standards, but language which sent readers by the droves to my stunned managing editor Olson.

When the onslaught subsided, a bedraggled Olson sauntered over to my desk and allowed as how I'd better stick to political and educational reporting and leave movie reviews to others. And, like editorials, suddenly movie reviews started to be run by the publisher.

Throughout these challenges, I had the stalwart support of the newspaper's longtime society editor, Joy Morrison. She was held in such high regard that her support no doubt saved my job. It didn't hurt, either, that Joy years earlier had been a classmate and good friend of my mother.

I also managed to be in the right place at the right time on several important occasions. One day, I dropped by the office during the afternoon, only to hear there was a student sit-in demonstration on campus, protesting the CIA being allowed to recruit on campus. They had occupied the office of ISU president William E. "Bud" Davis. I grabbed a camera and arrived on campus in time to snap a photo of the president lost in thought, smoking his pipe while standing in the midst of a sea of students sitting on the floor of his office. The Associated Press sent the photo and story nationwide.

But, politics was what I most enjoyed and to that end, I did my best to immerse myself in Bannock County politics. Due to a railroad legacy and the presence of several phosphate producing plants, Bannock County was one of only three strong union counties in the state. Organized labor, coupled with the traditional liberalism found on most university campuses, served to make the county reliably Democratic while surrounded by a sea of Republican, Mormon-dominated counties.

Bannock was a single-party county. Though I would often attend county central committee meetings, I soon learned there were factions within the party built around strong personalities, either former or current legislators, or individuals prominent in the state labor movement. I tried to figure out who the players were. I strove to write fairly about the issues of the day and where each member of the legislative delegation stood on those issues.

One day in early November 1969, my phone rang. It was Bob Lenaghen, a former state representative from Bannock County. He was now the dominant labor leader in the county. He growled into the phone in his remarkably Godfather-like voice, "Kid, meet me at the Bannock Hotel's coffee shop at 3 p.m. I got someone I want you to meet." I said I would be there.

I was about to start down a road not yet discernible but nonetheless life-changing. Waiting at the hotel was State Senator Cecil D. Andrus.

I knew Senator Andrus was contemplating another run for the Idaho governorship, having lost the race in 1966. Andrus was keenly aware of how that election had been splintered among four candidates. He grabbed a napkin from the table, pulled out a pen and proceeded to show me how he would win a two person race. I dutifully reported the "numbers game" he outlined on that napkin, which is exactly what he was seeking.

Though favorably impressed with Andrus, I retained my objectivity and dutifully reported on visits to central committee meetings by other potential candidates, including that of State Representative Vernon Ravenscroft of Tuttle and State Senator John V. Evans from Malad. Andrus, though, was the one that intrigued me most. He had the look of a winning horse. Whenever he came through Pocatello I would find an excuse to report on his activities in the *State Journal*. It was clear to me that he would announce for governor after the end of the 1970 session of the Idaho Legislature.

I had also covered the incumbent, Don Samuelson, whenever he was in the area. Though a nice enough guy, most reporters were less than impressed with his administrative abilities and I was no different. Once, while covering Samuelson on the nearby Shoshone-Bannock Reservation, I witnessed him reading a speech. Without breaking stride, he said, "turn the page, look up and smile." I reported the gaffe, which brought an angry call from the Governor's chief of staff, Doug Bean.

It also earned me my first call from Don Watkins, the "godfather" of Idaho journalists, who complimented me on the article. Watkins was ostensibly State Schools Superintendent Del Engelking's director of communications, but over the years he had accumulated influence by befriending and offering useful guidance to reporters around the state. During legislative sessions he and his wife, Anne, would often host dinners on Friday or Saturday night, and there were always sparkling political discussions around the dinner table.

Shortly after the New Year, I was off to Boise to cover the start of the 1970 session of the Legislature. Though not able to stay once ISU resumed classes, I arrangeed my schedule so that I could cover key events at the Legislature and be present on Fridays.

I recall sitting in on a committee session of the Senate in which no other reporter was present. Two state senators in particular took to berating the State Superintendent. One of the senators was from Declo and the other from Soda Springs. Both cities were in the *State Journal's* circulation area. In my story, I rather self-righteously termed the session a "kangaroo court," and wrote with an obvious bias about what the two "redneck" conservatives had done in subjecting the superintendent to an "inquisition."

Watkins, of course, loved it, but the two senators rightly took exception and I learned a hard lesson about not using such value-laden and judgmental terms in my writing, especially words which inflicted

damage on people's reputations. Years later, one of those state senators, came into a position of leadership. He had a long memory, and
was almost able to exact some sweet revenge.

In 1981, I was nominated to be the first member of the Northwest
Power Planning Council from the state of Idaho. Each state had two
council members whose primary charge was to develop plans that
would protect the declining salmon runs while still ensuring that the
region's economy could move forward. The senate *Pro Tempore* was
Reed Budge from Soda Springs, one of the two senators I had branded
a redneck years before. My new post required confirmation by the
Senate.

Senator Budge had his Bowie knife out and was waiting with keen
anticipation. This was further confirmation of the truth of one of Andrus' political maxims, "there is no road in politics so long that it
doesn't have a bend." I never did undergo a confirmation vote.

I learned another hard lesson by inciting the ire of a protective
mother, one Carol Andrus, the wife of the future governor. Pounding
out one of my "potpourri" columns one day in which a reporter includes little items, including rumor and gossip, I referenced the rumor
that Andrus' campaign for governor just might have a special "in" on
the ISU campus because his oldest daughter, Tana, was said to be dating the politically savvy student body president at ISU. Carol made
it clear to me in a phone call that references to children, unless the
campaign is actually using them to speak, are considered off-limits.
Even after the future governor later hired me, he let Carol find out by
reading the announcement in the morning newspaper. It took a few
years for Carol to warm up to me.

Meanwhile, Andrus was methodically wrenching the governorship
from Don Samuelson, who thought he could easily dispatch Andrus'
challenge. Having learned much from his disorganized effort in 1966,
Andrus was putting into place a series of tactical moves to ensure a
victory. First, he and Ed Williams traveled the state to meet with prospective Democratic candidates, trying to entice at least one of them
to challenge Samuelson. For example, they met with Idaho State University president William E. "Bud" Davis and discussed his potential
attractiveness as a Democratic standard-bearer. Davis demurred, but

he, like others that Cece and Eddy contacted, was flattered by the attention.

This search served several other purposes: It garnered considerable personal admiration from potential challengers; and, it permitted Andrus to showcase his skills while subtly intimidating potential primary challengers by implied comparison.

When Cece finally entered the race, he had ensured a broad base of support in most of the key counties. He had further cemented his relationships with various fellow state senators, many of whom became life-long loyalists who worked diligently for his election. Good examples were Pocatello State Senator Diane Bilyeu and her husband, ISU speech professor Chick Bilyeu, who succeeded her as state senator, and who worked tirelessly on behalf of Cece's candidacy each time he ran.In Bannock County alone, other future campaign workers included attorney Herman McDevitt, former State Representative Darrell V. Manning, Charlene Shou, Beverly Bistline, Steve Lee, Margot Briggs and Pocatello State Representative Patty McDermott ---all became loyal supporters. In later years their ranks were joined by Tom and Bessie Katsilometes.

Another deft move was reaching out and grabbing the services of a tall, rangy cowboy from Corral, Joe McCarter, who had previously run Vern Ravenscroft's primary campaign, to work in his campaign following Cece's defeat of Vern and Lloyd Walker (from Twin Falls) in the 1970 Democratic primary. It helped to ensure a united Democratic party in the campaign.

In addition, Cece and Eddie recruited Idaho Bank & Trust chairman Robert Montgomery to handle his campaign's finance duties. Eddie once again was the chairman, but this time Andrus provided some talented help to work in the Boise office, young guys by the names of Roy Haney and Larry Meierotto. Perhaps the smartest hire was KLEW-TV reporter John Hough, who became the campaign's press secretary, traveling aide, driver, and bag carrier.

Andrus and Hough quickly established great personal rapport ,and both had quick minds for turning almost mundane campaign items into stories carried by the various news outlets across Idaho. Jean Taylor, a socialite spouse of a successful Nampa physician, Sam Taylor, signed on as the scheduling secretary.

Montgomery proved adept at fundraising and Bob MacFarlane, along with Lenaghen, made sure organized labor did its part to provide campaign workers and hefty contributions. The state's teachers also provided a cadre of key supporters and contributions delivered through the Idaho Education Association, not so much because of Andrus' past support for the sales tax, but also because of his promised support for establishing state-supported kindergartens.

Andrus also chose a brilliant campaign slogan for the 1970 race: "A Governor for ALL Idaho." The slogan identified one of Don Samuelson's many weaknesses – he was seen as a divisive figure that catered primarily to the special interests and not the public interest. As the fall campaign wore on, another issue emerged that reinforced that perception of Samuelson and played into Andrus' hands.

The ASARCO Company had proposed the development of a masssive molybdenum mine in Idaho's scenic Boulder-White Clouds wilderness, with a tailing pond to be established near the base of majestic Castle Peak. Samuelson supported ASARCO's proposed mine; and, Andrus opposed it. While Cece lost Custer County, where the proposed mine was to be located, by a twelve-to-one margin, in the counties with most of Idaho's increasingly urban population, Andrus's view carried the day. It was a clear black-and-white difference, and Andrus later would observe that "Castle Peak was the mountain that elected a governor!"

# Photo Gallery

*Andrus family file*

Cecil Andrus's graduation picture from Eugene High School, class of 1948.

*Andrus family file*

The young Cecil Andrus at age eight.

*Andrus family file*

One of the earliest photos of the future Idaho governor and Interior Secretary. He and older brother Steve, pose somewhere on the family farm outside of Junction City, Oregon. Andrus, on the left, was about six at the time.

Carol's stepfather, Homer May. He formally adopted Carol while she was still an infant.

Carol's mother, Mildred May.

An Andrus family picture. From left, older brother Steve, sister Margi, father Hal, mother Dorothy and the Governor.

*Andrus family file*

The young lumberjack poses on a log landing outside of Orofino in the late 1950s. Andrus liked to say he grew up in the "slab, sliver & knothole" business.

*Andrus family file*

Cece and Carol in early 1949. Still newlyweds, residing in Eugene, having been married the previous August in Reno.

*Barry Kough*

*Andrus family file*

A devoted fly fisherman, Governor Andrus displays some fine trout taken from a private reservoir in southwestern Idaho (No-Tell-Um Lake) on a day away from the office during his second term.

Campaigning on the streets of Lewiston during his return to office campaign in 1986. In 1974, he won by the largest margin for a governor's race in Idaho history, garnering 73% of the vote, a record which still stands. In 1986, it was a squeaker. He won with just a 3,000-vote margin.

As a freshman at Oregon State University, the young Cece was a member of the school's Army ROTC program and poses in his uniform sometime during the 1948-1949 academic year.

A formal portrait of the young Navy enlisted man, probably taken in 1954.

Cece and Carol pose with Tana in Eugene, when Andrus was on leave from the Navy.

*Andrus family file*

The young Naval air crewman relaxes in front of his tent early in his posting to the Iwakuni (Japan) Air Base, during the latter stages of the Korean War.

*Andrus family file*

The Navy airman poses in front of a Lockheed P2V Neptune aboard which he served flying the eight-hour-long "Triangle Route" up the east coast of the Korean Peninsula from Iwakumi Air Base in Japan, across the 38th parallel, and down the west coast of Korea.

*Andrus family file*

*Andrus family file*

The young, newly-elected State Senator from Clearwater County.

Cecil Andrus's favorite photo of Carol, his bride of over sixty years.

*Andrus family file*

As the youngest newly elected member of the Idaho Senate, Andrus receives a toy donkey from Lieutenant Gov. Bill Drevlow on the first day of the 1961 session.

*Andrus family file*

Andrus poses on the Capitol steps on the morning of his first inauguration ceremony in 1971. This photo was also used in Idaho highway maps along with a "drive safely" message from the Governor. Shortly thereafter, Andrus also launched a "Idaho is Too Great to Litter" signage campaign on state highways.

83

*Andrus family file*

The about to be sworn-in Governor and the first lady on the Capitol steps in early
January 1971.

*Andrus family file*

First Lady Carol Andrus and press secretary Chris Carlson, entering a stage coach during the Payette Days parade in 1973. The Governor rode a horse. The tongue on the stage broke en route causing the horses to panic and a runaway that ended with the coach rolling and minor injuries to the First Lady and the young child on top. It was the first and last stage ride for both Carol and Chris.

*Photo courtesy of AP*

Andrus and "Otis" pose in 1973 at Morley Nelson's home in the Boise Foothills, where Nelson helped injured birds of prey and convinced the Governor to support the creation of a National Birds of Prey Natural Area, protecting habitat and prey base for majestic birds like this golden eagle.

*Andrus family file*

Labor was always an important constituency for Andrus, and long-time State AFL-CIO leader Bob McFarlane (on left with Andrus) was a loyal Andrus supporter. Here he introduces the Governor to National AFL-CIO President George Meany during Meany's visit to Boise in 1974.

*Barry Kough, Lewiston Morning Tribune*

Governor Andrus and his staff on election day 1974. Andrus received the largest margin of victory in Idaho history, with 73% of the electorate voting to send him onto a second term. Seated from left: R.J. Bruning, assistant for natural resources; John D. Hough, deputy chief of staff; William J. Murphy, chief of staff; Chris Carlson, press secretary; and Pat Vaughan, assistant for human resources.

*Andrus family file*

Governor Andrus and his staff during his second stint as governor of Idaho from 1987 to 1995. Photo taken in 1994. Pictured clockwise starting with the Governor to his left, Clancy Standridge, legislative liaison; Marc Johnson, chief of staff; Scott Peyron, press secretary; Jon Carter, legal counsel; Julie Cheever, special assistant for human resources: Andy Brunelle, special assistant for natural resources (back to camera); Chuck Moss, budget director; and, Clareene Wharry the Governor's personal secretary

*Barry Kough*

Andrus family photo taken in 1972 at the Governor's home just off of State Street. From left: Tracy, Governor Andrus, Kelly, First Lady Carol and Tana.

*Andrus family file*

Interior Secretary Andrus in 1980, making his case to actor Robert Redford to support his plan for the creation of a Birds of Prey Natural Area surrounding the Snake River in Southwestern Idaho..

*Andrus family file*

Washington Governor Booth Gardner meets with Governor Andrus in Spokane on the Centennial Trail in 1990. In 2008, Gardner was the chief advocate and lead spokesman for Initiative 1000, which legalized physician assisted suicide.

*Andrus family file*

Serving in his fourth term as governor, Andrus and Carol pose at the last Idaho Governor's Cup he presided over in the summer of 1994 at Sun Valley. The charity golf tournament, begun by Andrus in his first term, raised more than a million dollars over the years to provide full scholarships to entice Idaho's best and brightest high school graduates to pursue higher education in Idaho.

John Hough, Andrus' campaign press secretary in 1970, later his resource aide, then chief of staff. A sportsman in his own right, he now lives in semi-retirement on the Kitsap Peninsula in Washington state, where he spends a fair amout of time stalking and catching salmon like this one.

Marc Johnson, Andrus' press secretary and later chief of staff during Andrus' second stint as governor, the best of a very good group.

Larry Meierotto, a brilliant political advisor in all of Andrus' succeessful gubernatorial campaigns. Former deputy mayor of Seattle, former key aide at Interior, and also one-time chief of staff, he joined Chris as an original founding partner of The Gallatin Group. His tragic suicide in 1993 stunned and saddened all who knew him.

Mike McGavick who was hired as Chris' deputy for government affairs at Seattle's Rocky Company in 1982. He went on to engineer Slade Gorton's 1988 comeback Senate campaign, joined The Gallatin Group in 1990, and then turned to the insurance industry, where as chairman and CEO of Safeco Insurance he engineered that company's dramatic turnaround. Today he is chairman and CEO of the XL Group.

*Chapter 8*

# Washington, D.C.,
# Cece, and me

There are few things in life more satisfying and ego-stroking than seeing one's newspaper by-line. The psychic satisfaction often has to compensate for sparse paychecks. Unless one writes for the handful of major national newspapers, wages for journalists are not high. Working with A. Robert Smith, though, was to afford me many by-lines and provide a status for me at the age of twenty-four that was head-turning.

Bob Smith invited me to join his independent D.C. News Bureau following a November 1970 dinner in Spokane. I had obtained my Master's from ISU in June, had married Marcia in St. Maries (Idaho), also in June, and had gone to work at the *Spokane Daily Chronicle* as a copy editor.

Still nursing a desire to report and write, I had freelanced several articles for Sam Day's liberal Boise weekly, *The Intermountain Observer.* Bob Smith, being an old friend of Sam's, subscribed to the newspaper and happened to see and like some of my columns. He flew to Spokane to talk, and following a long evening's discussion, invited me to join his bureau. After a long chat with Marcia, I accepted.

Bob Smith was a wonderful mentor. He gave me a copy of a book he had written on the nation's capital which helped to delineate the major spheres of influence and players. Bob also showed me the city, walked me around the Hill, and introduced me to the members of Congress he had covered for years. He had me read his fine biography of Oregon's maverick Senator Wayne Morse, entitled *The Tiger in the Senate.* In addition, Bob gently edited my work in the beginning and taught me much about how to write a good column.

It was heady stuff for a native of the mining town of Kellogg in northern Idaho to be meeting and dining with legendary Senators like Washington state's "gold dust twins," Henry M. "Scoop" Jackson and Warren G. Magnuson, Oregon's Mark Hatfield, Idaho's Frank Church, and Montana's Mike Mansfield. It was obvious, too, that these Senators held Bob Smith in high regard, trusted his word, and knew he was a reporter who did his homework and understood discretion.

There were others, too, in those days just beginning to make their mark: Alaska's Ted Stevens would go on to become chairman of the Senate Appropriations Committee and the Republican Senate *Pro Tempore* before finally falling from the grace of Alaska's voters in 2008 after forty years in office (the longest serving Republican senator ever). Tom Foley, from my "hometown" of Spokane, where I went to junior and senior high school, would later become speaker of the House of Representatives. James McClure from Idaho would move on to the Senate where he later would work with my future boss, Cece Andrus, on a variety of initiatives critical to the future of Idaho.

Bob Smith hired me to provide day-to-day coverage of federal issues important to Alaska. The major issue confronting lawmakers was resolving Alaska Native land claims, something promised in Alaska's Admissions Act in 1958. These claims had to be resolved in order to commence with the construction of a pipeline from Prudhoe Bay, on the north slope of Alaska, to Seward on the south coast. Seward was an ice-free port from which tankers would carry the crude oil to the nation's refineries in the Lower 48.

Before such legislation could be passed, an additional player had to be satisfied – the nation's then nascent but growing environmental community, which was pressing for language in this and any other bill that would also set aside large parts of Alaska as new national parks, wildlife refuges and wilderness areas. Resolution of these issues in a fair and balanced manner was critical to the future well-being of the state. Alaskans eagerly followed the political saga.

Almost everything I wrote was featured on the front-page of *The Anchorage Daily News,* often with a banner headline at the top of the page. Likewise, the papers in Ketchikan and Sitka gave my dispatches prominent play.

My articles were also carefully scrutinized by the hyper-sensitive members of Alaska's congressional delegation in the early 1970s:

Senators Stevens and Mike Gravel, and Congressman Nick Begich. In addition, Alaska Governor Bill Egan, a frequent visitor to Washington, carefully followed stories out of D.C. None of them was shy about calling me or buttonholing me when I came to their office on my daily rounds, particularly if they felt my coverage was inaccurate or unfair. Senator Stevens particularly was known for his hair-trigger temper.

As a reporter for the Smith News Bureau, I broke several major stories. One, in particular, was of national interest. I was the first to report the plane carrying Rep. Begich and House Majority Leader Hale Boggs of Louisiana, which had disappeared on a flight between fundraisers for the Alaskan congressman, was not carrying the required locater beacon transmitter. This meant searchers would have little chance of locating the plane, which turned out to be the case. It has never been found.

I also happened to be sitting in a poorly attended Senate hearing on the creation of a Hells Canyon National Recreation Area. The Legislation was sponsored by Oregon Senator Bob Packwood, who, under questioning from Idaho Senator Len Jordan, who had lived on a sheep ranch for nine years at Kirkwood Bar in Hells Canyon, refused to guarantee the primacy of upstream water rights. In a water-sensitive state like Idaho, such a refusal was tantamount to a death wish and was big news. The *Lewiston Morning Tribune* ran the subsequent column as a front-page, banner-headlined story. Shortly thereafter, I had several additional Idaho subscribers to my weekly column.

In the summer of 1972, Smith sent me to Miami to cover the Democratic Convention. It was there I witnessed one of the weirder events in national politics, the effort by Alaska Senator Mike Gravel to nominate himself for the vice presidency and force himself onto the ticket with South Dakota Senator George McGovern. Rarely have I felt so embarrassed for the voters of one state, and I wrote a scathing account of the senator's futile effort.

Earlier that year, I also received my first offer to be a political candidate's press secretary. I admitted to myself that the more I covered politics, the more intrigued I was by the thought of "going over to the other side."

Idaho State Representative Ed Williams of Lewiston called me one night to entice me into returning to Idaho to be his campaign press secretary in a race for Idaho's First District congressional seat. A teacher and a coach, Ed had a reputation for being a sharp political strategist and a dedicated public servant. More importantly, he was the single closest friend and political advisor to newly elected Idaho Governor Cecil D. Andrus. Ed had helped manage Andrus' successful 1970 campaign.

I had covered Andrus during several visits he had made to Washington, D.C. and knew he viewed Ed as a brother. He had actually tried to talk Ed into running for governor himself, and was keenly interested in Ed's political future. The thought had already occurred to me that were I ever to see politics from the inside, Andrus was the figure I was most intrigued with. Thus, I instinctively knew I had to handle the overture from Ed with tact and diplomacy.

As usual, truth was the absolute defense. I told Ed I just wasn't ready to leave Washington, D.C., having been there only for little over a year. Nor did it make much sense for me to pull up stakes, move back to Idaho, and then, if Ed won, turn around and head right back to DC with him. I offered to help from afar *pro bono* by drafting a kickoff statement and press release. The conversation ended amicably with Ed harboring no ill will.

At the time, Ed thought he would be challenging Republican incumbent Jim McClure for the seat, but there was another variable which few had foreseen. Idaho's junior Senator in 1972 was Len B. Jordan, a former governor from 1951-1955, former member of the International Joint Boundary Commission, and a former sheep rancher immortalized in a book by his wife, Grace, entitled *Home Below Hells Canyon*. The book chronicled the nine years the Jordan's survived the Depression running sheep in Hells Canyon, the deepest gorge in North America.

A person of integrity, character and intellect, one who reflected strength and personified the successful rancher-businessman, Jordan was assumed to be seeking another term in the Senate. Earlier that year, the senator gained notoriety within the Beltway when he was accosted in an elevator by a man seeking money. The assailant had a weapon. The senator fought the assailant and knocked the guy cold.

I was caught by surprise in the late spring of 1972 when Senator Jordan invited me into his office and asked me to become his press secretary. While flattered because I greatly admired the Senator, I was quick to tell him it made a difference to me whether the job was to be a six-month one with the Senator leaving office after the November election, or a six-year one with the Senator seeking and winning relection. The Senator told me that was fair, and to come back in two weeks for an answer.

Two weeks later, Senator Jordan informed me he was not going to seek re-election. He then asked me to respect his right to let the people of Idaho know his decision at a time of his choosing and asked me to pledge confidentiality. So here I sat, with no choice but to sit on the biggest political story of the year for Idaho. Sit I did, however, for like the Senator, I had learned early in life, your word is your bond -- in politics and life.

Several months later, the Senator made his decision known and Idaho politics shifted into what would be one of the more momentous political years in the state's history. In the meantime, I settled back into concentrating on my Alaska issues, as well as producing my weekly political column for Idaho newspaper clients. My dabbling in Idaho politics was not yet finished, though, nor was I through receiving overtures to be a campaign press secretary.

Shortly after Jordan made his announcement, a friend from my days at Idaho State University, the school's president, "Bud" Davis, paid a visit to Washington, D.C. Davis, a former Marine officer, was a popular president, a gifted storyteller, and an excellent speaker. He had traveled the length and breadth of Idaho making a good name for himself while spreading ISU's story.

After lunch with Davis, I took Bud up to the Senate pressroom and out into the press gallery overlooking a deserted Senate floor, where I pointed out Senator Jordan's seat. Knowing a good potential candidate when I saw one, I looked Bud Davis in the eye and told him that chair could be his.

Caught by surprise, Davis demurred, but I persisted and at last Davis allowed me to put a speculative item in my next column saying he was entertaining the notion of possibly running for the U.S. Senate. With that we parted. I then sat down and wrote the column. Before Davis arrived back in Pocatello, the column had been bannered across the frontpage of the hometown newspaper, *The Idaho State Journal,* announcing Davis' possible candidacy. The news caught even Davis' wife, Polly, by surprise.

The die was cast, however, as Davis was soon inundated with calls of support and folks offering to assist his campaign. In a matter of weeks, he took a leave as president and declared his candidacy for the Democratic nomination.

It wasn't long before Davis was back on the phone to me saying in effect, "You got me into this, now you've got to come help me by running it or being the press secretary!" I declined yet a third offer, citing again that I just wasn't ready to leave D.C. I did, however, know just the person to be Bud's press secretary: my old friend, Jay Shelledy, with whom I had taught and coached at Kootenai High School during the 1968-1969 school year. The two of them talked, and Jay decided to resign his post at the Associated Press in Boise (he had left teaching a year earlier to join the AP) to take on the challenge of Bud's Senate campaign.

I again found myself caught up in the campaigns with one of my columns having an impact on the GOP primary. During the early summer, I noticed Idaho's two congressmen, James McClure and Orval Hansen, had voted differently on the so-called "prayer amendment" to allow public prayer in school. I visited each office to interview the congressmen and allow them to explain their reasoning which I intended to report in my next column.

Both were bright, articulate, dedicated public servants who could handle themselves with ease. McClure, however, was also running for Senator Jordan's seat and had three primary opponents, one of whom was former congressman George Hansen (no relation to Orval). McClure was also an eminently logical person, and in the course of the interview, I said to him something like "Well, if you really believe that, Congressman, then philosophically you have to be opposed to release time." McClure replied that was correct. Release time was the practice, prevalent in southern Idaho school districts with large populations of Mormon students, where students were released from school an hour early in order to walk to a seminary across the street and attend, for credit, religion class conducted by a Mormon lay teacher.

As I walked out the door of the congressman's office I told his administrative assistant, Dick Thompson, "I have to tell you that your boss just said he was philosophically opposed to release time." Thompson, who had never been to Idaho, replied "What's that?" I simply said, "In about three days, Jim Goller (McClure's chief of staff, who resided in Idaho) is going to call you and explain it to you."

Since I went into the interviews on the subject of the Prayer Amendment, I played it straight and actually buried McClure's statement towards the end of the column. It wasn't long, though, before Goller was on the phone to me explaining his congressman had misunderstood the question and had written me a note explaining the misunderstanding and setting the record straight.

Goller later told me he had to spend part of the summer trailing former Congressman George Hansen to various LDS wards and stakes throughout southern Idaho as Hansen tried to use the column to convince his fellow church members that McClure could not be trusted. McClure easily won the primary and went on to defeat Bud Davis in one of the closer senatorial contests in Idaho history. McClure's eventual winning margin was approximately 20,000 votes.

In Idaho's First Congressional District, a baby-faced apple farmer by the name of Steve Symms easily defeated Andrus' good friend, Ed Williams, in the race to succeed McClure. Symms used a simple gimmick in his TV ads where he took a bite out of one of his apples, looked at the camera, and said, "Let's take a bite out of government!" His campaign signage also showed an apple with a bite out of it. The voters loved it.

In some of his campaign speeches Symms also dropped a line that always went over well, saying, "Government serves the people like a bull serves a cow."

In December, 1972, I finally received the call I had hoped for. On the other end was Governor Andrus: "There's a ticket with your name on it waiting for you at National Airport. I'd like you to come on out to Boise and have a talk with me about a job." Shortly, thereafter, I was on a plane headed back to the West with some words from my wife Marcia still echoing in my ears: "I don't care if he offers you a janitor's job, you take it. I want to go home to Idaho!"

*Chapter 9*

# Press Secretary
# to the Governor

For years, often to the embarrassment of our children, I had a habit of singing the state song of Idaho, "Here We Have Idaho," whenever we crossed back into my native state. To say I was a chauvinist when it came to my native state would be an understatement. I also taught our children some words from one of Sir Walter Scott's poems:

> *Breathes there the man with soul so dead,*
> *Who never to himself hath said,*
> *'This is my own, my native land!'*
> *Whose Heart hath ne'er within him burned*
> *As homeward he hath turn'd*
> *From wandering on a foreign strand?*
> *If such their breathe, go, mark him well!*
> *For him no minstrel's rapture swell;*
> *For the dog, doubly dying shall go down to the vile dust from whence*
> *he sprung*
> *Unwept! Unhonored! And Unsung!*

As I crossed into Idaho airspace on my journey to meet with Governor Andrus such sentiment was far from my mind. I was too busy trying to keep airsickness from soiling the only sport coat and shirt I had brought, and mortified at the thought I might walk into the Governor's Office the next day smelling like a sick puppy. As luck would have it, I had a several-hour layover in Denver, aka "Coors Country." I quickly downed several of the "golden bullets" on an empty stomach, jumped back on the next leg of the flight to Boise, and promptly encountered some of the usual severe Rocky Mountain turbulence which soon had the beer regurgitating.

I was met at the Boise airport by the Governor's then-press secretary, John Hough, who had served as Andrus' campaign press secretary. I ate my eggs sunny-side over with a fork, not my spoon, since while in D.C. as a reporter, I once had breakfast with John and the Governor, and made the social mistake of eating my eggs with my spoon -- something both loved to recall to my constant embarassment over the years.

Hough backgrounded me on what had led to the Governor giving me a call. Basically it came down to John wanting to move to the administrative side of the office, in part because he had developed a fairly testy relationship with some in the Idaho media. He and the Governor recognized his talents might be better applied towards office management. In addition, Hough wanted to spend more time working on issues, such as providing protection for the Hells Canyon area and keeping central Idaho's Chamberlain Basin from being logged.

As Andrus would later note, "The team that helps to elect you is most often not the team that helps you to govern." In Andrus' case, within six months, there were only two campaign staffers remaining on his personal staff, Hough, then the press secretary, and Jean Taylor, the scheduler. Different skills were needed, and the Governor saw that.

When I met with Andrus he got right to the point. He offered me the job of press secretary, explaining that while the pay was not much, the opportunity to learn and grow with him could lead to bigger and better things in my future. I accepted the job on the spot. After the agreement in principle was reached and a time set for me to report -January 1, 1973- Andrus also casually looked at me and said, "Oh, by the way, get a haircut! I personally am not hung up on such an issue, but I don't need to spend my time with a diversion where people in a conservative state like ours are questioning me about why I have some long-haired hippie on my staff." I got a haircut.

Andrus was a marvelous mentor. He taught me a great deal about politics, as well as how to live responsibly and be accountable in a tough, competitive world. I have told many people, "Cece Andrus is the finest graduate program in political science one could ever take." Fortunately for me, the Governor was patient. While demanding in his

102

expectations of what he wanted from his press operation, he was also willing to let me make a few mistakes, as long as I learned from them.

The day-to-day press operation was fun and challenging, but not always demanding. I developed and maintained good relations with the state's media and made a point of cultivating the older journalists, not to mention the godfather of Idaho journalists, Don Watkins, who was then the State Superintendent of Public Instruction's communications director. I always returned phone calls, and quickly mastered the art of knowing when to speak on the record, for background only, or off the record. I paid careful attention to reporters' deadlines while feeding them timely tidbits.

While aggressively expounding the Governor's position on issues, I also kept my ear to the ground and took the time to listen to reporters and to what they said they were hearing. I traveled with the Governor almost all the time and kept track of and ghosted numerous thank-you notes, which went out after each trip to nearly everyone with whom the Governor had met. I oversaw a program of congratulatory notes sent by the Governor to those achieving a success in some area, which were gleaned by the staff from various newspapers we scanned every day. Early on, I recognized the immense power of television and the importance in staging artful "photo ops" that reinforced messages without coming across as too contrived. It helped immensely that Andrus was as close to "a natural" as there was in using the medium to deliver messages and doing so in a manner that allowed his candor and sincerity to easily show through.

I once heard Andrus say to a television reporter who had asked a question: "do you want the thirty second sound bite, the fifteen second sound bite or the five second sound bite?" He could condense his response and get his message across that quickly if he had to do so. That can't be taught. Furthermore, he instinctively knew not to repeat a reporter's question, for it often was cast negatively. He understood the importance of always making positive statements. He knew how to do what is called "block and bridge" – briefly answer the question, but block the thrust and then bridge to your message.

He knew he could control the interview and that television presented an unrivaled method through which he could connect with the voters. He made it easy to be his press secretary.

We also made good use of radio, dropping in on stations across the state wherever we were traveling and sending out taped versions of the "Governor Reviews the Year" and the "Governor Looks Ahead" columns I had ghosted by former AP writers like Earle Jester. These columns went out to the numerous weekly newspapers in Idaho.

Traveling with the Governor provided time for me to watch, listen and learn. Gradually, I absorbed how he analyzed issues and reached conclusions. Before long, I knew I was beginning to think much like he thought, which in turn led to him increasingly valuing my advice and counsel. I was always reading, studying, learning, and like the Governor, would often pick up the phone to call supporters simply to ask them what they were hearing. I knew the Governor, depending on the issue, sought discreet counsel from others both inside and outside government.

Andrus also possessed a knack for popping swollen egos and for reminding his staff they were there to serve the Idaho public, not to lord it over anyone. He set a good example.

One day I looked up from my desk, and there stood Andrus at the entrance to my office, looking at the name plate on the door. He then turned to me, smiled and said "There are a lot of names on doors around here, aren't there?" He waited a moment, then added, "Just remember, there's only one name on the ballot!"

Another time, he called me into his office, closed the door, sat me down and reached for his billfold. He pulled out what he liked to call a "shotgun shell," a $100 bill, and handed it to me.

"What's that for, Governor?" I asked.

"Take that and walk down the street to Jacque Pen-nay's (J.C. Penny's) and buy yourself a new raincoat. I can't stand that old World War II Navy coat you've been wearing!" Startled but obedient, I walked down the street to the store, thinking to myself I could find a raincoat for $50 and pocket the difference. Andrus must have known and already checked it out. There was exactly one raincoat my size in stock, and it cost $99.

On a different occasion when responding to a question from the Governor, I replied "Well, I assume, Governor..." Cece held up his hand and said, "Stop right there. Has anyone ever diagrammed the word 'assume' for you?" I said no. Cece took out a pad and broke the word down, saying to me, "When you assume something, you make an 'ass' out of 'u' and 'me'." I never forgot that lesson, either.

Another time, I knew the Governor was deliberately holding back some information given him in confidence, and dying of curiosity, I tried to get him to tell me the secret. Again, he took out a pen and some paper and wrote the numeral 1 on the paper. "When you have a secret, and you are the only person who knows it, that's the numeral 1. Now, if you tell someone, write the numeral 1 next to the first one. What do you have? You have the numeral 11. And if you tell one other person, write the numeral once again, and what do you have? 111, don't you? That's how fast a secret spreads if you tell one other person."

Occasionally, I got in my own licks. During my years at Columbia, I had sworn I would never have a job where I had to wear a tie. I could get away with that while being a D.C. journalist, but couldn't as the Governor's press secretary. My compromise was that I never *learned* how to tie a tie. I prevailed on my dear, sweet wife, Marcia, to tie the ties for me using a slip knot, and the few ties I had were all hanging in my closet with the slip knots already done.

That worked fine until, one morning while traveling with the Governor, I put on my tie, the knot slipped, and there I stood in front of the mirror, untied tie in hand, wondering what to do. I had no choice but to knock on the Governor's door. When Cece opened, I stood there with tie in hand, looking plaintive and pathetic. Fortunately, he was in good humor but made a point of trying to teach me how easy it was to tie a tie, not understanding this idiosyncrasy of mine. The episode has been worth a few laughs between us over the years.

The Governor also assigned me to be the lead on some policy duties, the most challenging of which was to help him fashion the state's response to a document being circulated by the Atomic Energy Commission (AEC), entitled WASH-1539. The document basically was a plan to locate and then send the nation's nuclear waste to one permanent repository, with Idaho being a prime target.

As the location of the Idaho National Laboratory, the largest aggregation of active and inactive nuclear reactors in the world, and with several large communities (Idaho Falls, Blackfoot and Pocatello) somewhat dependent upon the significant federal funds being expended at the site, Cece knew Idaho had to move cautiously. His political instincts, though, told him Idaho voters simply would not accept their state being designated as the nation's nuclear garbage dump.

After conferring, I drew up a list of distinguished Idahoans to serve on a "Blue-ribbon" panel, which Andrus would name to review the AEC plan and to hold hearings to obtain public input from around the state. At my suggestion, Andrus named the still-popular William E. "Bud" Davis, who had returned to the presidency of Idaho State University, as the chairman of the panel. The panel proceeded to hold hearings in most major communities of the state and, to no one's surprise, the people spoke clearly: They wanted nothing to do with the AEC plan. Davis presented the findings at a final hearing in Germantown, Maryland, and offered some constructive suggestions on how best to handle and dispose of the material.

Over the years of Andrus' tenure, the position he adopted in those early days of the 1970s stood him in good stead through his record-long career as governor. From that day forward, Andrus adamantly opposed Idaho being dumped on. His stance forced the AEC and its successor agency, the Department of Energy, to deal with Idaho.

During the early years of my tenure as press secretary, I had organized and accompanied the Governor on several visits to the Idaho National Engineering Lab (INL) where Cece quickly honed in on the numerous barrels of low-level (transuranic) waste improperly stowed and partially buried. He recognized the material had to be reclaimed, repackaged, and removed from above the Snake River Aquifer that underlay the site. He told me one of his recurring nightmares was that a cartoonist back East might portray Idaho potatoes being irradiated by contaminated water in the aquifer. In a nano-second, it would devastate the Idaho potato industry, something he knew must be avoided.

To that end, he also helped force the federal government to construct a repository for transuranic waste in the salt caverns of New Mexico. During his second stint as governor (1987-1995), the federal government tried to renege on the agreement and ship more waste to Idaho after all. Andrus reminded the then Secretary of Energy what their deal had been, and what the Secretary should be doing to ensure federal government cooperation. Eventually, Andrus ordered the Idaho State Police to block access to the site. A picture of a stocky state trooper standing with his arms folded, in front of his squad car parked across some railroad tracks, ran in the *New York Times* and got the message across to the folks at the Department of Energy.

I took great pride over the years in helping keep my beloved native state free from additional nuclear garbage and was proud to help Andrus direct Idaho's poorly buried transuranic wastes to be dug up, repacked and shipped out of state to New Mexico. Likewise, I took pride in my role in putting together and staffing the Davis commission.

At about the same time, Cece also agreed to a request from the Idaho Potato Commission to make several television commercials touting the state's best-known agricultural product. He was shrewd enough to condition his starring role on the commercials not being shown in Idaho, knowing that would invite political criticism from Republicans who would allege he had coerced the Potato Commission into financing what they would claim were "thinly disguised election ads" that would be appearing just as he was gearing up for his re-election run.

Andrus also knew more than enough Idahoans would see the ads during their travels, that word would get back to the state, and chances were high that television stations would show them as a news item, which is exactly what happened. The ads were produced by a first-rate firm out of San Francisco, Foote, Cone & Belding. It was my first exposure to a blue-chip advertising agency. I learned a great deal as I worked with the agency and the Governor in reviewing scripts and then watching as the ads were filmed. All three commercials were dynamite.

One had Andrus walking through a potato field in Teton County with the Grand Tetons in the background, talking about how the right convergence has to occur between water, soil, and air to produce an Idaho No. 1 baker. The second ad was shot in a kitchen where the Governor was slicing, dicing and preparing potatoes to accompany a meal. At first I balked when the agency wanted to put the Governor in a pink apron for the filming, but I relented and later admitted that Andrus' smiling wink at the end made the ad a great success.

The third ad was produced at a potato warehouse near Boise. A crane was used to perch Cece atop a huge pile of potatoes, which the viewer was not initially allowed to see. The ad started with a tight-in shot of the Governor, and slowly the camera pulled back as he delivered his spiel.

During one of his trips to the nation's capitol, Cece had stopped off in a hotel bar for a nightcap when one of the commercials came on. Another customer sitting at the bar watched the ad in silence, and as it finished said out loud to no one in particular, "You'd think they would pay that guy enough as governor that he wouldn't have to moonlight!" Andrus loved retelling the story.

In subsequent years, the Governor took to his role as chief spud salesman with relish. Often, when he and I were traveling, Cece would order a baked potato, and he would always ask if the spud was an Idaho No. 1. If he had any doubts, he would ask to see the box and more often than not, follow the server into the kitchen to verify the origin of the spuds. He would then introduce himself to the chef. I always half expected to see a chef, swinging a meat cleaver, chasing the Governor out of his kitchen, but it never happened.

What the spud ads demonstrated again to me was what a natural Andrus was. For a lumberjack without media training, I always marveled at this god-given gift to communicate. In Andrus' case, the medium was not the message, the *messenger* was the message.

Nor was Andrus afraid to put the media in its place when it stepped out-of-bounds. For most politicians this is high-risk behavior because if a reporter feels the criticism to be unfair, or that the politician does not recognize and respect the media's role in a democracy, the newshounds can and will turn collectively against that poor soul.

Once, Cece and I landed by helicopter in Rexburg on the campus of Ricks College (now BYU-Idaho) after inspecting the devastation wrought by the collapse of the Teton Dam. A herd of media converged on him. One TV reporter, from KSL-TV in Salt Lake City, thrust a microphone in front of the Governor and asked, "Governor, are you going to rebuild the dam?" Andrus looked at him and forcefully said "That's the dumbest question I've ever been asked and if you don't get that mic out of my face I'm going to jam it down your throat!" (There may have been a couple of swear words I have omitted.) Needless to say, the rest got the message.

Years later, former Oregon Governor Tom McCall, himself a former TV newsman, told me the only person he had ever seen handle the media and the medium better than Andrus was Ronald Reagan. Part of Andrus' unique appeal was that his sincerity carried through the television and attracted people from across the political spectrum. Because the Governor worked at solving problems and avoided sharply partisan politics, when it came time to run for re-election he was able to call upon many Republicans to publicly support him.

While at a Pacific Northwest Commission meeting in Salem, Oregon, in late 1973, I listened to both McCall, a Republican, and Dan Evans, the Republican governor of Washington, offer to help Cece in his re-election bid. On the drive back to the Portland Airport, I convinced him his colleagues were sincere and he should ask for their help by inviting them to attend his premier fundraiser in Boise on March 16, 1974.

Reluctant at first, he finally did call. Both men agreed, and McCall did actually appear and speak at the enormously successful fundraiser.

As press secretary, I also played an instrumental role in helping Andrus shut down the last remaining "houses of ill repute" in Idaho. These businesses, left over vestiges from the days when mining was a major employer in my native Shoshone County, still operated in the community of Wallace, near my birthplace. They were tolerated by local authorities who preferred that prostitutes be checked for disease and who also felt the houses were legitimate business enterprises that contributed to the economic well-being of the community. A "live and let live attitude" prevailed among a solid majority of the local citizenry.

Neither Andrus nor I had planned to take on this delicate issue. Rather, his hand was forced by a young, and idealistic worker for the State Department of Health and Welfare's North Idaho regional office, who wrote a white paper advocating the "girls" be given some training as "counselors" to help direct their clients to appropriate professionals for assistance.

Someone took it upon himself to take the report to a member of the news media, who promptly wrote a story about it. Here was an "official" document of the state of Idaho acknowledging the existence of an illegal and illegitimate activity. Andrus had little choice but to call the attorney general and the head of the Idaho State Police, both of whom notified the local county authorities that the houses had to be shut down, or the county would face serious repercussions; further, the houses were to stay closed.

This being the 1974 re-election year, we both recognized the issue could potentially do some damage to the Governor, particularly with LDS voters in southern Idaho. Nor did we believe we should let resentment fester in Shoshone County, for the county was a historically strong bastion of Democratic support. My solution was to propose the Governor and I fly to northern Idaho and do a "Capitol for a Day" visit to Kellogg and Wallace, that he walk the streets, talk to voters, answer questions, and quell any lingering resentment.

Former State Representative Bill Murphy, serving as a deputy chief of staff to Andrus at the time, vehemently objected to my plans, but the Governor saw the wisdom in confronting the issue head-on and overruled Murphy. I made sure Spokane television was notified of the visit, hoping that at least one of the three commercial stations which dominate the northern Idaho market would end up covering the visit. KHQ-TV, the NBC affiliate, decided to send a reporter and a cameraman to follow the Governor.

In my mind, the best scenario was for the Governor to be walking the street and have someone stumble out of a bar, spot him, walk up and demand to know why he had shut down "their" houses. The governor could then politely but firmly explain the law was the law and he had taken an oath of office to uphold and enforce the laws of the state. I could not have scripted it any better. While walking the main street of Kellogg, the Governor was confronted by a rather rude and snooty voter who walked out of a bar and who demanded to know why the houses had been shuttered.

During the 70s I was witness to both poignant moments and funny incidents. On the poignant side, shortly after I went to work for the Governor, his good friend and chief of staff, Ed Williams, tragically drowned when his jet boat swamped in the high water of the Snake River during an Easter outing in Hells Canyon. Several other staff members from the governor's office were on board, but mercifully they were wearing life jackets.

Those with life jackets were swept quite a distance downriver and were suffering from hypothermia before being rescued. Ed and his cousin, Jack, were not wearing life jackets and were never to be seen again.

Governor Andrus personally searched for Ed's body by helicopter up and down the river. When he returned to Boise, he summoned his staff to a meeting at his home where he broke down and wept over this deeply personal loss.

One of the reasons many Idahoans identified with the Governor was he loved to hunt and fish. The Governor was also good at both and took pride in his skill.

Thus it was that one morning I was awakened by a call from the Governor who, in a very cold and stern voice said, "Well, what do you have to say for yourself?"

"About what?" I groggily asked.

"About the front page of today's *Statesman!*"

I hurriedly signaled to Marcia to get the paper off the front step, telling the Governor I needed to retrieve it and look.

"Take your time," he said sarcastically.

I looked at the front page, where there was a story about a recent deer hunt the Governor had been on, in which he had shot at a deer but had apparently missed because the deer did not go down. Normally a crack shot, the Governor shot six more times before the deer finally went down. Andrus could not believe he had missed so badly so often. Of course, he hadn't. He hit the deer with all seven shots and pure adrenaline had kept the deer moving.

The UPI reporter played the story along the lines of "Governor Shoots Bambi – Seven Times!"

"It wasn't me," I told the Governor.

"Then who?" he asked.

Not wanting to be a ratfink, I said just that to the Governor, then added a question: "Who else did you tell the story to?"

Suddenly saying, "That damn Hough, I'll kill him," the Governor slammed down the phone.

I was convinced John Hough, then the deputy chief of staff, was a dead man walking. Somehow, though, Hough was able to get the Governor to see the humor in the situation and he survived.

The time for the Governor's run for a second term was rapidly approaching and I began to shift my focus to the re-election effort. The Governor took the position that, like himself, I was on duty twenty-four hours a day. One could not separate my communication duties between the Governor-as-governor and the Governor-as-candidate for re-election. Along with another staffer, Larry Meierotto, who had labored in Andrus' first successful campaign in 1970, I became the *de facto* communications director and co-manager of the campaign alongside my state duties as press secretary.

One of the first things Meieretto and I did was cook up the already referenced program called "Capitol for a Day," in which the Governor traveled to all forty-four of the state's county seats, declaring each town "Capitol for A Day." He would spend the morning walking Main Street, visiting with the druggist, stopping by the local coffee shop to palaver, dropping in on the grocer and the jeweler. At noon, he usually spoke to a service club, and then dropped by the newspaper and/or the radio station to report on what he had been hearing that day from townspeople before heading back to Boise.

(Andrus' successor, John Evans, continued the program, but it lapsed when Phil Batt and Dirk Kempthorne served as governor. The program was resurrected by Jim Risch and continued by Andrus' long-time Lieutenant Governor, Butch Otter, after his election in 2006.)

We also designed a 3x5 card for the Governor to hand out, especially if someone got too long winded with him. He would invite the citizen to write his or her name and to describe succinctly the issue. When he got back to Boise, he would pass the cards out to his staff with instructions that the citizen was to receive an interim response within two weeks, with an answer and, if possible, a resolution within one month.

During one Capitol for a Day visit to the Idaho County seat of Grangeville, I feared for a second I was going to be confronted with a press secretary's nightmare. I saw the Governor's eyes flash and thought surely he was going to punch out a constituent! It was no ordinary constituent, either, but rather a colorful, almost legendary character named Buckskin Billy, who was a squatter on federal land along the Salmon River, far from the end of the nearest road.

We had been walking Main Street and had stopped by the Washington Water Power office when Billy, who had heard the Governor was in town, confronted him. Billy wanted the Governor to order the Forest Service to quit harassing him and to convey to him title to the place he felt he had homesteaded. The Governor patiently explained to Billy the laws covering his case and why he couldn't and wouldn't intervene. At some point Billy called the Governor a liar and that was when I saw the Governor's eyes flash. I thought for sure the old gypo logger in Andrus was going to overwhelm the governor in him and Billy was going to be laid out by a right cross. I saw the headlines: "Governor Decks Constituent" with a subhead of "Loses Temper at Legendary Buckskin Billy." I knew it wasn't going to be pretty, and knew it might cost us our jobs.

Somehow, Andrus checked his temper, told Billy they were just going to have to agree to disagree, gave him the card, and said he had to be moving on. Billy walked off still complaining bitterly about all forms of government.

The Capitol for a Day program was enormously successful and was one of many reasons Andrus was re-elected by the largest margin in Idaho history, 73% of the total vote. Though not a particularly taxing campaign, I internalized a lot of stress and worry about the future, for upon coming home following election night I slept for three solid days.

As the Governor embarked on his second term, it dawned on me he was getting bored. Always one to draw up lists, Andrus had drawn up a list of what he wanted to accomplish while in office, and by the beginning of his sixth year as governor he had largely achieved each and every goal. He had obtained funding for kindergartens, reorganized and streamlined state government, obtained a series of local land use laws that would enable Idaho counties concerned about growth to plan and manage their growth, provided circuit breaker property tax relief for senior citizens -- in all, he had ten goals he kept on a slip of paper underneath his desk pad, and he had checked off all of them.

Always one with an uncanny capability to look over the horizon, the Governor, unbeknown to anyone, was quietly plotting his next move. He was eyeing the position of a cabinet officer in the Democratic administration he was sure, because of Watergate, would be elected in 1976. The post he most coveted, Secretary of the Interior, was one that would allow him to continue to work for Idaho.

Andrus was also pretty sure who would be the next president – his good friend and the former Governor of Georgia, Jimmy Carter. There was only one complicating factor, and that was the looming candidacy of another good friend, Idaho's senior U.S. Senator, Frank Church. Andrus had to walk a fine line of being loyal to Church as long as he was in the race, while assuring Carter he would help him whenever Senator Church ended his candidacy. Carter understood and respected

Andrus for his loyalty to Church and the skill with which he handled this ticklish situation.

Andrus thought the Senator early on had made a fatal, strategic error that would inevitably doom his candidacy. He urged the Senator to abandon his divisive hearings into the rogue behavior of the CIA and to commit himself to campaigning early, so as to establish himself as the clear liberal alternative to the more conservative Carter. Andrus correctly predicted that if Church stayed on to chair the investigation, by the time it concluded, it would be too late for the Idaho senator to win sufficient primaries and convention delegates despite whatever good press the hearings might generate.

Once Carter had dispatched Church just as he had Senator Henry M. Jackson and Rep. Morris K. Udall (earlier liberal challengers), Cece was free to help the Georgian. And help him he did, not only at the Democratic Convention in New York City, but also when Andrus and I barnstormed across the state of South Carolina for the Georgia peanut farmer.

Carter intrigued me from the start. I can easily recall watching Andrus and Carter work together at a National Governor's Association (NGA) gathering the summer of 1973 at Lake Tahoe. Each served on the Health and Welfare subcommittee of the NGA and had worked to put together a policy statement on welfare reform. It was a balanced statement and received the unanimous support of the other governors present.

However, as the meeting got underway, California's Governor, Ronald Reagan, arrived and let it be known he objected to the policy statement. Carter, with the help of Andrus and Oregon Governor Tom McCall, then orchestrated the presentation of the policy to all the governors. When Reagan objected, Andrus and McCall began asking the California governor a series of questions, first and foremost among them: "Isn't it true, Governor Reagan, that the subcommittee of which you are a member met seven times and that not once did you or any of your staff ever attend a session?"

With Carter and Andrus standing at the podium, a series of embarrassing questions were asked with Carter quietly smiling while Andrus and McCall publicly humiliated Reagan. When the vote came it was 49 to 1 in favor of the proposal. Reagan, of course, was the lone no vote. Following the vote, Reagan immediately got up, left the room,

114

held a press conference, and departed the meeting altogether. When Cece returned to his seat, I remember whispering in his ear, "You better hope Reagan never becomes President, because that man's not going to forget what you and Governor Carter just did to him." In one of the few political misstatements I ever heard him make, he smiled and said he doubted Reagan would ever be president.

Andrus seemed to think that Carter had possibilities. I quickly read the Georgia governor's short political biography, *Why Not the Best?* Andrus and I also journeyed to Pocatello and Idaho Falls when the now ex-Governor Carter visited Idaho in his role as chair of some national Democratic endeavor. It was clear to me how serious and methodical Carter was as I answered numerous questions from a Carter aide regarding the press that were covering these events and the other folks who attended. Carter was also quick to point out to folks and press that he had been to Idaho before, when he was in the Navy being trained as an officer on a nuclear submarine under Admiral Hyman Rickover. The Naval Propulsion Lab, which had perfected the nuclear reactor for submarines, was located in the Idaho desert at the National Engineering Lab, and Carter, like many Naval officers, as part of his instruction, had been stationed there.

The only surprise to me was that after Carter received the Democratic presidential nomination, the only place the campaign asked Andrus to campaign for the Georgian was South Carolina. It seemed far from Andrus' natural turf, but away we flew to Charleston to begin a four-day barn-storming trip around the Palmetto State in October 1976.

I remember two things about the trip. One was South Carolina Governor Jim West saying to Andrus as we drove down the road late in the afternoon "I feel a sinkin' spell comin' on Cecil!" That was Governor West's way of saying it was time for a drink, and the South Carolinian quickly demonstrated he had a God-given capacity for quite a lot of John Barleycorn. That Carter later made West ambassador to the dry kingdom of Saudi Arabia simply boggled my mind.

The other item was meeting a savvy, articulate State Senator, Richard Riley, when we were in Greenville. Like Andrus, I was beginning to spot what Andrus called "solid horseflesh." Riley went on to be elected governor of South Carolina, and then served as the Secretary of Education in President Clinton's cabinet.

Within a few weeks of the November, 1976, election of Jimmy Carter as the next president of the United States, I found myself, along with John Hough and the Governor, winging our way to a meeting in Plains, Georgia.

## Chapter 10

# The Return to Washington, D.C.

I n early December, President-elect Carter invited Andrus to come to his hometown of Plains, Georgia to discuss the post of Secretary of the Interior. For several weeks, whenever press speculation focused on the Interior post, Cecil Andrus was at the top of the list and he was considered a prohibitive favorite to get the nod. I was already fielding inquiries from national media, as well as calls from folks who wanted to work for Andrus at Interior, some of whom were brazen enough to make it clear that they thought they had better credentials than me to be the communications director.

I also gained a new insight into a move the Governor presciently had made during his 1974 re-election race. With two weeks until Election Day and comfortably ahead in his race against his Republican Lieutenant Governor, Jack Murphy, Cece ordered Meierotto and me to pull all of his television spots except the final weekend's "ask for the vote" ad, and to turn the already paid time slots over to the Democratic candidate for lieutenant governor, State Senator John Evans of Malad.

At the time, I thought the gesture was primarily motivated by revenge. Evans' opponent was a turncoat former Democratic State Representative, Vern Ravenscroft, whom Cece had defeated in the 1970 Democratic gubernatorial primary. After the election, Ravenscroft promptly switched parties, leaving several good Democrats holding the bag on campaign debt, and began to transform himself into a stalwart Republican. Andrus detested such moves, and for years thereafter, calling Ravenscroft the "right kind of enemy" to have, went after him unmercifully at every opportunity. It was nothing personal, it was just good hardball politics.

Though Evans was trailing slightly at the time, the infusion of a massive television buy did indeed turn the tide for him. While Andrus was re-elected by the largest margin in Idaho history, Evans squeaked by Ravenscroft and now I understood the real reason. Always one to look over the horizon, even in 1974, Andrus was farsighted enough to see that the Democrats would probably retake the White House, but that he would only have a shot at a cabinet post if he could turn Idaho's gubernatorial chair over to another Democrat. He left little to chance.

Nor did he leave anything to chance as he prepared for his interview with the president-elect. He researched the issues he thought Carter might want to talk about, and when we flew to Plains, he was fully prepared to discuss almost any topic. Both of us knew one issue, if not the leading issue, was going to be resolution of the so-called section 17(d)(2) of the Alaska Native Land Claims Settlement Act. This was the "bargain" section whereby proponents of Alaska's pipeline agreed to a *quid pro quo* that would set aside at least eighty million acres of pristine Alaska lands into the four protection systems – national parks, wildlife refuges, wild and scenic rivers, and national recreation areas. And Idaho's governor just happened to have on his staff someone intimately familiar with the act, the players, and the backroom deals that had been cut.

To make connections work and to be in Plains by the time the President-elect wanted to interview Andrus, John Hough and I had chartered Boise Cascade's corporate jet to fly to SeaTac Airport in Seattle where we boarded a Northwest "red-eye" flight to Chicago. There, we had to talk ourselves onto the oversold flight from O'Hare to Atlanta because the Governor had snagged the last available seat. We succeeded.

In Atlanta, we were taken by the Georgia State Police to the private side of the airport, where we boarded a single engine Cessna 172 for the flight to Plains. Ninety minutes later, we landed in a cow pasture, and, as the plane bucked to a stop, we looked up to see a contingency of the White House press corps, led by UPI's Helen Thomas and ABC's Sam Donaldson, stampeding across the field, eager to consume the "new meat" which had just arrived.

Fortunately, before any "foot in the mouth" could occur, we were rescued by Carter's press secretary, the late Jody Powell, who drove us to the Carter home, a modest, one story rancher on the edge of Plains.

We were graciously greeted by the President-elect and Mrs. Carter, and, after some pleasantries, the two governors got down to business in Carter's study. John and I stood in the kitchen chatting with Mrs. Carter and Powell.

That night, John and I sauntered over to the complex of trailers serving as a mobile newsroom for the media following the President-elect. There also was a lounge trailer where the hard-working members of the media could enjoy an adult beverage. John and I thought we would "spin" these veteran sharks on the merits of the new Interior Secretary -- on background, of course.

In particular, we thought we would hustle crafty old Helen Thomas. We found her enjoying perhaps a few too many drinks with Donaldson. Not fooling her one bit as to what we were doing, she asked me if I knew how to write on the teletype machines UPI used.

"Of course," I fibbed.

She handed me the key to her teletype and said "Here, go file a piece with the new Interior Secretary's background and credentials."

Hough and I about fell over, but I didn't hesitate a nano-second, grabbing the key and heading off to the newsroom. In that way, UPI subscribers worldwide first learned about the "probable" nomination of Idaho Governor Cecil D. Andrus to be Carter's Interior Secretary along with a wealth of information about his background, skill, successes, and what a great choice the President-elect had made.

Andrus and Carter met privately twice. The next morning, in a press briefing in Americus, Georgia, the President-elect announced his selection of Idaho's twenty-sixth governor as the nation's forty-second Secretary of the Interior. It was during one of these interviews that Andrus, knowing the President-elect to be an avid fly-fisherman, invited President-elect Carter and his wife, Roslyn, to float and fly-fish the Middle Fork of the Salmon River during one of the upcoming summers. Andrus promised a wonderful time both shooting rapids and fishing for westslope cutthroat.

A couple of summers later, the President-elect accepted the invitation, did indeed come to Idaho to enjoy one of the world's unique floating and fly fishing experiences. It killed me not to be able to accompany Cece on that trip, but a few years later, when our children were older, our family floated the Middle Fork and had a wonderful time.

After the second meeting between Andrus and Carter the next morning, John and I rode with Powell to the press event for the Andrus announcement. I will never forget Powell railing about the Secret Service while we were racing along one of just three routes to Americus, which they always varied. Powell compared the Secret Service to ancient Rome's Praetorian Guards and predicted that someday history would repeat itself with the Secret Service making and breaking future presidents, just as they had once made and unmade Roman Emperors.

With the President-elect's announcement, the Secretary-designate and his two aides were soon on their way back to Boise to be greeted by a tumultuous airport welcome, led by, among others, former Governor and U.S. Senator Len B. Jordan, about-to-become Governor John V. Evans (Evans was almost giddy in anticipation of achieving his long-desired goal), other statewide elected officials, members of the legislature, and many of the Governor's friends. Idaho itself seemed proud that day to have its governor become the first Idahoan ever designated to serve in a President's cabinet.

Unbeknown to anyone, in a private moment with Cece, I tried to talk him out of taking the position. Having been in D.C. before, I knew what a cutthroat, sharktank of a world it is, and that Andrus was a straight-shooter who operated in a trusting way. I felt the Governor ultimately would be frustrated and disappointed by the dishonesty, the moral corruption, and the many ego-driven jerks who held positions of prominence in the national government.

As Andrus always did, he listened politely to my argument, and then quietly replied: "This is a wonderful opportunity to do some real good not only for the people of Idaho, but for the people of the United States. It's a door opening. If one refuses to go through such a door, that's the day he starts to die, Chris. I don't know about you, but I'm not ready to start dying. I'm stepping up to this challenge and opportunity and going to D.C. and you're going with me!"

And so I did.

In those days, the federal government did not pay for a move to Washington, D.C., so I had to engineer a bridge loan from a banker friend, Harry Magnuson, to underwrite my moving expenses. Because I was soon consumed in my new work, Marcia and I decided to once again settle in Gaithersburg, buying a home which literally backed up to the 10,000-acre Seneca Creek State Park, which we had enjoyed living close to during our earlier stint in D.C.

I would be the first to admit that the secret to the success I achieved in managing the Office of Public Affairs was that after reviewing my new staff, I picked out one veteran, Harmon Kallman, who I made my chief deputy and charged with the day-to-day running of the office. Harmon was superb, not afraid to challenge me when he thought I was going down the wrong path, and always a source of wise counsel. Having been a journalist at the *Denver Post* before coming to D.C., he had high regard for the craft as well as a deep love of the West, and a wealth of knowledge about the Interior department and its multiple public affairs offices. Together we made a great team.

The other astute move I made was cultivating the mumbling – almost bumbling – minor official who delivered Interior's press releases around town, Harry Thomas. Harry had a heart of gold, often offered shrewd insights on the ways of D.C., and personified loyalty to both the Secretary and me.

It turns out there is a large, primarily African-American network of lower-echelon civil servants who do most of the nitty-gritty work in Washington ensuring that the government works on a day-to-day basis. If one is astute enough to be aware of and smart enough to accord them the respect they deserve, they can do much to help make the tenure of outsiders like Andrus and his Idaho mafia be a successful one.

Harry, with the assistance of his talented wife, Romaine, was a major wheel in this below-the-radar-screen operation, and shortly after we left, he was elected to the D.C. City Council from Ward 5, the poorest, toughest African-American ward in the city. Harry remained the man for that ward for many years, holding the seat until ill health dictated he retire – and pass the seat along to his son.

Whenever the Governor and I visited D.C., even long after we left office, Harry saw to it that we had a discreet police escort, and he kept a kind and watchful eye on us. I'll always remember his first words to me when we were first introduced: "Thank God Almighty, the Democrats are back, Mr. Carlson!"

I was also aware that some folks in D.C. are attracted to power and will use sex to entrap. I carefully sized up my staff and kept as my personal secretary a talented but matronly woman, Ruth Edmondson, who had served my Republican predecessor. I asked Ruth one question: Would she be as loyal to me as she had been to my Republican predecessor? She answered yes, and she was true to her word.

I further recognized that a certain attractive young woman, who obviously knew she was attractive, could become a source of temptation and trouble. So along with six others, I sent her over to the new Department of Energy which Jim Schlesinger was creating.

Somehow, Andrus learned about this person before I made my final decisions on what personnel to cut or designate for reassignment. Shortly after opening shop, he had mandated that his "direct reports" (those who reported directly to the Interior Secretary and not through another senior official) reduce their personal staff by 25% and their budgets by a like amount. He asked to see the list of the six folks I had designated for assignment to Energy.

I went down the stairs to the sixth floor (the Office of Public Affairs was on the seventh floor), and into the Secretary's office and presented the list. He looked it over, looked up at me with a smile, and quietly said, "You're learning, Chris."

The Governor also taught me, both in word and by example, the importance of standing up for what one believes to be right. It came about that I defied the legendary California Representative Phil Burton, knowing I was right and that the Secretary would back me up. Much to the consternation of Andrus' director of legislative affairs, Gary Catron, I balked at "layering in" to the bureaucracy a Burton staffer.

Burton had an office director in San Francisco whom he decided he wanted placed into the position of communications director for the newly created Golden Gate National Park. The only glitch was that I, as the director of the office of public affairs, had to sign off on the appointment. I refused to do so. The reason was that on an earlier visit to San Francisco with the Secretary, Burton's office director was to introduce Cece at a breakfast gathering, something he was barely able to do because at,7 a.m., the office director was drunk.

While at home one evening, I received the inevitable call from the congressman. At first, Burton was polite, but before long he was angry and threatening. I, however, wouldn't budge. Burton harangued me with several more late-night calls, but when Secretary Andrus refused to intervene, his legislative affairs director soon approached me to see if a compromise could be reached.

I insisted the congressman's office director first undergo an alcohol rehab program, that he be sober for six months, and then reapply for the position, which would be kept open. Burton accepted the compromise, and to my knowledge the individual remained sober and was able to capably fulfill his new duties.

While I did the right thing in that instance, there were other times when I skirted the edge of truth. While striving to be an intrinsically honest person, like many, I was not always as honest as I might have been. It's amazing to me how, over the years I have been bowled over by the incredible mental machinations normally bright and intelligent people will go through to rationalize why honesty is not always the best policy.

One time, it had funny, if embarrassing consequences.

Gary Catron and I are big baseball fans. The schedule had the Interior Secretary flying again to San Francisco, and I realized if we departed on Sunday morning from the Baltimore airport we would arrive in San Francisco in time -- barely -- to see the Giants play Atlanta. Realizing how tight it would be, I decided to call the Giants' public relations office and say that Secretary Andrus and several of his aides would be in town and would like to see the Giants game. Then I asked if they could accommodate the Secretary with tickets.

One can guess what happened. Andrus, not even aware of the little scam I was working, expressed no interest in attending the game, and instead went right to his hotel room. Gary and I, not to be deterred, went right onto the ballgame, collected the tickets, and took the seats.

All was fine until the fifth inning. The Giants flashed on their scoreboard a big welcome to Interior Secretary Cecil D. Andrus, and the Giants' public relations director showed up at the seats with a television crew in hand that wanted to interview the Secretary. Keeping my cool, I explained that Andrus, not feeling well, had just left – a nice little white lie if there ever was one.

Another time, I orchestrated -- from my home -- the deft handling by the Park Police of a sit-in by Mitch Snyder, a self-styled champion of the homeless. Here also, in retrospect, I later came to wonder if I had acted in a manner consistent with my Christian principles. At the time, though, I had convinced myself Mitch was nothing more than a publicity hound using homeless people as a pulpit to spew his other beliefs. Never having met the man, I nonetheless self-righteously questioned his sincerity and convictions.

I had just gotten home when Larry Meierotto, whom I had encouraged to seek the powerful position of Assistant Secretary for Policy, Budget and Administration, was on the phone. The Park Police were reporting Mitch had led about fifty homeless people into Union Station and they were conducting a sit-in until forcibly removed. Once I established they were not blocking the passage of commuters and customers to trains, I told Meierotto to direct the Park Police to leave them alone until midnight.

He asked why, and I explained it was the media picture of the police carrying the homeless to paddy wagons that Mitch wanted, and we were not going to let him have it. At midnight, after the late evening news was over, I told Meierotto to have the Park Police gently pick each demonstrator up and carry them out of the station. End of story. So that's what happened.

Shortly after midnight, however, I was awakened by Meierotto again. He reported that the homeless protestors had promptly lain down in the street in front of the station, and the police wanted to know what they should do next. I told Larry to tell them "Nothing – the street is the responsibility of the D.C. police, not ours, and it's now their problem." Within minutes Meierotto was back on the phone, saying the situation commander on the scene for the D.C. police was asking if we had any advice for him on what he should do.

"I suggest they block off the street and leave the protesters there. It is going to be below freezing tonight, and once they realize they're not going to be arrested, they'll all get up and leave before the sun rises." That's what happened.

The next day I was the toast of the Secretary's staff meeting for handling the situation in a manner which garnered no bad publicity for the department. Even I realized, though, that the issue of the homeless was real and needed to be redressed in some way. While I had been a good soldier in denying media coverage, I wasn't so sure I had necessarily been in the right.

I refined and postulated some political axioms while in D.C. that, while not original with either Andrus or me, nonetheless nicely covered many of the situations that occur in the nation's capitol, a place we felt was surreal most of the time. To wit:

*1) "In politics, there are no coincidences."* Over the years, almost every time I saw something or heard something in the political arena and was struck by "the coincidence" of that with something else, there was in fact no coincidence. I later came to realize that the two were related and I just had to figure out how.

*2) "The ship of state is the only ship that most often, most frequently leaks, from the top."* Whenever a leak occurred in D.C., which was frequently, since the town lives and thrives on leaked information, I was able to convince the Governor not to look down the organization, but instead up. Leaks most often were carefully calculated and came most frequently from high-ranking officials and not from the professionals within the civil service.

*3) "He who tooteth not his own horn, the same shall not be tootethed!"* This was my way of saying in a town full of ego-maniacs, if one wanted to be heard one had to toot his own horn loudly, if not often. I was selective and thoughtful, but there were several times when I carefully scripted and orchestrated such "tooteth" exercises to keep the Interior Secretary in the news.

Two outstanding instances of this were when I had the Governor release a couple of peregrine falcons from the top of the Interior building in D.C. This resulted in a wonderful front page picture in the *Washington Post* of Andrus holding one peregrine with another perched on his shoulder. The second instance was when Andrus dedicated a small unnamed park across from the U.S. Information Agency in the name of one of television journalism's patron saints, Edward R. Murrow. Murrow's widow, Janet, attended the event, as did Eric Sevareid and CBS brass. Andrus received five minutes on the *CBS Evening News* that night.

*4) "Pigs get fat, but hogs get slaughtered."* This was vintage Andrus and covered so many situations perfectly because it went right to the heart of what's wrong with ego-maniacs – fundamentally, they are just greedy souls who will never be satisfied with what they get out of life, whether it is more money, more sex partners, more power, more whatever. Inevitably, not being satisfied with being a pig, these personalities overreach, become hogs, get caught because the overreach often crosses ethical or legal lines, and the individual gets lead to the slaughterhouse. Politics, whether local, state, or national is replete with the skeletons of practitioners who overreached because they could never be satisfied with just being an ordinary pig.

*5) "There's no road so long that it doesn't have a bend in it."* Another vintage Andrus expression that is so true. Today's enemy is tomorrow's ally, and if one has burned a bridge, or stepped on someone while headed up the ladder, the worm always turns and the offended party has a shot at wreaking vengeance. Just in discussing this axiom one can see how many of these clichés have become part and parcel of everyday conversation, but one most often sees them in the context of politics. The issue for me with regard to this axiom was whether to pull the trigger on the metaphorical gun I might hold when someone who had crossed the Governor appeared in my boresight. Trying to remain a good person in the rarified air of D.C., I did have to remind myself the truth in the Biblical saying: "Vengeance is mine. I will repay,- saith the Lord!" The temptation to be the Lord's avenging angel, though, can be overwhelming.

*6) "Denial is not just the name of a river in Egypt."* Another observation the Governor and I drew was how many people in Washington, D.C., lived in denial of obvious truths, especially facts existing beyond the Beltway. It was like living in a surreal world enabled one to deny all that may be real or true, especially when it came to the real-life impacts of decisions made by agencies with no thought of impacts in places like North Fork, Idaho.

7) *"They never go back to Pocatello!"* This axiom was first postulated in the mid-1950s by a U.S. senator from Oregon, Richard Neuberger, and was the title to a piece he wrote for *The Saturday Evening Post.* The Senator used it to explain the phenomena of how few congressmen, upon leaving office, ever returned home. With the passage of time, it has become increasingly true. It's not just true for members of Congress, but is also for many of the staff they bring with them from the home state. Both member and staff alike get trapped by the attraction to being close to the seat of power and by the salary they make. In D.C., Congress has done an incredible job of taking care of its members in terms of salary and benefits, and much of this has spilled over into the civil service. People simply get trapped. They fantasize about returning home, but the truth is they can't afford to do so. Few will command the kind of salary they earn in Washington. Keenly aware of this, the Governor and I planned our exit strategies, literally from day one. Unlike many Idahoans who had gone to Washington, we successfully made our return to the Northwest. We did go back to Pocatello.

8) *"Rode hard and put up wet."* Another Andrus expression which referred to the many long, hard days his staff and he put in at Interior. Andrus and the Idaho crew were not the typical D.C. 9-to-5 workers. Most, like the Secretary, were at their desks by 7 a.m. and often did not leave until 7 p.m. Most also took home a brief case of memos to read in the evening after dinner. This sort of work ethic was not typical. To his credit, though, Andrus was insistent that staff, especially those with family, spend their weekends at home. He knew families bore the brunt of the long hours during the week and the numerous travels. He underscored how important it was that staff keeps

personal relationships with spouses and children in good shape. This I dutifully obeyed, seldom going into the office on the weekend.

*9) "It is easier to chuck a spear than to hold a shield."* Another truism that the Governor often used while noting how easily and quickly yesterday's allies would toss a barb or criticism at him if he wasn't in their corner on all of their issues all of the time. Defense, holding the shield, required one to stand there in one place and hold up the shield to deflect the incoming missile. Preferring to be on the offense and to force antagonists to respond to his initiatives, the Governor did not particularly like having to hold up the metaphorical shield and deflect criticism. He sometimes would smile while saying, "You know, it's hard to hit a moving target." The challenge for staff, however, was not only to keep moving, but also to keep critics on the defensive by chucking a few spears of our own.

*10) "There's nothing like a hanging in the morning to focus one's attention."* Another of my favorites, Andrus would invoke this saying to underscore the importance of certain meetings, that there would be no excuses for mistakes, and there would be no surprises to him. Surprising the Governor, either in a meeting, or by his learning something through the media he should have been first informed of, would inevitably lead to the "hanging in the morning." Anyone violating the "no surprises" rule would be shown the door immediately.

There were several other defining moments which tested our mettle during those years in D.C. One of the most prominent involved the columnist, Jack Anderson, and another involved a well-crafted effort to create a Department of Natural Resources which went awry.

Jack Anderson was for many years a classic, "muckraking" columnist. Through his column, which ran in more than 600 newspapers across the country, he felt it was his purpose to expose corruption and hypocrisy on the part of politicians and fraud, waste, and abuse in government wherever he could document it. A devout Mormon from Utah, he had a self-righteous streak to him. He wrote his columns in a pejorative manner, carrying on the tradition of his mentor, Drew Pearson.

One day, my secretary at the Office of Public Affairs stuck her head in the door and said a Dale Van Atta was on the phone. I knew Van Atta was an associate writer for Anderson and my guard instantly went up. My caution was warranted.

Van Atta began peppering me with a series of questions related to an old and unproven story from Idaho which had first circulated in the mid-1970s, alleging Governor Andrus had ties to mob-connected gaming interests. Allegedly, a firm out of Buffalo, New York, had channeled thousands of unreported dollars into Andrus' successful 1970 election campaign and the alleged *quid pro quo* was that the Governor would work behind-the-scenes to foster the legalization of gaming in Idaho. The earlier charges also alleged the Governor's first director of law enforcement, former Kootenai County Sheriff John Bender, had been a part of the conspiracy and that he too had ties to "the mob."

There were several problems with the story, beginning with the fact none of it was true, which I explained to Van Atta. A right-wing attorney from Nampa, Stanley Crow, had taken it upon himself to become a self-ordained investigative reporter. Since he had an agenda, namely to discredit Andrus, he set out looking for information he could selectively use, as most smear artists do, and present it as the "truth." Crow sold several weekly newspapers on running a series of articles he would produce, and though built entirely around circumstantial "evidence," the weeklies would publish.

Most mainstream news media in Idaho did their own checking, then dismissed the story for the balderdash it was. Then, for reasons neither Andrus nor I ever really understood (perhaps they were merely trying to build circulation?), Dick Hronek, the managing editor of the state's largest newspaper, *The Idaho Statesman,* decided to buy the series and start running it.

As I referenced earlier, while Andrus is a politician with an exceptionally thick skin there is one thing he will not tolerate – anyone questioning his integrity. At the Governor's behest, I scheduled an editorial board in 1975 with the Boise newspaper. We went immediately to the paper, confronted Hronek and the board, and presented facts which rebutted all the allegations. It did get quite heated and at one point I wanted to knock Hronek's block off, he was being so insulting. Andrus, though himself angered, kept his cool while I stewed. When it was done, the publisher ordered the series dropped. I thought we had seen the last of this claptrap. It was also the last we saw of Hronek, who shortly thereafter left the *Statesman.*

To my surprise, though, Jack Anderson was recycling these old unsubstantiated charges. Even after a detailed explanation to Van Atta, it was clear Anderson intended to run with the story. Once briefed, Andrus wanted to know what could be done to stop this calumny from being printed. When told nothing was going to stop it, he directed me to find a libel lawyer, for he intended to sue Anderson and the *Washington Post,* which distributed Anderson's column.

I found an excellent libel attorney with whom the Governor and I met to discuss the Governor's concerns. It was an interesting meeting in that the attorney told Andrus he thought given the Governor's excellent reputation, it would be very difficult to prove that the Anderson rehash in any way caused damage to the Governor's reputation. The attorney said he seriously doubted any jury would give substance to the allegations Anderson would allege and that a jury would, in all likelihood, conclude the Governor had not been damaged. In a nice way, he said he could take the Governor's money, but at the end of the day nothing would come of the story and the Governor would not be harmed.

He turned out to be correct. It was a one-day story to which no one else in the media gave any credence, and clearly there was no damage done to the Governor's reputation.

While serving the public from Interior, there was one serious policy setback which the Secretary felt could have been a victory if the Georgia Mafia and the President had listened to Cece's counsel. This policy issue related to President Carter's desire, supported by the Interior Secretary, to create a Department of Natural Resources that would house all land management and environmental agencies, with the exception of the Environmental Protection Agency, under one roof and one secretary. Carter and Andrus thought it absurd, for example, that the U.S. Forest Service was housed in the Department of Agriculture when it more naturally should be housed at Interior and combined with its sister agency, the Bureau of Land Management.

The President wanted to do it legislatively. However, after studying the matter carefully and assessing the politics of the issue, the Governor and his team concluded the only path to success was for the President to use his executive authority and by Executive Order create the new department. Andrus, with my help, concluded that while Congress had sixty days to undo the order, the odds were infinitely greater that the Carter team could block any potential legislative challenge, whereas the reverse were true if the President tried to legislate the action. Entrenched bureaucracies and those concerned about turf and kingdoms could easily thwart any affirmative legislative action, but if confronted with an executive order, they could howl and cry foul but would not be able to undo it.

The wisdom of Andrus' advice was soon borne out. Always the good soldier, the Secretary had me put together a "campaign" plan to sell the merits of the DNR to the key constituencies through editorial board visits to the nation's major papers and by appearances before major interest groups who would hopefully in turn lobby members of Congress. The game plan saw us make visits together to the editorial boards of *The New York Times, Washington Post, Wall Street Journal, Denver Post,* and *Los Angeles Times,* to name a few.

Support from the various editorial boards was lukewarm at best, with some seeing the merits and others not. Almost universally, the major constituencies, water conservation districts, wildlife protection groups, and resource-consuming firms uniformly opposed any change in the order with which they had comfortable dealings.

Finally, the day came when the Interior Secretary set up an appointment with the President, walked up the street to the White House, and told President Carter and the inner coterie of five Georgians that he was going to have to withdraw his DNR proposal or have his head handed to him. Reluctantly, the President accepted Andrus' counsel.

As the one term of the Carter Administration began to wind down, I turned my attention to thoughts of how to orchestrate a move, paid for by Uncle Sam, this time back West. Following the Secretary's admonition that four years would be it and sharing Andrus' belief that the Carter Administration was in dire trouble because of inflation and Iran, I formulated my exit plan.

131

My former gubernatorial colleague John Hough had never "gone back East" with the rest of the "Idaho Mafia." Hough chose instead to take and expand a position called the "Western Field Director" for the department, acting as the Secretary's personal representative of the far-flung agency in the West where many of its numerous functions occurred. Hough had closed the office, which then existed in Portland, and reopened it in Seattle because he wanted to live on Bainbridge Island. In 1979, Hough decided to take a position as the Northwest government relations director for ITT Corporation, thus opening the post and creating an opportunity for me, among other things, not to have to borrow money to move my family back "home."

I laid out a plan to the Secretary whereby I would add Hough's title to my other titles, move west, and continue to fulfill those other duties while strongly relying on my deputy, Harmon Kallman, to keep running the public affairs shop efficiently and effectively. The Governor agreed to the plan in part because it made a lot of sense, and in part because he had a couple of ticklish tasks he wanted me to tackle that had long been festering.

"OK. You move West and add that office to your other roles, but while you're out there, there's a little issue with BPA I'd like you to resolve. I'd like you also to come up with a proposal to the long-lingering issue of settling the claims of the Colville Indian Nation over taking of salmon runs by the building of the Grand Coulee Dam," Andrus said. I knew neither of the tasks he was asking me to tackle would be easy.

Before heading West, our growing family had the rare opportunity to attend a Mass on the Mall presided over by the still relatively new Pope John Paul II. Because the National Park Service controls the Mall, my family, along with the other Catholic members of the Secretary's staff, were able to obtain seats close to the altar and view the Pontiff up close. Like many, we were infatuated with the man and his story and saw the Divine Hand in his election and the subsequent role on the world stage over the next twenty-six years. For years, a picture we obtained of the Pope while at the Mass held an honored place in our home.

A year later, as Cece and Carol were preparing to head back to Boise, on the morning of the inauguration of Ronald Reagan as president, the *Washington Post* had two editorials. One welcomed the new

Administration, and the second singled out three people in the outgoing Carter Administration who warranted special praise for performing their jobs exceptionally well: one was the late Warren Christopher, the Deputy Secretary of State; another was Charlie Shultze, head of the Council of Economic Advisors; and, the third was Interior Secretary Cecil D. Andrus.

Over the years I've been asked to explain why Andrus has been so successful as a governor and Interior Secretary. I usually cite his exceptional personal qualities – his intelligence, integrity, humanity, decency and problem solving skills.

Andrus also had a set of his own political axioms that instinctively he operated by. Among those axioms the following six stood out:

> *1) A win is better than a loss.* Andrus always understood that politics is a contact sport, and, winning is what counts. It helps to be right, and it is great to win fairly, and how one wins is important, but voters like to identify with winners, not losers. Successful leaders are most often leaders who win contests. The news media also likes to identify with winners and can't help lionizing political winners and finding fault in or even demonizing political losers.

> *2) Hope is better than fear.* Like Ronald Reagan (remember "It's morning in America"?), Andrus has always grasped the notion that voters prefer optimists over pessimists, and that they want and need to believe problems are solvable and better days are ahead. In this respect, Reagan was almost unique among Republicans, most of whom have long had the corner on pessimism, fear mongering and sheer demagoguery. Andrus, though, is one of those rare public office holders who know how vital hope is to folks and how important it is that a leader not just feel a constituent's pain, but also provide that constituent with a sense of hope for getting their problem or challenge solved. He has always had faith that the voters most often reward those who appeal to their better rather than their worst instincts.

*3) Being for something is better than being against something.* This follows from the second axiom. Be *for* something. Too many people and too many campaigns make the mistake of starting off by pronouncing what they are against. Andrus always knew that people responded to leaders who were for things, for solving problems, and for finding solutions, as opposed to those who could only talk about what they were against.

*4) A specific is better than a slogan.* Here also, Cece's intuition told him to cite specific accomplishments when he was governor and Interior Secretary. What did one do, what did he accomplish with the trust placed in his hands to advance the public good while serving as a steward of the public interest? Andrus could always tick off ten things his administration had accomplished or ten accomplishments of his Interior Department. These specifics would always trump bumper sticker slogans that critics liked to bandy about. The voter, however, can tell the difference between a man of few words who can talk about what he's done and the bloviator who can spout slogans and sound bites, but in reality is just the proverbial bag of hot air.

*5) An improving economy is best of all.* Cece has always understood that the number one requirement for a holder of high public office was to use his office to help to keep the economy growing and generating new jobs for the new talent flowing constantly into today's labor pool. First you have to have a job, and then you have to have a living that's worthwhile. To that end, while governor he was constantly seeking new businesses to come to Idaho, as long as they paid their way and paid their fair share of public obligations. As one Republican dairy farmer noted when Cece mounted his comeback campaign to the governorship in 1986, "I don't know how he does it, but the economy is always good when he's governor." The lifelong Republican made it clear he was going to vote his pocketbook and vote for Andrus.

And that's what it is all about – it's really no great mystery. Most voters vote self-interest and vote for whom or what they deem to be in their best economic interest. Thus, with inflation at 18% and no peace in the Middle East and therefore a threat to the oil supply and rising energy costs, Andrus knew Carter was toast when it came to being re-elected long before most other observers saw the outcome.

When one looks at the first five, they all make common sense. What makes them so uncommon is how few politicians understand and appreciate the basic nature of these five axioms and apply them in their own careers. Inevitably, if they don't get it, it's not long before the voters figure out that they don't get it, and they find someone else who does get it. Thus, a sixth axiom should be added:

> *6) Always respect the collective judgment of the body politic and the "voter."* Andrus often said the voter can smell out a politician who doesn't respect them or give deference to their views, fears, or concerns in a nano-second. And woe to those who make that mistake, for they seldom get a second chance. He would lace his own remarks with self-deprecating humor to make sure folks knew he didn't take himself too seriously. He reminded folks that he put his pants on one leg at a time just like everyone else. He never put on airs, and he always understood he was a public servant. And it wasn't an act; it was true and genuinely him, which is why to this day he is still one of the most beloved political figures in Idaho.

# The Washington Post
# ...And the Old Order

This is a wistful, melancholy time for the government just turned out of office. There is something in the pathos of the moment that can generate compassion even in this hardhearted town, especially when you measure the glum expressions of the outgoing crowd against the celebrations and high hopes of the new bunch–and remember how happy and confident the newly fallen were four years ago when *they* took the town. Jimmy Carter's government was always odd in certain respects, one being that it never quite seemed a government at all, but rather a kind of confederation of bright people. But this had to do with the president's own conception of an administration, and whatever its other effects, the Carter style of governing did produce some notable acts of good government by good people.

We are not going to go through the buildings one by one nor the agencies desk by desk. We are not even going to mention some of those whose labors we admired greatly. But a few individuals can be taken as representing the best of certain virtues of the Carter administration. We start with Vice President Mondale, who managed the next to impossible feat of staying loyal to his principal without sinking into the idle, slavishly sycophantic and generally somewhat embarrassing life style an ungrateful nation imposes on its vice presidents. Surely one of the innovations Jimmy Carter promised and which he must be given credit for delivering on was his promise to raise the vice presidency to a useful, dignified office. He did.

There is the whole realm of environmental and consumer concerns, for which the Carter administration took a goodly amount of abuse, the charge being that it was in the thrall of extremists and loons. Yes, there certainly were excesses. But they were not and will not be the chief legacy of the Carter administration in these areas. As an example of an administration official who will be remembered for distinction and success, we cite Secretary of the Interior

Cecil D. **Andrus**, who gave over endless hours of productive attention to the Alaska lands bill. Enactment of that legislation was a momentous achievement, and Mr. Andrus was largely responsible for it.

As an exemplar of the patient, professional, supremely devoted worker there is Deputy Secretary of State Warren Christopher, who has been an uncomplaining and tireless executor of Carter policy and a man whose legal and diplomatic imagination helped get the country (and his president) out of more than one bind. Mr. Christopher had a somewhat old-fashioned approach to government service–he did not seek a whole lot of notoriety or public praise, being content to accept responsibility as distinct from credit and to remain in some respects nearly anonymous at the center of power.

As an example of candor and honor under pressure we give you that much kicked around figure, the chairman of the Council of Economic Advisers, Charles L. Schultze. We are aware that no one could call the Carter years a triumph of economic prescience. But these are truly terrible times for economic schools and theories and predictions, and no one comes off as a sterling example of insight or capacity to manage the economic forces loose in the country and the world today. Say this for Mr. Schultze: he and his colleagues chose a policy designed above all to create jobs, and in that regard they succeeded. Had they moved more rapidly and forcefully to restrain inflation, the country might well have paid a substantial penalty in lower employment. Though some of the administration's decisions turned out very badly, you still must say they were taken for substantial reasons well grounded in the past generation's experience with unemployment and its costs.

That idea can in fact be transposed to many other fields of policy in which the Carter administration failed to live up to its promise and its own hopes. But it was not for a lack of good and honest people doing the best they could to tame and manage the unfamiliar world in which we live now.

*Chapter 11*

# The Waning days &
# the Northwest Power
# Planning Council

E arly in 1980, I began working out of the Federal Building in Se-attle as the newly minted western field director for the Department of the Interior and the personal representative of Interior Secretary Cecil D. Andrus. I retained my other titles, assistant to the secretary and director of the office of public affairs, and continued to fulfill the duties required, though I did much more over the phone. I also continued to take the lead in responding to press inquiries directed at the Secretary from major news organizations.

I embraced those responsibilities while maintaining close contact with the Secretary, as well as my deputy at the office of public affairs. With the absolutely invaluable assistance of an aide in the western field office, Dave McCraney, I took on the tasks the Secretary had given me and was able to fashion solutions to BPA's desire to put a new transmission line across a wildlife refuge and to develop a framework for settling the Colville claims.

If anything, I traveled even more than before, mostly throughout the Northwest, and often I would meet up with Andrus when his travels brought him west. I found the additional work fascinating, and, frankly was glad to have escaped D.C. as easily as I had.

On one occasion I met Andrus in Boise, where we were also joined by actor Robert Redford. Together, we were going to float a portion of Idaho's Snake River which flowed through southwestern Idaho. The river in this area is surrounded by high desert country and attracts one of the world's largest collections of birds of prey – bald eagles, golden eagles, peregrine falcons, and various types of hawks.

Since Andrus' early days in the governorship he had been a strong supporter of providing this unique area with protection that would preserve the prey base for the birds and keep it from being gobbled up by encroaching irrigated agriculture. A good friend of his, the late Morley Nelson, had been instrumental in enlisting the Governor's support. Staff aide John Hough worked closely as the pair's go-between while in the Governor's office and then during his stint as western field director. Now, as Interior Secretary, Andrus was in a position to do something about the issue because much of the land needing protection was managed by the Bureau of Land Management.

Andrus also enlisted the help of some good friends at The Nature Conservancy, which specializes in purchasing conservation easements and private property deemed valuable for aesthetic or wildlife reasons. The organization often holds the property until it can be traded or sold to the federal government. To draw media attention to the need for a Snake River Birds of Prey Area, the Nature Conservancy, using its relationship with the Interior Secretary and Redford, helped sponsor the float trip.

For my part, I had the Office of Public Affairs poised to issue an educational booklet on the subject once the trip was completed. Of course, with Redford along there was little challenge in attracting considerable press coverage. The party spent the better part of two days floating through the area with a wonderful night of camping under gorgeous stars, which afforded much time for talking around the camp fire.

Later, in the fall of 1980, I took another trip almost as nice along the Bruneau and Owyhee Rivers of southwestern Idaho courtesy of a BLM helicopter. I called these trips "resource inspections", and while some might view them as junkets, employees within bureaus were always glad for the opportunity to better educate political appointees on the issues they confront in managing the often conflicting demands over resources.

I especially enjoyed this trip because we flew along much of the rivers' length, often just a few feet above the river. I had a genuine bird's eye view of things and always cherished the special feeling the perspective provided.

During a trip to Wyoming with the Interior Secretary to visit a ranch Senator Alan Simpson wanted to be considered as the Western "Camp David", Cece and I talked about the future. Andrus indicated he was going to the private sector as a consultant, make some money to secure his family's future, and sit on some corporate boards. He told me if he ever ran for public office again, it would be a return to the Idaho governorship ten years hence. He urged me to look to the private sector as well.

I also had my eyes on one public sector fallback position in case I couldn't find immediate private sector employment. As January 1981 rolled around, I set the plan in motion. I flew down to Boise where I met with Governor John Evans, with whom I had worked over the years when he was a state senator and then Andrus' lieutenant governor. I explained to Evans an obscure aspect of a new law which had just been passed, called the Northwest Power Planning and Conservation Act. Buried in the details was the creation of a Northwest Power Planning Council that would include two representatives from each of the four Northwest states. The council members would be appointed by each state's governor. This council was to oversee the development of power plans, fishery improvements, and the operations of the BPA. It was going to have a remarkable amount of power.

I asked Evans to name me to one of the two Idaho seats and said I would move to Boise immediately to make clear I was still an Idahoan. (Throughout my time at Interior I always maintained my voting residence in Idaho). As I explained the act and the role of the council, Evans' chief of staff, Bob Saxvik, became intrigued with the idea of securing the other appointment for himself. Afterr taking a night to sleep on it, and with some gentle lobbying on my behalf from a mutual friend, Wayne Mittleider, Governor Evans offered the post. I quickly accepted.

I drew up the executive order creating the position and the press release announcing the appointment. Knowing the Act also set the compensation at the equivalent of a federal pay grade GS-18, I included that in the order also. Overnight, Saxvik and I became the two highest-paid public employees in Idaho!

I also had to finesse the issue of confirmation by the Idaho Senate, still dominated by a set of conservative cowboys who had never liked Andrus and were no doubt relishing the thought of carving up the mouthpiece for the former governor. This group was led by Senator Reed Budge of Soda Springs, about whom Cece had once quipped, "Reed Budge can't read and he won't budge." The Senator had not forgotten. Nor had he forgotten that years earlier, when I was the young, know-it-all, political editor of the *Idaho State Journal,* I had characterized him as a "redneck" state senator conducting a kangaroo-court hearing on the Department of Education's budget. What goes around comes around.

With the help of some legislative allies and David Leroy, the Republican lieutenant governor and former attorney general, I was able to get confirmation postponed for a year, which I felt would give me the necessary time to visit and woo members of the Senate.

What I didn't foresee was a downturn in the Seattle housing market. Our house didn't sell and didn't sell. While I had an apartment in Boise, it was no secret to those familiar with the council that I was flying to Bainbridge on weekends to be with my family. Some people began to wonder if Washington didn't really have three folks on the council and Idaho just one. I knew if I didn't have my family with me by the time the Legislature convened, my prospects were toast.

Nevertheless, I enjoyed my nine interesting months on the council and was able to exercise some influence in shaping the future of the council and the office of the Idaho members. Knowing the council had two critical issues to decide immediately, that of selecting a chairman and selecting a place for the permanent office, I orchestrated a meeting in Idaho Falls with Montana's two newly designated members, Keith Colbo and Gerald Mueller.

I explained that the two downriver states, Washington and Oregon, were going to want the chairmanship and the permanent office. I also pointed out that the two upriver states did not have large state energy offices to support their council members and that the enabling legislation allowed the council to set budgets for the state offices financed by BPA revenues. What the upriver states of Idaho and Montana needed was for the council to establish decent budgets to enable us to operate, but I knew we would have to leverage our votes on the two critical questions.

When the day came for the organizational meeting, I first nominated my colleague, Bob Saxvik, to be chairman. Washington member Chuck Collins nominated his colleague, former Governor Daniel J.

Evans, to be chairman. The vote was a 4 to 4 tie. At this point Collins moved for a recess. During the recess he and Evans approached me to discuss the deadlock. I explained what Idaho and Montana were seeking. Evans explained rather nicely that he never "made deals" while governor and he wasn't about to start. Collins, on the other hand, took me aside and basically asked what it would take to make Evans the chairman.

I told him the upriver states would vote for Evans for chairman and for Portland to be the main office location if Washington and Oregon went along with a generous BPA-financed budget for the state offices. Collins agreed, and the deal was ratified when the council resumed its meeting. The whole process, though, soured Oregon member Roy Hemmingway on me. He forever thought I had tainted the council's beginning with slightly unsavory politics.

When Bob and I returned to Boise, we began to build a staff and outfit an office. In a twist of fate, we hired a long-time supporter of Governor Andrus' to be staff director – Bob Lenaghen, the former Pocatello labor leader who had first introduced me to then-State Senator Cecil Andrus some eleven years earlier.

I picked up the phone one September afternoon in my Boise office and took a call from a gentleman named Jay Rockey. Jay ran one of the largest public relations firms in the Northwest, and he wanted to talk with me. Somewhere Rockey had heard good things about me, and, needing an account executive to manage the firm's Northern Tier Pipeline account, he thought there might be a good fit.

At last, I had a chance to do as Cece had suggested and move to the private sector. I submitted my resignation to the council. In a sense, I was the first one on the council and the first one to leave.

My time at Rockey, where I was given the task of setting up the public affairs division of the firm, led to meeting another person who was to have a profound impact on my life and, to a lesser degree, Andrus', in subsequent years.

My first hire at Rockey was the young and talented Mike McGavick. He not only would soon be one of the founding partners of The Gallatin Group, but also would go on to head Safeco Insurance Company, where he engineered one of the great business turn-arounds ever accomplished by a single CEO. Mike was and is one of the finest political minds I ever encountered, second only to Andrus', as well as an incredibly gifted speaker. Years later I strongly supported Mike's bid to unseat Washington Senator Maria Cantwell in 2006, even though he was running as a Republican. Friendship trumps partisanship in my book any day.

When change comes in life, it often comes swiftly and with little warning. We had journeyed to Spokane to visit with my mother and sister and Marcia's family towards the end of August 1984. It was to be a brief vacation for us, but once again, a phone rang.

On the other end was Jess Erickson, a senior vice president in the Oakland headquarters of the Kaiser Aluminum and Chemical Corporation. He invited me to fly to Oakland the next day to meet. He told me I had been recommended by Ralph Cheek, another Kaiser executive, as a possible replacement for the company's departing vice president for Northwest public affairs in Spokane.

I knew my old hometown's largest employer was in trouble, and the thought that I might be given the opportunity to do something about it was appealing. It also was possible that at last, despite a couple of detours, I might have a shot at a senior communications role for a major private corporation. It was tempting.

In Oakland I met with several members of the Kaiser senior management, but my most memorable interview was with Erickson, who calmly looked over my resume for a few minutes, offered that it was an impressive resume and said he had just one question: "Who are your enemies?" It is the most insightful question I had ever been asked, and I have never since forgotten the value in asking such a question when conducting my own interviews.

My answer must have satisfied Erickson, and I must have satisfied the others, because I left Oakland with an offer to become Kaiser's regional vice president for government affairs. The terms, however, were to be negotiated with Ralph Cheek. I had one non-negotiable condition: Kaiser had to buy our home on Bainbridge, something it normally did not do for first-time employees. The housing market on Bainbridge remained slow, and I was not going to run the risk of carrying two mortgages when we could barely afford one.

After some wrangling, however, the condition was accepted. It was fortunate. The house remained on the market for almost eight months.

As the regional vice president for government affairs for the area's largest private employer, I was the public face for the company. While

I worked with the two plant managers for Kaiser's facilities at Mead and Trentwood, I was the most visible executive and the company's representative to much of the community. In this role, I sat on major civic and charitable boards and handled the company's relations with governmental entities and the news media.

Despite my many years working with and for Andrus, I did not fully appreciate at first how much importance others attached to the position, and early on I was not as careful as I should have been in offering opinions and comments. Soon enough, I realized anything I said was almost always repeated and often distorted. What would circle back to me about what I had supposedly said just boggled my mind. I soon learned to be much more circumspect in what I said about things and where I said it and to whom.

I had been hired to fashion a political solution, if possible, to Kaiser's energy cost challenges. As one of the region's largest consumers of electricity purchased directly from the BPA, which marketed the government's hydroelectric power generated by the region's federally-built dams, Kaiser was sensitive to the cost of that power. Few people realize that when holding an aluminum beer or pop can in their hands, they are holding fused electricity. One third of the cost of producing a pound of aluminum is due directly to the cost of electricity.

When Kaiser's power bill surged almost 900% overnight, because the Bonneville Power Administration had to absorb the costs of its disastrous venture helping build five ill-fated nuclear plants to serve future predicted regional load growth, Kaiser began to bleed money.

It was hoped, using the skills I had learned while working for Andrus, that I could help find a solution, and save Spokane's largest employer (Kaiser employed almost 5,000 people). I set to work on the challenge. With the considerable help of Kaiser's regional power manager, John Bracher, and the Direct Service Industries Association's executive director, Brett Wilcox, we hit on the idea of convincing BPA and the other regional energy players to implement a variable power rate tied to the price of aluminum on the London Exchange.

The theory was that when the price of aluminum was high, companies could afford to and would pay more for their electricity. When the price was down they would pay less, but the lower price for energy would allow the plants to keep operating and not become the swing plants for the industry.

Mounting what was in effect a political campaign, much like the one I had been involved with when Andrus successfully won re-election in 1974, we achieved the goal. I called on all my past political campaign skills to mobilize public support across the region, working closely with the plant unions to ensure management and labor had speakers at BPA hearings. The entire family worked at the union sign shop to produce campaign yard signs which folks could place in their yards, letting their neighbors know there was "Another Kaiser Household" in the neighborhood.

Indispensable to the success of this unusual labor-management coalition was Al Link, who was serving as the vice president of United Steelworkers of American Local 326 at Kaiser-Mead. Al went on to be elected and serve for many years as the secretary-treasurer of the Washington State Labor Council – the second most powerful labor position in the state.

My years with Governor Andrus, and the high regard in which he was held by labor throughout the Northwest was of considerable assistance to me after I left his employ. Their respect for him rubbed off on me, something I was always conscious of and grateful for.

We further mobilized support by developing a call-in show which ran on Spokane's PBS station soliciting donations for the campaign and garnering names and addresses for viewers to receive material providing them with more background as well as outlining "talking points" they could use in letters to the editor and letters to BPA. The campaign committee placed ads in various regional newspapers and lined the route from the Spokane airport to the hearing room with signs and Kaiser families waving hand-held signs for the visiting BPA officials to see.

The committee we formed also produced bumper stickers with slogans and stickers to go on checks which said, "This bill paid with Kaiser dollars." All this served to reinforce how widespread Kaiser's economic impact was in the Spokane and Tacoma communities. The Kaiser effort was replicated in other plant communities across the region. Out of all of this, I also developed a thirty-minute program called "Inside Kaiser Aluminum" which copied the highly successful news magazine format utilized by programs like Entertainment Tonight. Amazingly, I was able to purchase, for a relatively inexpensive fee, the half hour leading into CBS' highly successful and highly rated

*60 Minutes* Sunday night broadcast, which gave our program a big audience. As the host of the show, I also became one of the more recognized figures in and around Spokane.

BPA never stood a chance. The committee pushing the variable rate proposal had done such an effective job of building a broad base of public support while minimizing criticisms that the outcome was inevitable. We made sure the voice of the public was heard. The exercise reinforced for me that building a solid base of public support pays dividends, even for controversial proposals.

Another project I undertook to help Kaiser's northwest facilities reduce their costs to produce aluminum involved obtaining better pricing for natural gas. In particular, the casting stations at Kaiser-Trentwood, where the firm remelted aluminum ingots, defective products, and large rolls of coiled aluminum used as beverage can stock, consumed large amounts of natural gas.

To help achieve a savings, I turned to a talented consultant who had done considerable work on natural gas and the pipelines that transport it -- Cece Andrus. Having always been a smart negotiator who did his own homework, Andrus, working closely with one of my future successors, Pete Forsyth, hammered out a new contract with Kaiser's gas pipeline carrier that saved the company considerable capital.

I tapped my old boss for another critical role – that of starring in Direct Service Industry ads. Our polling had turned up the disturbing information that a substantial majority of the region's voters thought that because aluminum companies paid less than homeowners, or even other industrial users, it meant the citizens were subsidizing a dying dinosaur of an industry. For most of the public, it was a zero-sum game with the majority tilting against the industry.

The critical perception that needed turning around was that the industry was being subsidized when, in fact, it was the opposite that was true – the industry actually subsidized the residential user. Because of the high-volume usage, the receipts were applied to BPA's revenue needs. Without the aluminum companies' revenues, everyone in the region would have to pay at least a third more for their power.

Andrus' ability to convey a complicated message succinctly came through like gangbusters, and by the end of the media campaign, the numbers were reversed. People across the Northwest now acknowledged the industry subsidized their lower power rates. Without the old boss's skill, this kind of rapid turn around would have been impossible to achieve.

When the variable power rate formula kicked in and Kaiser saved over $100 million on its power bill the first year, I first gave thought to becoming a consultant. If I had achieved that goal as a consultant and charged a small percentage of whatever savings were obtained, I would have been able to retire early.

As it was, all I and others did was stave off the day of reckoning for Kaiser. While the company was able to beat back a takeover bid by the English buccaneer, Alan Clore, it was sufficiently weakened so that when the Houston financier and takeover artist Charles Hurwitz came after the company, he was, after a lengthy fight, able to succeed.

For the almost five years I was with Kaiser, circumstances and events were interesting and exciting. I also found the ethics of the business challenging. While the company generally had upstanding, forthright and honest senior management, its ducks and dodges when it came to owning up to serious environmental pollution it had created always bothered me. I am a great believer in the benefits of corporate transparency.

From my days as Governor Andrus' press secretary, I always tried to follow the admonition of never lying to the media or any audience. As things worsened for the company, I had to become more artful in how I answered questions. One incident in particular stayed with me.

As things at Kaiser were deteriorating, I received a rare visit from Jess Erickson, who had a retention agreement which provided a sizable bonus for me to stick with the company during the hard times. Few of these agreements were offered and when their existence became public knowledge, there was understandable anger, especially among the union folks who worked at Mead and Trentwood.

Always accepted by the unions because of my work with Andrus and my perfect attendance at the annual labor picnic each year, I was scheduled to speak to a combined meeting of the two union locals shortly after the news of the retention agreements broke. Unfortunately, one condition of the agreement was the recipient could never disclose he had one.

I was beside myself trying to be truthful and somehow dodge the question I knew would come. Until it came, however, I didn't really know what I would say. As the question was being asked, I suddenly knew what to do. Looking at the questioner, I quietly said, "Do you think this company values public affairs so much they would even think about offering me one of those deals?" "Hell no!" someone shouted from the back of the room to the applause and cheers of the others. I dodged the bullet, but I didn't feel good about it.

*Chapter 12*

# The Return of Cecil Andrus to Idaho's Governorship

During my years with Kaiser, I remained close to Andrus, who, in late 1985, began planning his return to the governorship. He asked to meet me for breakfast when we both were in Portland on business. I knew what he wanted to talk about, but I had come to breakfast with a slightly different agenda.

As he started to lay out the comeback campaign, I stopped him with another proposal. Instead of the governorship, I urged him to run for the U.S. Senate seat in 1986, then held by Republican Steve Symms. Once he won it, I suggested, he should keep right on running to secure the Democratic nomination for the presidency in 1988. I felt the nomination was going to be a wide-open affair, and I truly felt he could win both the nomination and the election. I laid out my thoughts on how it could be done, how the money could be raised, and who the key supporters would be.

As usual, Andrus listened patiently. When I was through, he looked me in the eye and said, "I don't want to be President of the United States. The best job in the world is being governor of Idaho. That's what I want and you're going to help me get there."

End of discussion.

Andrus said he was bringing Larry Meierotto back to Idaho from his job as deputy mayor of Seattle to run the comeback campaign. I then gave the Governor a memo I had drafted and urged him to share it with Larry. The memo laid out how many new voters there were in Idaho who in the last twelve years had never had the opportunity to vote for him. In many respects it was going to be almost like running as a brand new candidate.

I did my part during the campaign season of 1985-1986. I served on the unofficial steering committee that ran the campaign, talked almost daily with Meierotto, and I had a hand in selection of the pollster, the media team, and the campaign press secretary, Marc Johnson. I also helped to raise money, working my business connections in Spokane, as well as securing support for Cece from Kaiser, the region's other aluminum companies and other normally Republican business establishments such as Spokane's private power utility, the Washington Water Power Company (now Avista).

Andrus' 1986 opponent, David Leroy, and his campaign manager, future Congresswoman Helen Chenoweth, were stunned when they approached WWP for support only to find out Andrus and I had secured the company's support months before. One key to garnering that support was the friendship and loyalty of Tom Paine, the head of Avista's government affairs. Tom had lived across the street in Lewiston from Cece when Tom's father was WWP's Idaho lobbyist and Cece was the state senator from that district. Politics is all about relationships.

As the November election approached, it became increasingly clear to Meierotto, Johnson, and I that Andrus was in for a real fight. It was going to be a tight race. Republicans had nominated Leroy, the ambitious lieutenant governor and former attorney general. Leroy was doing a masterful job of turning the race into a contest between his youth, thirty-nine, and Andrus' age, fifty-five. Leroy was helped, in part, by Andrus being one of those people who photograph ten years older then they really are.

Idaho was becoming ever more Republican, a state that revered Ronald Reagan, and one that increasingly was the retirement destination for thousands of California Republicans who were flocking into Ada and Kootenai counties. The GOP was well-organized with a solid machine that was great at mobilizing voters. Cece was running against a tide.

Still, Meierotto, Johnson, and I believed he would win, despite a last-minute Republican smear alleging Andrus would give away Idaho's water. The basis for this canard were political contributions to Andrus' comeback campaign from water-dependent agricultural interests (largely cotton) in far-away southern California. Secretary Andrus had, late in his term at Interior, reversed himself on the issue of whether these agri-businesses should be held to acreage limitations contained in the original 1902 Reclamation Act, and a major revision in 1979. Republicans tried to suggest it was a short step to his supporting the export of Idaho water. Unfortunately, because this distortion was being pushed by the so-called "Committee of Nine," the nine water masters on the Upper Snake River irrigation projects, it had currency, especially with potato farmers and members of the LDS Church.

On election night, I was in Walnut Creek, California, on Kaiser business. Every hour, I spoke with either Mereiotto or Johnson. As the evening wore on, Andrus remained slightly behind.

Andrus kept examining the precincts reporting and realized many key precincts in the northern Idaho (traditionally Democratic-leaning country) had not reported. He started asking, "Where's the north?" An apocryphal story has it he called his good friend, State Senator Mike Mitchell of Lewiston, and asked the same question: "Where's the north, Mike? Where are the votes from the north?" Mitchell reportedly replied "How many votes do you need, Cece?"

Finally, at 2 a.m., Mereiotto called to say almost all the ballots were in, and the Governor appeared to have a 3,000-vote lead. We discussed a couple of key counties where the sheriffs were active Republicans. I suggested Meierotto get supporters to go to where the ballots were collected just to ensure there would be no tampering. We expected a recount, but in the end, Leroy graciously conceded. Cecil D. Andrus had been elected to the office of governor for a third time, ten years after having left "the best job in the world" to be Jimmy Carter's Secretary of the Interior.

In January of 1987, I flew down to Boise for the inauguration. While there, my friend Meierotto, the new chief of staff, asked me into his office. There, to my surprise, he indicated he was only going to stay with the Governor for a year at most. He said he planned to help get the administration up and running, but then he would pursue plans to start a consulting business. He wanted to know if I would consider joining him, making it a partnership with offices in Spokane and Boise.

Intrigued by the thought, I mentioned that I had been thinking about orchestrating a graceful exit from Kaiser and going into business for myself. I told Meierotto I would get back to him shortly.

As I ruminated on the plane ride home, it started to crystallize that what the region needed was not a Carlson-Meierotto partnership covering just Spokane and Boise, but a truly regional public affairs/government affairs firm spanning the four economic capitals of the Northwest: Seattle, Portland, Spokane, and Boise. I knew just the folks I wanted to enlist.

I told Meierotto my refinement on the idea and who else I was thinking about. We agreed to get together in the next few months. I then ran my thoughts by my attorney friend from Bainbridge Island, Mike Patterson. He was enthusiastically supportive. I asked if he would consider letting the group assemble at his cabin on Lake Coeur d'Alene and join us. I wanted Patterson to become the new firm's legal counsel. He agreed, and so I went to work assembling my future partners and finding a date to gather at Mike's cabin.

In late March of 1987, the initial meeting of what was to become The Gallatin Group gathered. Besides Patterson and me, the group included Meierotto, who would run the Boise office; Gary Smith and Mike McGavick, who were planning to form their own partnership and we hoped would agree to run a Seattle office; and, Joe Piedmont, a Washington Water Power vice president for communications and a former deputy regional government affairs director for Kaiser. I hoped to entice Piedmont to run an office in Portland if he and his wife moved back to their native Oregon, as they were then contemplating. I would run Spokane.

One glitch became apparent, however. Smith and McGavick had already made plans to form a firm to handle former Senator Slade Gorton's comeback campaign in 1988. Gorton's good friend, former Washington Governor and then-Senator Dan Evans, had decided not to run for a second term. Evans had left the Northwest Power Planning Council after the sudden death of Senator Henry Jackson and had won a race in 1983 against Congressman Mike Lowry to finish the five years left on Jackson's term.

Andrus and I had played a minor role in that Evans-Lowry race by helping to form a group called "Democrats for Evans", which took out ads and held press conferences around the state explaining why so many Democrats were supporting Dan Evans. Besides knowing Evans was far and away the better man, we also considered it payback for Dan Evans' constant and loyal support for Cece over the years. Along with Oregon Governor Tom McCall, they formed a trinity many believed were the three best governors ever to serve at one time in the Northwest.

(For my efforts on behalf of Evans, I was the subject of a resolution from the King County Democrats and their then chairwoman, the late Karen Marchioro, formally drumming me out of the Democratic Party. For years, I proudly displayed the resolution in my office.)

In 1986, former Congressman and Carter cabinet member Brock Adams had upset Senator Gorton in his race for a second term. When Evans decided not to run in 1988, Gorton decided to try again and pressed McGavick and Smith into duty. McGavick had previously run then-Attorney General Gorton's Senate campaign in eastern Washington in 1980 when Gorton upset the legendary Democrat Warren Magnuson. He and Smith were committed to the race, which meant the group would have to stagger the opening of its various office if the pair were to join us.

All at the Patterson cabin agreed the "one for all, all for one" model made sense if the regional firm were to be established; that the goal was worth it, and worth the wait. The potential partners strongly embraced the concept that we all had to share equally in the revenues. We instinctively knew the firm would not survive the so-called "eat what you kill" model. We knew some offices would have down years while others had up years. Over time, however, things would most likely even out. The group was establishing a key principle: The future partners believed in each other and their relationship with each other. Certainly everyone was expected to do his part, but each recognized that others would be operating in different markets with different time schedules to manage. What counted was the vision and the culture we were creating.

We proved prescient on this point, even though a few years later growth dictated that the model change. But the culture we established and the priority of investing in people while valuing relationships foremost stood the firm in good stead over the years. Plans were made for Meierotto to launch the Boise office first, which he did in the spring of 1988; I was to launch the Spokane office in January of 1989. We hoped that Smith and McGavick would be able to open a Seattle office after the Gorton campaign. Piedmont indicated his plans would take longer to mature, and it would probably be 1990 before he could launch a Portland office. The uncertainty dictated a so-called rolling start. The group also agreed Patterson would be the firm's outside legal counsel. And the group resolved that, once up and running, Meierotto would be the president, and the business office would be located in Boise.

As the meeting drew to a close at day's end we had a surprise drop-by visit from Governor Andrus and his press secretary, Marc Johnson, who were in Kootenai County on official business. Later, they figured significantly in the growth of the firm.

With one exception, the "rolling thunder" staggered office opening schedule came about. The next glitch, when it came, was once again in Seattle. McGavick and Smith engineered a successful comeback campaign for Gorton, who promptly got on the phone to me. He said he needed McGavick and Smith to go to Washington to set up and run his office for eighteen months to two years. Would I release them from their commitment to join our new firm after the campaign?

I appreciated the courtesy call, but I knew McGavick and Smith were headed to D.C., Mike as chief of staff and Gary as communications and legislative affairs directors. They set up the Senator's office, got it running smoothly, and when they returned home in mid-1990, they, along with Joe Piedmont, accepted our offers to open Seattle and Portland offices on July 1, 1990. On that date, the basic structure of the firm took shape.

I had another goal for myself as I moved into my early 40s: to climb the highest mountain in each of the states where the new firm would be operating.

I started with Mt. Borah, the highest in Idaho, at 12,662 feet, and the second highest in the Northwest. I chose a late September day in 1989. As it turned out, I lucked out with a clear blue sky and no wind, a perfect day for climbing. Borah is considered more of a scramble except for two spots where some risk is apparent. It is considered a non-technical but nonetheless challenging hike by professional climbers.

I was accompanied by my brother, Corlan, who as a member of the Seattle Mountaineers knew much more about climbing than I did. We camped the night before on the other side of the fault line of an earthquake that had rocked the region in the early 70s, literally raising the mountain an additional eight feet.

All was well for the first 10,000 feet. Corlan then began to experience altitude sickness. The only cure is to return to a lower altitude, so Corlan started back down to camp. I pressed on, eventually arriving at the summit about noon. I carried with me an Andrus bumper sticker which I slapped on a tube at the top of the mountain that contained notebook paper for climbers to leave messages or thoughts. Still miffed at David Leroy, who in the 1986 campaign not only made a point of talking about his jogging, but also bragged about his having climbed Mt. Borah (as if Andrus couldn't), I left a message for Leroy.

I knew Leroy was thinking about a rematch with the Governor, and I took an educated guess that someone would read the message and relay it to him within a few weeks. The message said: "By Chris Carlson, done on behalf of his friend, Governor Cecil D. Andrus, as a message to David Leroy. There are thousands like me who will climb any mountain and do whatever it takes to return the champion to the ring for another term! You better think long and hard before seeking a rematch!"

I still cherish a photo taken of me by another climber on top of Borah holding the tube with the Andrus bumper sticker on it.

Within three weeks, Leroy was on the phone saying he understood I had left him a message on top of Mt. Borah. "Indeed I had," I said, and repeated it. Leroy and I kidded each other. When 1990 rolled around, Leroy did not challenge Andrus.

Over the next three years, I set out to bag the highest peaks of Washington and Oregon. For good measure, I also threw in a climb up the region's third highest peak, Mt. Adams. After climbing Mt. Adams, I added Mt. Hood, Oregon's highest peak.

Finally, I set my sights on Washington's Mt. Rainer, a splendid bulwark of glacier ice and rock that on a clear day dominates the views south of Seattle and east of Tacoma. For years I had flown by the mountain, wondering what it would be like to stand on its top.

For this venture, I hired a good friend, the world renowned mountain climber, John Roskelley, to serve as guide. Rainer requires roping up and carries more risk than most mountains in the region. The day we summitted in mid-May was a windless, clear, bluebird day. The views were fantastic and our joy unbounded at having conquered the mountain. The only glitch was Corlan again developed signs of altitude sickness while at the top. He remained sitting on a small ledge off the false summit while the rest of us walked around to the real summit.

Upon returning, we found Corlan nursing a few cuts and bruises on his face. He had fainted while we trooped over to the summit. We quickly started back.

At the top of each mountain, I always took time to offer a prayer of thanksgiving for my health and ability to climb, for the beauty of the mountains around me, for the views from up high, for friends and family.

I launched the Spokane office on January 1, 1989, with one major contract in hand – my former employer, Kaiser Aluminum, good for one year for "advice and counsel on various matters." While it was a start, in and of itself it would not be enough to sustain the office. I knew I had to market my services aggressively. I especially appreciated those folks who came through in the early days with issues or projects, such as Mark Crisson, executive director of the Tacoma Public Utilities, and now president of the American Public Power Association.

For a number of years, until Kaiser declared bankruptcy in the late 90s, my annual contract was renewed, which I attribute in part to the good work we performed and to President Steve Hutchcraft's loyalty to those in the public affairs arena who, while employees of the company, had put their jobs and their livelihoods at risk during two nasty takeover attempts. In addition, I always received strong local support from my former deputy, Susan Ashe, and from one of my successors at Kaiser, Pete Forsyth.

As 1990 rolled around, I again started focusing on Governor Andrus' upcoming run for an unprecedented fourth term. Meierotto floated by Andrus' now chief of staff, Marc Johnson, and me the idea of enlisting a young Coeur d'Alene attorney, Brad Stoddard, to run the campaign. Stoddard had been the Governor's coordinator in 1986 in Kootenai County and had done an excellent job of getting out the Democratic vote in an increasingly Republican county. Johnson and I liked the idea of putting the campign in his hands, and I had even taken Stoddard on an overnight backpacking trip along the Idaho-Montana state line in the late summer of the previous year to sound him out. The final recruiting was not difficult and Stoddard, his wife

Catrin, and their children picked up and moved to Boise to live while he ran the campaign with some advice from a rump steering committee consisting of Johnson, Meierotto, and myself.

There was one issue – abortion – I knew was going to dominate the 1990 session of the Idaho Legislature; a classic "wedge" issue designed to divide people. Like Johnson, Meierotto, Stoddard and the Governor, I was aware that national Right-to-Life leaders had targeted Idaho as a state where they could pass a draconian measure restricting almost all abortions. They knew it would pass the Legislature and because Andrus was a self-described pro-life governor, they thought he would sign it without hesitation. They saw it as an opportunity to get a test case before the U.S. Supreme Court which would attract the support of the key swing justice, Sandra Day O'Connor.

In early January, I wrote Andrus a long memo outlining and clarifying the nuances of the issue as I saw them. Andrus and I had discussed the issue before. Andrus is a practicing Lutheran and firm in his opposition to abortion as the Supreme Court's *Roe vs. Wade* ruling allows. He believes abortion should not be countenanced nor permitted except in cases of rape, incest, or to save the life of the mother. Only in those relatively rare instances does he think that the right of the individual transcends the right of life for the child.

Andrus strongly holds the view that the first law of society, and the primary reason people band together to form a society, is to protect life and to protect the weak from the strong. He believes people, especially couples who freely engage in sex, should be accountable for their choices and responsible if the outcome is a child. He also believes life begins at conception, and that once the egg is fertilized, all the potential for that child in the womb is in place. This position, while not a pure pro-life position, puts him at variance both with the majority of pro-choice Democrats and with pure pro-lifers who argue for no exceptions.

Most people assumed that Andrus would end up signing the legislation when it came before him. They were wrong. It was Johnson, who, to his credit, suggested the Governor take the time to carefully study the implications of House Bill 625. Despite his pro-life position, what Andrus read appalled him. There was little flexibility, no mercy, and no compassion in the legislation.

Supporters of the legislation in Idaho made the tactical mistake of never coming to see Andrus to determine what he might or might not accept. They assumed he would quickly sign it, but they never verified that assumption.

Andrus had always been a successful politician, in part, because he wasn't afraid to take and hold to a difficult stance. He knew that as long as he could articulate his reasoning, thinking voters would support him. Despite his affinity for the sentiment behind the bill he knew he could not sign it. It was simply too punitive. A young woman having suffered from the trauma of a rape had only seven days to report the crime to police. Andrus knew for many women the trauma of being raped required more time to deal with and report. He also felt the language around threats to the mother's life was too narrowly drawn.

Finally, he resented the national interests that had brought the issue to Idaho to get what they wanted, believing they could influence him into signing. Thus, threats of Idaho potato boycotts only served to make him angrier at those who would so transparently use a state to push such a controversial issue.

Personally, Andrus felt conflicted by the issue in part because all three of his daughters harbored pro-choice views. As a good Lutheran, he was on record as being pro-life. Cece does feel strongly there are instances where one simply has to let a woman and her doctor decide if her health is threatened or her pregnancy is the result of rape or incest. He knows the life in the womb, which can survive outside the womb after as little as twenty-one weeks (fetal viability), has rights also.

I had once passed along to Cece a phrase I had heard that the definition of a true tragedy was not the conflict between right and wrong with the wrong winning. It was the conflict between two equally valid rights. I further conveyed to him sentiments eloquently written by A. Barlett Giamatti, a renaissance scholar, former president of Yale, and at the time of his premature death, the commissioner of baseball:

"As I think back and look forward, I see how nothing is straightforward, nothing is unambiguous. Salvation does not come through simplicities, either of sentiment or system. The gray, grainy complex nature of existence and the ragged edges of our lives as we lead them defy hunger for a neat, bordered existence and for spirits unsullied by doubt or despair."

It goes without saying that Andrus recognized the ambiguities of this complex issue. I was not surprised when, after uncharacteristically letting the debate and pressure grow because he thought the process would help voters educate themselves, he vetoed the legislation. The Idaho legislature, knowing a loser when they saw one, sent him the legislation at the end of the session and promptly adjourned. Republican leadership guessed he would veto it, and knew they didn't want to deal with the issue again.

Andrus' Republican opponent in 1990, State Senator Roger Fairchild, famously said he would have signed the legislation "in a baby's heartbeat" and predicted he would win in the fall on the abortion issue alone. He was wrong. He went down to defeat, 69% to 30%, in the second-worst slaughter in Idaho history (the first being Andrus' massacre of Jack Murphy, by a 73% to 26% margin in 1974).

Subsequent surveys I have studied only reaffirmed that there was a slight silent majority who, while they might want abortion available in the rare instances of rape, incest, and risk to life of the mother, were nevertheless, very uncomfortable with abortion on demand. The general public might agree with Bill Clinton, that abortion should be "safe, legal and rare", but many voters suspect the Bill Clintons and Bob Packwoods of the world, who use women to feed their egos, support abortion on demand for some transparently personal reasons.

Andrus falls back to the first rule of the society: people band together to protect life. He recognizes he has to react with compassion and charity to those who feel so desperate as to have an abortion. Nonetheless, it is "anti-life" and people of conscience have to be more forthright in standing up for life from conception to natural death.

Thursday April 5, 1990

# The Washington Post
## Showdown in Boise

NO POLITICIAN in the country would have envied Idaho Gov. Cecil Andrus at the end of last week. Faced with making a decision on an extremely controversial abortion bill, he was sure to infuriate voters in either camp. Abortion is a subject on which there are deeply held views, moral divisions and a great deal of emotion. Very few of his constituents will fail to note or remember his position when they decide whether to reelect him in November. But in the face of all this pressure, he made the right choice.

The Idaho legislature had passed the most repressive abortion law in the nation. Opponents said it would have banned about 90% of the abortions performed in Idaho. It would have allowed abortion in only four circumstances: cases of rape, if reported within seven days; incest, if the victim was under 18; profound fetal deformity; and cases where the life or health of the mother was at stake. Though the governor is a declared opponent of abortion, he vetoed the bill. The provisions on rape and incest, he said, were "drawn so narrowly that [they] would punitively and without compassion further harm an Idaho woman who may find herself in the horrible, unthinkable position of confronting a pregnancy"

that resulted from either of these two causes. He also said that he had consulted legal scholars of both parties who told him that the bill was almost certainly unconstitutional.

Over the past three weeks, there had been an unusual amount of pressure on Idaho officials. This bill was drafted and supported by the National Right to Life Committee. It was its best shot at attacking *Roe v. Wade* on the broadest grounds. Abortion opponents wanted to take this one to the Supreme Court, and they thought they had a formula that would garner the necessary five votes.

By the same token, the stakes were high for abortion rights groups, which are moving from one state legislature to another trying to put out the brushfires that have been flaring up since the Supreme Court decided the Webster case last year. Tens of thousands of individuals contacted the governor's office, national figures on both sides spoke out, and the spotlight on Boise was intense, as it has been on statehouses in Florida, Pennsylvania, Maryland and elsewhere this year. Politicians had hoped to duck the abortion issue, but they can't. Like Gov. Andrus, each of them will have to take a stand sooner or later. The governor made the right decision.

## Chapter 13

# The Wit & Wisdom
# of Cece

E arly in his political career, Cece discovered the value of self-deprecating humor. He also instinctively understood, however, that there was a critical difference between people laughing with you as opposed to people laughing at you. Humor, he realized, served a useful purpose in getting both the audience and the speaker to relax and be more at ease.

He became a master of the self-deprecating quip. He also came to understand that good anecdotes, jokes, and stories can easily stand re-telling, and even when an audience may have heard a joke before, they can still appreciate the delivery of an effective punch line.

Often the best jokes and stories derived from actual events or happenings. These particular anecdotes were part and parcel of what I liked to call the "verisimilitude" test: does it resemble the TRUTH? When it did, it almost always guaranteed a good laugh.

One of Cece's best stories came out of his second campaign for governor in 1970. He and John Hough, his campaign press secretary, were working the streets of Challis, the county seat of Custer County. It's a sparsely inhabited, ranch-dotted area in central Idaho that also happens to be home to the majestic Castle Peak, located in the midst of the Boulder-White Clouds roadless area east of the scenic Sawtooth Basin.

The mining conglomerate ASARCO was pushing a proposal to develop a molybdenum mine at the base of the peak and to utilize nearby Frog Lake as the tailings pond. In a move clearly ahead of its time, and at somewhat of a risk to his campaign, Andrus had come out against the proposed mine on environmental grounds. Nonetheless he was campaigning in Challis, even though the good folks in that small community felt that they stood to benefit greatly from the mine's development.

Thus, Andrus' reception as he campaigned up and down Challis' one main street was anything but warm. "People literally sicced their dogs on me," Andrus would recount. "And when I walked into the town barbershop and introduced myself and said what I was running for, the barber said, 'Yeah, we were laughing about that earlier this morning.'" No one would even shake his hand.

Finally, Cece had enough. He told John to start the car, and they headed south out of town. They hadn't gone very far before they came across an old sheepherder trailing a band of sheep across a fence along side the road. Cece told John to stop the car. He was going to make a last try at winning at least one vote. John stopped the car, Cece got out, jumped the fence, and walked up to the old sheepherder.

He immediately launched into his campaign spiel about who he was and why he was running. He hadn't gotten very far when the sheepherder held up his hand and stopped him, "Who else is running, young fella?" Cece, having long ago learned not to mention the name of his opponents, briefly described each of his opponents then started to resume his pitch. Again, the sheepherder held up his hand and stopped him. "Well, young fella, you're my second choice!"

Given his reception in Challis, Cece felt this was at least a step up. So he thanked the sheepherder, and then asked, "If I'm your second choice, do you mind me asking who your first choice is?" Without missing a beat the old sheepherder replied "Any one of the other three." Cece lost Custer County overwhelmingly the following November, but he won the overall vote and ever after referred to Castle Peak as the mountain that elected a governor.

1970 General Election Results, Custer County: Andrus 135, Samuelson 1,164
1970 General Election Results, statewide: Andrus 128,004, Samuelson 117,108

Those who are married know how easily one's spouse masters the ability to issue a blistering put down with a well-timed barb. Each spouse knows the other's weaknesses, as well as which buttons can be pushed to keep the other humble, especially if one of the spouses is an office-holder starting to get a little over-inflated. So it is with Cece and Carol. Cece has a habit, when introducing Carol at public events, of referring to his "first wife" which invariably causes folks in his listening audience, especially women, to look puzzled for a second. One can see the gears start to turn and read their minds – "I didn't know he had been married to someone before Carol?" He hasn't. He quickly smiles as he identifies his bride, and his pride is obvious.

A couple of zingers from Carol stand out.

Early in his first term as governor, Cece and Carol returned to Orofino to do some steelhead fishing on the Clearwater. Ever the good teacher, Cece was giving Carol some pointers on what to do. Almost immediately, she caught a nice steelhead and was understandably pleased with herself.

Cece continued fishing, but he wasn't getting a bite. As the day wore on a role reversal took place, and Carol began to make suggestions to her instructor as to what he ought to do, or not do. Cece is a great teacher, but nobody has ever commented on his being a great student when it comes to fishing or hunting. With a lifetime of experience he knows what he is doing.

Predictably, he started to take a dim view of Carol's efforts to be helpful, and let her know her counsel was neither sought nor appreciated. At this point Carol had enough. She looked him dead in the eye and said, "Well, if you're so darn good, why don't you just throw one of your business cards overboard and let the fish know who is up here!"

Being bald has also generated its fair share of jokes and comments over the years. Once Cece was giving a speech somewhere and he could not resist working in a joke about bald men. Looking out over the audience he ran his hand over his head and said out loud "You know, grass doesn't grow on a busy street!" From the back of the room came a voice saying loud enough for all to hear "Yeah, it doesn't grow on a rock either!"

Andrus has been good friends with former Wyoming Senator Alan Simpson for years. Each is lanky and tall, noted for their candor as well as their smarts, and each is bald. One time when they were together at a gathering, Simpson ran his hand over his bald pate and said to Andrus, "Cece, you know what this bald head is, don't you?"

Andrus bit, saying, "No. Go ahead and tell me you coyote-killing, arsenic lovin' old s.o.b." "It's a solar panel for a sex machine," Simpson laughingly said. Cece couldn't wait to get home to tell Carol. When he did, she looked at him and without missing a beat said, "Well, the sun sure hasn't been shining much lately!"

Cece could also be a skillful practitioner of the "Don't get mad, get even" school. While not a particularly vindictive person, he knew the importance of making people or organizations feel some real pain, make them pay as the expression goes, for crossing him.

In the late 1960s that group was the Idaho Judicial Council. Andrus often said to his staff that one of the dumbest things his predecessor, Don Samuelson, ever did was to give away the heretofore unrestricted ability of a governor to name judges to the various courts, including the State Supreme Court. Samuelson signed legislation in 1967 that created an Idaho Judicial Council, which reviews the qualified judicial candidates and then submits several names to the governor. The governor must select from that list. So it came about that a conflict soon arose between Governor Andrus and the Judicial Council.

A good Democrat and attorney from Idaho Falls, Bob Fanning, had challenged an elderly member of the eastern Idaho District Court and narrowly lost the election. Shortly thereafter the incumbent died in office, creating a vacancy, and Fanning, among others, applied. Like all the applicants, however, he had to go through the screening process of the Council.

Most inside players thought the interview process was largely pro forma. No one questioned Fanning's competence, and most everyone knew that Andrus expected to see Fanning's name on the list. However, most members of the Council were Republicans previously appointed by Samuelson. They had no intention of going along to get along with Andrus.

The Governor and I were in Pocatello attending an event put on by the Idaho Education Association when I saw the chair of the Council, Democratic attorney Bob Huntley, approach the Governor and hand him a list of three names for the vacant position.

For only the second time in all my years working with the Governor, I saw his eyes flash and for a split second thought to myself "Oh no, he's going to deck him!" Andrus knew not only had he been betrayed by Huntley, he had been set up.

The list contained the names of two solidly conservative Republicans who, not coincidentally, were members in good standing of the Mormon Church, the predominant church in eastern Idaho. The only Democrat was an African-American attorney allegedly living "in sin" with his white girlfriend. The Judicial Council was daring Andrus to appoint the Democrat, knowing it would generate lots of political problems for the Governor in Idaho Falls.

Thus, a process supposedly designed to remove the selection of judges from the taint of politics merely ensured that the politics of the legal community would be layered over more common partisan politics. The Governor was quiet for most of the flight back to Boise that night.

Just as we touched down he turned to me and said "We've got to figure out a way to make those S.O.Bs pay for their gamesmanship and blatant partisanship. Put your fertile brain to work and see if you can come up with some idea that will cause them so much grief they'll never dare to cross me again."

"Will do, Chief," I replied, sounding far more confident than I really was, because, at the time I didn't have the foggiest idea what he could do.

As the next week went by, I pondered the challenge off and on when time allowed. The following Sunday evening, I was taking a bath, lounging in the hot water, when I had one of those "eureka" moments, a flash of insight that I was sure would meet the Governor's charge. I asked Marcia to get a copy of Idaho's Constitution that I kept around the house and from time to time would peruse.

I carefully read and reread the section on the appointment of judges and the requisite qualifications. My memory was correct: the Idaho Constitution said absolutely nothing about judges having to be trained as lawyers or being members of the bar. The constitution only stipulated that judges be "citizens in good standing and capable of exercising good judgment".

I could hardly wait for Monday morning to come. I bounced into the Governor's office bright and early, telling him excitedly that I'd figured out a way to create the consternation he wanted and a way to deliver the "don't mess with me, you bastards" message he wanted to send.

We both knew time was of the essence, because a vacancy was about to be created on the State Supreme Court, and it was going to be the traditionally Democratic North Idaho seat. Andrus already knew whom he wanted to appoint, but the challenge of ensuring that the Judicial Council didn't play games remained.

"So what's your idea? " Cece asked.

"You hold a press conference, and you tell the Judicial Council they are going to interview lay as well as lawyer candidates for the Supreme Court vacancy, because the Constitution does not require judges to be lawyers. Indeed lawyers do not have a monopoly on the ability to render justice and good judgments. To underscore the point, you'll throw out a few names of folks who are clearly qualified like former state senator and gubernatorial candidate Perry Swisher who has written half the laws in the state or Kay Pell who heads up your Office of Aging and is two-thirds of the way towards her law degree, and there are others."

At first he looked at me like I had lost my marbles but in about fifteen more seconds, he had run the political calculus through his head, and quietly said "I like it. Let's do it."

The next day he held that press conference and announced what he was calling for and why. He urged any citizen who felt they filled the constitutional criteria to apply, and promised they would be interviewed and evaluated on the same basis as lawyers: character, intelligence, an understanding of the law, but most importantly, the ability to display judicial temperament and render sound judgments.

Lawyers across the state protested. They wrote letters to the editor comparing themselves to physicians and saying a citizen wouldn't want a non-doctor operating upon them, would they? But the public loved it. As Andrus well knew, most lawyers are held in low esteem by the public, rating only slightly above used car salesmen in numerous surveys.

Letters and calls to the Governor's office ran four to one in favor of his demand, with people loving the way that Andrus had clearly gotten the goat of many attorneys and twisted their tail in the truest metaphorical sense. In all some thirty-seven non-attorneys applied, including former Senator Swisher and Kay Pell, and the Judicial Council dutifully interviewed every one of them.

When it came time to submit the three names for the vacant Supreme Court seat, lo and behold, there on the list was the name of Stephen Bistline, the person Andrus wanted to appoint and subsequently did. The Judicial Council played no further games with judicial appointments and for all the remaining years Andrus served as governor, no Judicial Council ever double-crossed him again. They knew he knew how to get even.

Former Andrus press secretary and chief of staff Marc Johnson remembers a funny story from the Governor's final term. For some time, Andrus had been locked in a political struggle with the legislature that involved the sometimes arcane, but always important issue of "separation of powers." Under our system, the legislature creates law (with the governor's approval) and the executive branch has the responsibility to carry out the law.

The legislature had adopted the notion that it could amend, as it saw fit, the various rules and regulations the executive branch – the governor's branch – promulgated in order to carry out a statute that had been created by the legislative branch. Andrus thought that if legislators objected to a rule they should, under the Constitution, pass another law that the governor could then review and approve or reject.

The issue came to a head over an otherwise innocuous bill dealing with, of all things, tinted windows in automobiles. The legislature had slipped into the bill a clause saying the law would not go into effect unless and until the legislature first approved the executive branch rules required to enforce the provisions. It was widely believed that Andrus would veto the bill on "separation of powers" grounds.

Nonetheless, the bill's senate sponsor, long-time Republican State Senator Denton Darrington of Declo, who had always enjoyed cordial relations with Andrus, wanted to make the case directly to the Governor as to why his bill was worthy of the Governor's signature rather than the red ink of his veto stamp.

Andrus politely and quietly heard Darrington out and thanked him for coming down to make the case. The senator was escorted out by Andrus aide Clancy Standridge and the big door of the governor's office swung shut behind them. Seconds later, Darrington and Standridge heard a particularly loud thump sounding ominously like the Andrus veto stamp coming down hard on the senator's bill.

167

Darrington smiled and said to Standridge, "I think the governor just vetoed my bill." It was a case of the gubernatorial trial being courteously held, followed by a swift and final verdict.

In Rudyard Kipling's poem "If," he talks about the importance of being able to fill the unforgiving minute of extra time one may find himself holding "with sixty seconds worth of distance run." It's a different way of saying one should seize opportunity when it presents itself and not be loath to go looking for worthwhile ways to fill extra time when one can.

During a trip to Washington, D.C., for the 1974 Winter Meeting of the National Governor's Association, an organization of the fifty states that Andrus was slated to become chairman of later in the summer, we found ourselves with a free afternoon in the nation's capitol. Cece asked for some suggestions on what we might do.

I asked if he would be interested in touring the new LDS temple that rises spectacularly next to the Beltway just outside the district in Silver Spring, Maryland. I told the Governor that I knew the temple was pretty well finished but had not yet been dedicated, so "gentiles" like the two of us could tour. I also knew from newspaper reports that the new temple was partly the product of generous donations from J. Willard Marriott, the hotel magnate.

I asked the Governor to give me thirty minutes to see if I could talk to someone in Mr. Marriott's office who might be able to give us a personal tour or steer us to someone who could. I called the corporate headquarters and was put through to the chairman's office. I explained who I was, and who I was working for, and what we were interested in doing to the receptionist, who then put me through to Marriott's personal secretary. The next thing I knew, I was talking to the man himself.

To my pleasant surprise, he said he would love to conduct the tour himself and he would be by our hotel in twenty minutes to pick us up in his personal limousine. When I called the Governor's room and told him that J. Willard himself was on his way over to pick us up and take us out to the temple for a personal tour, the Governor, as he had done on a few occasions, said he was shaking his head.

"Carlson, it's better to be lucky than good, and sometimes you are darn lucky." I readily agreed but I wasn't about to let a little good luck mar what I knew was a real p.r. coup just as we were about to launch the Governor's re-election campaign in a little over six weeks.

Right on schedule, Marriott pulled up to take us out to the temple. He was genuinely thrilled to be able to take the governor of Idaho through the temple, and I confess it was an absolutely fascinating tour for the both of us. Marriott was a gracious and charming host and we had a grand time.

When we got back to the hotel I told the Governor I would quickly pound out a little press release to be sent back to the Boise offices of the Associated Press and United Press International. To my surprise the Governor said "No, you won't, Chris. The LDS Church has a marvelous phone tree system, and unless I miss my guess, almost every bishop in Idaho will know within three days that I've toured the Temple in D.C. before its dedication. We won't have to say a word."

And of course, as usual, he was correct. For several weeks afterwards almost every LDS member in the administration, or other friends who were LDS, would begin a conversation with the Governor with the words "I heard you toured the new temple in D.C. What did you think of it?" There are some things better left unsaid, and some things that just don't require a press release.

That November Andrus rolled up the biggest margin of victory by any gubernatorial candidate in Idaho history, and he decisively carried virtually every one of the heavily LDS counties (see Appendix B) of southeastern Idaho. (The sole exception was Lemhi County---the one county in Idaho Andrus never carried in six gubernatorial primary and general elections). His tour of the Temple undoubtedly helped, but Cece personally conveyed genuine respect for those of the Mormon Church and some of his staunchest backers in southeastern Idaho were Mormon businessmen like Del Ray Holmes and Brent Bell.

Andrus also always maintained a cordial relationship with one of the few Democratic state senators from the upper Snake River Valley, Ray Rigby. When we traveled to and through Rexburg or Rigby we would often stay in the homes of the few LDS Democrats. While in these heavily LDS communities, Andrus and I would refrain from drinking coffee, and in other small ways, indicate our respect for their highly organized and obviously successful culture.

Andrus is also a fairly common name in southeastern Idaho. Cece would always greet any Andrus as a long lost cousin and immediately talk about an apocryphal "Grandpa Milo."

Two years later, Andrus forever won the hearts of most members of the southeastern Idaho LDS community through his masterful handling of the collapse of the Teton Dam, on June 5, 1976. He quickly mobilized state support and worked with LDS relief agencies to help the hundreds of Idaho citizens displaced by the calamity.

For several weeks following the disaster Andrus was constantly on the scene overseeing the state's effort, working with federal disaster agencies to get those rendered homeless by flooding temporary housing, and food and clothing vouchers. In particular, the people of Rexburg and the surrounding Madison County area saw their governor in action, leading as only a natural born leader could do.

Later that fall the people of Madison County and the church authorities running the town's largest employer, Ricks College (now BYU-Idaho), held a moving ceremony on the Ricks campus to honor those who had died, as well as to celebrate the community's response. (The collapse took six lives. That the death toll was not higher was a direct result of the LDS phone tree system that gave many people timely warnings to get out of the way of the oncoming waters.)

Andrus was asked to speak, which he gladly did. Few recall what he said that day, but many will never forget what occurred at the ceremony. In an extraordinary gesture the President of the LDS Church, Spencer Kimball, literally laid hands on Governor Andrus. He has been held in high esteem by most members of the Mormon Church ever since that day though this esteem has not always been reflected at the ballot box in Idaho's heavily LDS counties.

Relations with the Mormon Church were not always so good. Indeed, Andrus had to overcome a rough beginning. Shortly after he took office in 1971 one of the *Idaho Statesman's* legislative reporters, Jerry Gilliland, stopped by press secretary John Hough's office.

On his desk, John had the Idaho Constitution as well as some historical documents from the State Archives Office. The material dealt with the state's early history and the laws prohibiting voting by any professing member of the Mormon Church. Jerry asked John just what was he doing and John said he was researching early anti-Mormon laws.

Gilliland, a faithful member of the church , walked out of the office and proceeded to write a story that was bannered on the front page of the next day's *Statesman*. The headline was something like "Andrus Administration Researches Anti-Mormon Laws,". It appeared on the day the Governor was due to deliver his very first State of the State speech. Of course, it chased anything about Andrus' speech and what was anticipated right off the front page. Gilliland, to his credit, did not embellish the story. He simply wrote a brief, factual account of what he had seen. The headline in and of itself left open to a reader's interpretation just what they thought the new governor was doing.

An angry First Lady, Carol Andrus, marched into John's office that morning and proceeded to tell him, in no uncertain terms, that he had done more damage to the Governor than she could have had she decided to walk naked down the main street of Boise. John could not quite believe that this bit of innocent research was generating so much controversy.

He walked into the Governor's office and opined that this was a one-day story and folks were making a mountain out of the proverbial mole hill. Andrus disagreed and invited John to call a good friend of theirs, a judge on the State Supreme Court who was also a member of the LDS faith. John was quickly educated by the Judge as to the damage the story was causing among church members.

Over the next several years, Andrus' steadfast work as governor, as well as his ability to keep building relationships, gradually began to win over members of the Mormon Church first made skeptical by this incident.

Time heals all wounds, (or wounds all heels!), and by the time the 1974 election rolled around the incident had largely faded from memory.

An examination of Andrus vote totals over the years in Madison County and some of the other, LDS dominated counties of the upper Snake River Valley reflects the fact that, not only had Cece overcome the rough start, but that voters in these counties were generally pleased with the job Andrus was doing. So, despite the fact that he was a Democrat, and the vast major of LDS members typically vote Republican, many more LDS voters cast ballots for Cece in 1974 than in 1970.

Indeed, the 1974 Andrus vote total has never been topped by any Democratic aspirant for governor in the general election since that time. The numbers are as follows. A good example is Madison County; Rexburg is its largest community:

1970:  Cecil D. Andrus 1,765 votes  Don Samuelson  2.171 votes
1974:  Cecil D. Andrus 2,964 votes  Jack Murphy  1,634 votes
1986:  Cecil D. Andrus 1,912 votes  David Leroy  4,528 votes
1990:  Cecil D. Andrus 2,766 votes  Roger Fairchild  2,467 votes

Given the population growth between 1974 and 1990, not to mention the LDS Church turning Ricks College into a four-year school and renaming it BYU-Idaho (meaning it is a full branch campus of the massive Brigham Young University), the numbers reveal how many deeply partisan Republican voters there are in the Upper Snake.

Despite being almost as universally liked and admired in 1990 as he was in 1974, Andrus drew almost 200 *fewer* votes in 1990 than he did sixteen years earlier and won the county by less than 300 votes against a candidate who had been accused by his ex-wife of spousal abuse, drug use, and infidelity. It appeared not to make a whole heck of a lot of difference to many LDS voters, for whom party is of paramount importance.

The pattern was repeated in Jefferson and Fremont counties. The year 1974 was Andrus' high water mark there as well. Only in Bonneville County did Cece top his 1974 vote total both in 1986 and in 1990, and much of that gain can be attributed to a significant rise in population in Idaho Falls .

Early in his political career Andrus showed the rare ability to reach across the aisle and work with Republicans. In particular, during the historic 1965 session of the Idaho Legislature, when many moderate Republicans recognized the needs of education and the need for more funding for education, Andrus was the only North Idaho Democrat who supported having a public referendum on the issue of establishing a state sales tax, and for months was the only North Idaho Democrat who said he would support the establishment of the tax.

This ability to work in a bi-partisan manner, sometimes in a non-partisan manner, bore fruit a few years later when he became governor. On several occasions when Cece needed one or two Republicans to vote to sustain a veto he always managed to find that critical Republican vote. Sometimes it was future governor then State Senator Phil Batt, a Wilder farmer, who would listen to reason and vote for the public interest, not just the party interest.

Sometimes the needed Republican vote was provided by Boise state Senator H. Dean Summers, an insurance agent who loved to play cards with Andrus, and with whom Cece would sometimes have an adult beverage after a day in the office.

The record speaks for itself. During his four terms as governor, Andrus vetoed over one-hundred bills, and not until late in his last term of office was one finally over-ridden.

The truth is there were – and still are – many Republicans who just could not help liking Andrus. First, he was a fiscal conservative. Second, he had a well honed sense of humor. Third, he was a leader and most folks respond to real leadership. Fourth, he was a good listener. Fifth, his word was his bond. Sixth, he just made people feel like helping him was the right thing to do for the state.

There's no other way to explain Andrus' skill at getting things like state supported kindergartens, state land-use planning, circuit-breaker property tax relief for senior citizens, creation of a department of water resources, and dozens of other progressive measures enacted. "Success has a thousand fathers," he liked to say, and Andrus was always generous in sharing "success."

One particular incident was reflective of how Cece could get along with Republicans, even on the campaign trail, and even when the particular individual had defeated his best friend, Ed Williams, for the 1st Congressional District seat – the roguish Steve Symms.

During the late spring of 1974, we were back in Cece's hometown, Orofino, for a Capital for a Day program. Carol met the Governor and me there, having driven up from Boise. Since it was the old home town and there was going to be a fundraiser afterwards for Clearwater County's favorite son, Carol thought it best she be there.

The county Democratic Party decided to host the event up the draw headed east out of town in a place called Konkolville, near one of the few sawmills to escape Potlatch's predatory practices a decade earlier. By pure coincidence, Congressman Symms had also scheduled a visit to Orofino for his campaign. The problem for him was that most every politically inclined person in the county, regardless of their party preference, was planning on attending Andrus's fundraiser.

Not to be deterred, Symms decided to show up at the Andrus event. He saw me at the door and was smart enough, and polite enough to ask me to ask the Governor if he could join in the event. Always quick on his feet, the Governor told me to tell the Congressman he was welcomed to attend *if* he bought one of the $10 tickets.

Symms, instantly recognizing a dare, did not hesitate. He whipped out his checkbook, wrote a check made out to the "Andrus for Idaho" committee, and joined the crowd. Andrus, of course, graciously acknowledged Steve's presence, thanked him for his attendance and the two of them engaged in a bit of good-natured joshing that the audience loved.

We never did cash the congressman's check. Andrus had it framed and kept it in his office for a few years. I made a photo-static copy and put out a short campaign press release in which our campaign treasurer, Robert Montgomery, thanked the congressman for his contribution to Andrus' re-election campaign.

Indeed, as one drove around many of the communities in Idaho's First Congressional District during the 1974 campaign season, one frequently saw cars with an Andrus bumper sticker on one side and a Symms sticker on the other. I especially remember one cantankerous, and colorful character by the name of Rodney Hawes. Rodney published his weekly newspaper, *The Owyhee Nugget,* using one of the last of the hot-lead type-setting machines in the state.

Hawes drove into Boise from his home on the Snake River at Marsing in his big, old, brown Cadillac, sauntered into my office, and nicely but firmly suggested I grab the Governor for a minute so he could show Andrus something. Since I tried to accommodate the media whenever possible, I interrupted the Governor and we followed Rodney out of the office and down to the street where his car was parked.

There Rodney, a lifelong, die-hard, black-hearted Republican, proudly showed the Governor the rear bumper of his big car with Andrus and Symms stickers. Always quick with a quip, Andrus said "That's very nice, Rodney. . . But don't you think my sticker should be on the left side and Steve's on the right side instead of the way you have them?" We all had a good laugh.

There are too many good examples of Andrus reaching across the aisle to mention them all, but one in particular bears repeating. The story involves his successful collaboration with the Republican governor of Alaska, Jay Hammond. The pair worked together for months on setting boundaries for the legislation establishing the national parks, wildlife refuges, wilderness areas and wild and scenic rivers that would be included in the Alaska National Interest Lands Conservation Act – the so-called "Alaska lands bill."

In the summer of 1979, Andrus had me put together the mother of all resource inspection trips – a two week tour of most of the areas being proposed to receive special protection in Alaska. Months in advance, I had a team in the public affairs office working to put together a tight itinerary that would showcase what should be protected and why. We also tendered invitations to a cross-section of the nation's media, mostly major daily newspaper reporters who covered resource issues. We settled on a cost to each media representative, not only to help defray some of the cost of what would be an expensive undertaking, but to also mitigate the inevitable criticism we knew would be leveled at the tour by Alaska's cantankerous senior senator, Ted Stevens.

Unbeknownst to the reporters traveling with us during the well publicized tour, Andrus had been talking quietly with Governor Hammond, who in many respects was a fellow much like Andrus. Hammond was an honest-to-goodness Alaskan bush pilot, hunting guide and fisherman, who flew his own float plane and was married to an Alaskan native.

Like Andrus in Idaho, Hammond was revered by Alaska voters, in large part, because both called things as they saw them, were studious and knowledgeable on the issues, had phenomenal memories for names, and understood how to lead.

So it came about that early one morning during an R and R layover day for the touring group at Lake Iliamna, a solitary Cessna 172 float plane landed on the lake adjacent to the lodge, taxied up to the dock and a single passenger jumped quickly aboard. The pilot was Alaska's governor; the passenger was America's Secretary of the Interior, and off the two of them went.

The trip was both business and pleasure. Hammond, knowing that Andrus loved to fly-fish, had preselected a few places to land the plane where bountiful streams flowed into lakes full of fish eager to hit a fly. The governors landed at one lake where they could taxi close to the shore, sit down on some down timber and pull out their respective maps to discuss boundaries. Equally important to Hammond were access corridors for resource development firms with valid mineral rights that might end up inside of proposed protection areas. He wanted the corridors to be drawn in such a way as to guarantee access for those who truly had developmental plans. Andrus was not about to approve corridors where either he, or Hammond for that matter, suspected a company might only want to keep a mineral right for purely speculative purposes.

In recalling this trip Andrus reviewed my account and added: "We then landed at a big bend in some nearby river, taxied to the shore and refueled at his personal filling station which was two five gallon cans of fuel hidden behind a big log, put there in case he needed it. Great trip."

During his fifty years in public life, Andrus has worked with hundreds of talented individuals who, like he, demonstrated skill and ability as public officials and who also knew public service to be a noble calling. He also dealt with and frequently worked against a collection of rogues and less than exemplary holders of public office, but life is too short to dwell on the negative, so I'll simply list some of the good guys he worked with and ignore the occasional bad guys. Of course any such list is purely subjective and I will obviously leave some worthy indiviudals off. But this list provides further insight into the remarkable man and his career. After all the company one keeps is often a strong indicator of the kind of person one becomes.

Here's my take at a list of his favorites:
FAVORITE U.S. SENATOR–DEMOCRAT, FROM IDAHO:
    Frank Church
FAVORITE U.S. SENATOR–REPUBLICAN, FROM IDAHO:
    James A. McClure
FAVORITE U.S. SENATOR–DEMOCRAT, NOT FROM IDAHO:
    Dale Bumpers of Arkansas
FAVORITE U.S. SENATOR–REPUBLICAN, NOT FROM IDAHO:
    Alan Simpson of Wyoming
FAVORITE CONGRESSMAN–DEMOCRAT, FROM IDAHO:

176

Larry LaRocco
FAVORITE CONGRESSMAN–REPUBLICAN, FROM IDAHO:
Orval Hansen, Mike Simpson
FAVORITE CONGRESSMAN–DEMOCRAT, NOT FROM IDA-
HO:
Pat Williams of Montana
Syd Yates of Illinois
Norm Dicks of Washington
Mo Udall of Arizona
Tom Foley of Washington
FAVORITE CONGRESSMAN–REPUBLICAN, NOT FROM
IDAHO:
Don Young of Alaska
FAVORITE GOVERNOR–DEMOCRAT, NOT FROM IDAHO:
Wendy Anderson of Minnesota
Cal Rampton and Scott Matheson of Utah
Jimmy Carter of Georgia
Mike O'Callaghan of Nevada
FAVORITE GOVERNOR–REPUBLICAN, NOT FROM IDAHO:
Tom McCall of Oregon
Dan Evans of Washington
FAVORITE GOVERNOR–REPUBLICAN, FROM IDAHO:
Phil Batt
FAVORITE GOVERNOR–DEMOCRAT, FROM IDAHO:
John V. Evans
FAVORITE LT. GOVERNOR–REPUBLICAN, FROM IDAHO:
C.L. "Butch" Otter
Brad Little
FAVORITE LT. GOVERNOR–DEMOCRAT, FROM IDAHO:
Bill Murphy
Bill Drevlow
FAVORITE IDAHO STATE SENATOR WITH WHOM HE
SERVED–REPUBLICAN:
H. Dean Summers
FAVORITE IDAHO STATE SENATOR WITH WHOM HE
SERVED–DEMOCRAT:

Art "Pop" Murphy
Merle Parsley
FAVORITE IDAHO STATE REPRESENTATIVE WITH WHOM HE SERVED–DEMOCRAT:
Ed Williams
FAVORITE IDAHO HOUSE SPEAKER WITH WHOM HE SERVED–REPUBLICAN:
Pete Cennarusa
FAVORITE ATTORNEY GENERAL–DEMOCRAT, FROM IDAHO:
Larry Echohawk
Tony Park
FAVORITE ATTORNEY GENERAL–REPUBLICAN, FROM IDAHO:
None
FAVORITE CHIEF OF STAFF FOR ANY OFFICEHOLDER:
Verda Barnes (Frank Church)
Mary Bain (Syd Yates)
FAVORITE NEWSPAPER PUBLISHER:
A.L. "Butch" Alford of the *Lewiston Morning Tribune*
J. Robb Brady of the *Idaho Falls Post Register*
Bob Hammes of the weekly *St. Maries Gazette Record*
FAVORITE EDITORIAL PAGE EDITOR:
Bill Hall of the *Lewiston Morning Tribune*
J. Robb Brady of the *Idaho Falls Post Register*
FAVORITE PRESIDENT–REPUBLICAN:
Dwight D. Eisenhower
FAVORITE PRESIDENT–DEMOCRAT:
Harry Truman
John F. Kennedy
FAVORITE BOOK ON POLITICS:
*All the King's Men* by Robert Penn Warren
FAVORITE MOVIE ON POLITICS:
*The Candidate* with Robert Redford
*Primary Colors* with Kathy Bates

I will leave the last word on Cece's wit and wisdom to his middle daughter, Tracy, who points out that her dad is not really big on a lot of sayings, even as I make much ado about some of them. She correctly noted, "Dad is hugely consistent, though, in the things that he says and they tend to center more on a 'words-to-live-by' theme."

"He always used to tell us that we shouldn't do anything we wouldn't be proud to read on the front page of the *Idaho Statesman*. He would also say that anything that had the appearance of being inappropriate, even if it wasn't, was probably crowding the line. And the one saying I've heard him use multiple times throughout my life, both pointed in my direction and towards others, is that the first thing one needs to do when they're in a hole is to stop digging."

Be accountable for your actions. Have a sense of propriety. Quit digging yourself in deeper when in trouble.

Solid, common sense counsel and advice. What makes it remarkable is the one dispensing that common sense advice matched deeds to the words, "walked the talk" as the saying goes, and that in part helps to explain what made him such an exceptional person and such a marvelous mentor and teacher, not to mention one hell 'uv a successful governor.

*Chapter 14*

# Campaigning for Life

*"There's a grief that can't be spoken, there's a pain goes on and on..."*
– *Les Miserables*

This chapter is very personal. I have tried hard to write objectively about a controversial topic: physician assisted suicide. Does
one have a "right" to end their life? Should doctors be encouraged to assist in an act that by definition does harm? Should the state
incentivize the act? Can it ever be rational? Is it ever morally correct?

My feelings on the subject are strong because my life has been
deeply affected by suicide. I can personally testify that those who kill
themselves merely pass on their pain to their loved ones. As the line
above says, it engenders a grief that never ends. It is the pain that goes
on and on.

In August 1961 my father shot himself, leaving a grieving wife,
two sons who adored him, and at the age of 13 and 14 were utterly
bewildered, and a young daughter of three who never understood and
was scarred permanently. I chalked the suicide up to a number of factors: his horribly painful migraine headaches, his having been "given
away" to some shirt-tailed relatives by his mother when he was six,
his overly strict fundamentalist step-parents, horrible memories from
ten Pacific Theater battles while in the Navy during World War II,
bouts with depression, and, I learned some 50 years after his death, a
probable manifestation of his depression, a guilt-inducing affair with
a fellow school teacher. We'll never know; he left no note.

Some 30 years later, in July 1993, both Cece Andrus and I were rocked by the suicide of one of the Governor's "surrogate sons," and my friend, Larry Meierotto. Larry was one of the key, behind-the-scenes, players in Andrus' successful 1970, 1974, 1986 and 1990 campaigns. Meierotto and I together were also the founding partners of The Gallatin Group.

Somewhere along the way, I can only speculate that some wires crossed in this brilliant mind, and driven by whatever demons, he behaved in a way I never thought possible. On the day he was compelled by a federal judge to produce bank records and the books he administered as firm president, he shot himself. Larry left a grieving widow, a stepson who adored and loved him, a governor and a partner who loved him, and a long list of imponderable questions.

Those who loved and cared for him would have done anything to help him get the help he needed. Any problem could have been worked out. Yet Larry chose the option for which there is no turning back. Despite the threat he created for his partners and their families, I still miss him and still wonder why, as does Cece Andrus.

So, yes, I admit to holding strong views on the subject and make no apologies.

Fast forward a number of years to 2007. Andrus is still "of counsel" to the renamed Gallatin Public Affairs and is still generating lots of rain in his role with the firm. Marc Johnson is now the firm's president. Due to two serious health issues I am in the process of considerably reducing my role in the firm and trying gracefully to head out to the pasture.

Fate, though, provides one last opportunity for me to apply all the many things I have learned from Andrus regarding politics and campaigning. I undertake the lead role in what will be my final campaign, leading the charge against the state of Washington's adoption of an initiative that will permit physician assisted suicide.

On the other side, leading the campaign for the initiative, and also calling it his final campaign, is a fellow Parkinson's disease sufferer, the once popular and still charismatic former two-term Governor of Washington, Booth Gardner. Despite my diligent application of all that I learned from Andrus, I prove to be no clone of his, and my side ends up getting trounced.

It's a story worth retelling, though, because it demonstrates the power of money to overcome merit as well as fear to triumph over hope, insanity over sanity, and social responsibility to lose out to a glorification of self and selfishness. Apt a student as I was of Cecil Andrus', it also shows the truth that few acolytes are ever as good as the masters who instruct them.

Perusing the December 2, 2007, Sunday edition of the *New York Times,* I turned to the final section I always read – the weekly magazine. There, somewhat to my surprise, highlighted on the cover, was former Washington Governor Booth Gardner as the subject of the lead article entitled "Death in the Family." What I read appalled and alarmed me.

The article could not have turned out quite the way Gardner might have hoped. Like me, he suffers from Parkinson's disease, but instead of giving a sympathetic portrayal of his cause – advocating the misnamed Death with Dignity and promoting an initiative that would legalize Physician Assisted Suicide (PAS) – the article zeroed in on the tragedy his efforts were engendering within his own family. There was a serious rupture in the relationship between Gardner and his son, Doug, over this issue. In general, the article accurately portrayed Gardner's selfish interest in this subject and, while balanced, highlighted the threat PAS represents to the disabled, minorities, elderly, and especially vulnerable women.

The article's writer, Daniel Bergner, postulated that women in particular are more vulnerable than might be recognized, because many tie their identity to raising their children and helping to raise their grandchildren. When those roles diminish considerably due to illness, a sense of worthlessness can ensue which can lead to depression and a sense that life is no longer worth living. For women in this state the writer speculated that physician assisted suicide might begin to look like an attractive option.

I knew Gardner well, liked him, and had been a strong supporter when I served as the regional vice president for Kaiser. I also served on the Washington State Humanities Commission for several years, courtesy of an appointment by Gardner. At my request, he had appeared at a couple of events in Spokane with Andrus when their terms overlapped for two years. But after leaving the governorship, Gardner was diagnosed with Parkinson's disease, and slowly, it was debilitating him.

The last time I had seen and talked to Gardner was at a spring training game in Peoria, Arizona, where we sat watching a game between the Seattle Mariners and the Kansas City Royals. We spent much of the game comparing notes about how we were combating and managing Parkinson's.

I had no idea, though, that Gardner's reaction to the disease would be to become a leading advocate, the poster child for, and the chief spokesperson of, a campaign to put an initiative on the ballot allowing those diagnosed with terminal illness and given less than six months to live to opt out of life by having a doctor prescribe a lethal dose of medicines, which the victim would self administer.

With every fiber of my being, I knew I had to oppose the initiative and get involved. It felt like a calling, and I recognized it also presented an unusual opportunity to bring to bear the many things I had learned from Andrus about politics, issues, and managing campaigns. My initial research, much to my surprise, found there to be no formal opposition group to combat the initiative. It was clear to me that I had to start from scratch by organizing an opposition group and getting onto the playing field in a very short time.

My first call was to William Skylstad, Bishop of the Catholic Diocese of Spokane and chair of the U.S. Catholic Conference of Bishops. I asked him what, if anything, the Catholic Church was doing about the initiative. He introduced me by telephone to Sister Sharon Park, executive director of the Washington State Catholic Conference. As I looked back over the momentous year that was 2008, and reviewed what had gone wrong in our ultimately unsuccessful fight to defeat the initiative, one thing stood out: my good fortune in becoming acquainted with Sister Park.

As tough, smart, and talented as any politician I ever worked with, Sister Park commanded respect from all. She is a classic iron fist in a velvet glove: charming, witty, and outgoing, coupled with a great sense of humor. She is disciplined, focused, and dedicated.

It only took a short conversation to recognize we could help each other. Sister Park was looking for someone to identify and recruit a political consultant or a firm to handle the coming campaign. For a variety of reasons, it had to be kept separate from an education campaign she was planning aimed at parishioners. Obviously, a pollster had to be recruited, as did a fundraiser and a campaign manager.

Like most successful politicians, Andrus valued extensive, objective polling early in a campaign cycle. He instilled in all his "students" the value of research and the establishing of a baseline against which future polls could measure progress. He could read polls well, and took pleasure in digging into the crosstabs to understand differences in gender attitudes, income, and especially frequency of church attendance.

Lesson one was, "Research, research, research." Lessons two and three were the importance of selecting the correct finance chair and campaign manager. The two people holding those titles had inordinate influence within the campaign structure. Andrus believed one hired good talent, and then listened to what they had to say.

I volunteered to undertake these tasks. For my part, it was a relief to know some planning was being done. Sister Park brought to the table her experience in having been one of the co-leaders of a successful effort to defeat a 1991 initiative aimed at legalizing assisted suicide.

Another cardinal Andrus rule was to create a cohesive team for the campaign. Towards that end, Sister Park put me in touch with people who she knew would want to take an active role in fighting the initiative. Among this group were several doctors – Shane McCauley, Patricia "Paddie" O'Halloran, and Susan Rutherford, and a talented hospice nurse, Eileen Geller. Another crucial role was filled by Duane French, the charismatic leader of a disability rights advocacy group, "Not Dead Yet".

The name comes from a marvelous Monty Python skit portraying a couple of men during the Middle Ages when England and Europe were being ravaged by the Black Plague. A man leads a cart through a decimated village crying out in a mournful voice, "Bring out your dead! Bring out your dead!" The villagers then throw bodies on the cart with others they have collected for burial. Soon they are approached by a man carrying another man on his shoulder, wanting to dump his cargo on the cart, but this "victim" vehemently insists, " I'm not dead yet!" Hence, the name.

Circumstances dictated that we move quickly. Andrus liked to say "Keep moving. Keep moving. It is hard to hit a moving target." Reports were soon coming in that Gardner intended to personally file the request for a ballot title for the initiative by early January.

I quickly pounded out a press release announcing the formation of an opposition group and articulating some of the initial arguments we would use against the initiative. The release was to be distributed in a "blast" e-mail that would go to all the news media outlets in the state on the day Gardner filed. In addition, we made plans to have two of our group's spokespersons appear at the news conference that we knew Gardner would hold after the filing. We provided our own "talking heads" – in this case, two of our doctors – to counter Gardner's claims.

Another Andrus cardinal rule was the importance of responding to charges in the same news cycle to ensure that voters who read a charge could also read the rebuttal in the same article or see it in a television clip. Andrus intuitively knew that if one's response did not catch up with all the false charges in the same news cycle, a charge made and unrebutted, as he put it was a charge believed. The next day was simply not good enough in his estimation.

Our initial release quoted a statement from the Governor, Christine Gregoire, a practicing Roman Catholic, who, when serving previously as the state's Attorney General, had successfully defended the state's law against physician-assisted suicide. That law had been passed by the legislature following the 1991 defeat of a somewhat similar measure, and the U.S. Supreme Court later unanimously upheld the Washington ban.

Gregoire reiterated her opposition to the news media, only to back off a few days later after taking a call from Gardner, with whom she had served as the state's first Director of the Department of Ecology.

Nevertheless, our quick response succeeded. Gardner and the proponents, led by the renamed Hemlock Society, (now calling themselves "Compassion and Choices"), were caught by surprise.

Next, I turned my attention to finding a political consultant and a pollster, to establishing a Web site, and raising money. Knowing Gardner and his allies wanted the voters to see this as an issue being pushed primarily by pro-choice Democrats with the support of that party's traditional constituencies, especially labor, women's groups and Planned Parenthood, I turned to my rolodex, which held the names of most of the leading Democratic campaign consultants. I found, much to my surprise, that almost everyone I contacted was already under contract to Gardner.

In the meantime, we also garnered one other early success by convincing the Associated Press to call the initiative what it was – a measure allowing physician assisted suicide rather than one of the euphemisms the proponents were advocating such as "death with dignity." Previous polls across the nation indicated that when voters focused on the issue as one promoting doctor's involvement in assisting a person to commit suicide, they were more likely to turn against the measure. When AP concluded the initiative involved suicide, it notified its subscribers it would refer to it as such in its dispatches.

After exhausting my list of prominent Democratic consultants, I turned to a prominent Republican consultant, Stan Shore, with whom I had worked when serving on the steering committee for the campaign of a good friend, Spokane Mayor Dennis Hession. Shore is a multifaceted talent who would be of immense assistance if we could recruit him. Initially, he hesitated, saying he wanted to discuss it with his wife. Fortunately, she blessed his role and Stan committed to help us.

Our group next agreed to flesh out our organization, agree on a name, incorporate, and file with the State's Public Disclosure Commission. I flew into Sea-Tac Airport in late January 2008 to meet what was becoming the self-appointed steering committee to lead the campaign effort. Joining the initial band of soldiers at this meeting was Marilyn Golden from the Disabled Rights Education League (DRED) from Sacramento. With Marilyn's addition, the steering committee membership was set for the campaign.

Our agenda included identifying what we thought the issues would be and which messages would resonate best with the public. Poll results later would reveal we had anticipated some, but had missed others, including the sheer emotional appeal inherent in the desire of many people to "control" their passage from this world.

I was named chairman of the group. I attributed this selection to two factors: my political experience from having been involved directly in several of Cece Andrus' campaigns, as well as my personal story of having been given six months to live in November of 2005. The initiative specifically cited as one of its qualifying criteria that a candidate for assisted suicide must have a diagnosis that there was a high probability that he or she had six months or less. The group recognized my personal story was a powerful counter to anyone prematurely giving up all hope.

It became clear almost immediately that Compassion and Choices had been plotting and planning the initiative campaign for years. They had raised a substantial war chest to fund the effort to obtain the signatures to place the measure on the ballot and then pass it. Using paid signature gatherers, who were initially paid $.75 a signature and later $1, they dispersed across the state appearing at shopping malls and sporting events. Many of the signature gatherers had only a nominal sense of what they were promoting and disingenuously would urge people to sign just so "the people could vote on the matter."

Proponents also released results from their early polling which they claimed showed voters statewide would support the measure by a two to one majority. Their strategy included securing early endorsements from the Democratic Party, the Washington State Labor Council, and Washington Women Vote, the political action committee for Planned Parenthood, a leading advocate for the "choice" argument.

Our steering committee set out to deny them these key endorsements. After obtaining from Dr. O'Halloran a copy of the initial fundraising letter mailed primarily to the national mailing list of the "old" Hemlock Society and signed by Gardner, I drafted and distributed an open letter to Gardner.

The letter read:

> *Dear Gov. Gardner:*
>
> *As we greet the arrival of spring, nature's promise of the renewal of life leading to a bountiful harvest in the fall, it seems fitting to respond to a recent letter you sent across the nation soliciting funds for the initiative you hope to place in the November ballot allowing physician-assisted suicide (PAS).*
>
> *First, please accept an apology. In an earlier interview I said you were acting selfishly. That was wrong of me. Much as I think suicide is an irrational and selfish act, I*

*should separate advocacy for the act from the person. I should not and will not question your motives. Not only do you and I share the same affliction, which is Parkinson's disease, we also share a love for politics and baseball. With respect for each other, we should agree to disagree, but avoid being disagreeable.*

*I do go you one better, though, in that I would qualify under the terms of your initiative to avail myself of a physician's prescription to obtain the lethal drugs the initiative would permit. In November, 2005, I was told I had Stage IV cancer and the probability was I would not last six more months. But 16 months later I'm still here which, in and of itself, identifies one huge problem with your initiative: doctors are usually just making an educated guess when they predict how long one might live.*

*Certainly you have a right to your opinion, and a right to express it. Where in my humble opinion you go badly astray is asserting that there is a human constitutional right to what you call "death with dignity."*

*Really, Governor? Just where does it say that in the Constitution or the Bill of Rights? As Seattle Post-Intelligencer columnist Joel Connelly recently said in a column: Isn't the correct expression that all are endowed by the Creator with inalienable rights including the right to "life, liberty and the pursuit of happiness"? That's a right to life, not death, or do you place this fictional right under the "pursuit of happiness" clause?*

*Let me ask a few other questions regarding claims made in the fundraising letter.*

*Where in the Constitution does it say we have been endowed with a right to "unfettered personal liberty"? Really? I thought in society we accept constraints because we all understand the chaos that would result if we all had "unfettered personal liberty"? Most people understand we have responsibilities to our fellow human beings, not an absolute right to do as we please.*

*The letter conjures up a picture for its recipients of their dying loved ones having to endure unbearable pain, anguish and suffering. Is that really the way it is? Most proponents of assisted suicide now acknowledge that modern palliative medicine has become so effective that claiming assisted suicide is needed to prevent unbearable pain is just no longer credible. And isn't it true, Governor, that in Oregon pain is rarely invoked as the reason for requesting the lethal concoction of drugs?*

*The letter claims the initiative protects privacy, requires informed consent and provides safeguards, Governor, but isn't it true there is no requirement to notify one's family of this request for a lethal prescription? Isn't it true, too, Governor, that studies show almost all those given a terminal diagnosis exhibit signs of depression with some even expressing a desire to hasten death, but that most change their minds when the underlying depression is treated? Isn't it thus deeply concerning that not a single person availing themselves of Oregon's assisted suicide law in 2007 was even referred to a mental health professional for evaluation and true assistance?*

*The letter claims the Oregon law works, but how do you know? Isn't it true there is no penalty for non-reporting by a doctor either in Oregon or under the proposed Washington initiative? So how can one claim it works when there's no checking and enforcement?*

*And how can you claim taking a lethal dose of drugs to kill yourself is not suicide? The definition of suicide is clear and unequivocal. Isn't claiming, as the initiative does, that the underlying cancer or incurable condition is the cause of death, and not the lethal dose, completely inaccurate and in fact disingenuous?*

*And by the way, aren't we all terminal? Life itself is a terminal condition, Governor. Following your logic, couldn't healthy people avail themselves of your proposal? Aren't current laws focused correctly on protecting life and wouldn't your assisted suicide initiative really shift the entire focus of the laws built over a period of 2000 years?*

*You say this is all about the individual having power over how their life ends (though none of us had any "power" over how, where or when we were born) yet aren't you really inviting government into a heretofore very private and personal situation and actually ceding power to doctors--who clearly don't want it – or to HMOs, which may very well want it?*

*How about a friendly wager, Governor, that your campaign will end up spending more than the $1 million your letter says is budgeted to try and convince the voters of Washington to sanction government getting into the business of killing people? An exaggeration? Haven't you said several times this is just a first step? A first step to what, Governor?*

*Sincerely,*
*Chris Carlson*

Gardner did not reply. And, of course, the campaign he spearheaded spent far more than $1 million. By the time the smoke cleared, *Compassion and Choices* had spent nearly $8 million, three times as much as our campaign.

Knowing that Gardner was planning to make a personal appeal before the Spokane County Democratic Convention to ask for the adoption of a plank in the state party platform supporting the initiative, I took several countersteps. I contacted several friends who were active Democrats, and asked that they form and publicize a committee called Democrats Against Assisted Suicide. A prominent member and the spokesman for the group was attorney Tom Keefe, a former Democratic candidate for Congress in Washington's Fifth Congressional District, a former deputy mayor of Seattle, and a former chief of staff to the late U.S. Senator Warren Magnuson.

Keefe has a knack for giving the press a quotable quote and concise sound bite and was well-known and well-liked by political writers. His speaking for the group gave it instant credibility. I also contacted two other good friends who I knew were delegates to the county convention. Both were key members of the local Obama for President organization, and though neither were against the proposed initiative, they agreed to speak out in opposition to the matter becoming a plank in the party platform.

On a cold Saturday morning in April, our second daughter Marissa and I stood outside the entrance to University High School in Spokane Valley passing out copies of my open letter to Gardner. Chances were excellent that during convention down time delegates would read the missive. Also, chances were good that someone would hand it to the *Spokesman-Review's* political editor, Jim Camden, and he would weave it into his Sunday story. And that is what happened. The Sunday morning coverage was extensive and a plus for our side.

Working the news media was a major part of our early strategy, because we were being heavily outspent and out-organized. We forwarded the open letter to one of the state's most read political columnists, the *Seattle P-I's* Joel Connelly. He utilized the letter extensively in a column shortly thereafter, which created howls of protest from the largely liberal audience on the west side of the Cascades.

Gardner failed to sway the Spokane County Democrats despite an emotional speech, and he subsequently failed also to sway the state Democratic Convention. The Democratic platform remained silent on the issue.

An even more critical thwarting was denying proponents the endorsement of the Washington State Labor Council. Our campaign owed this almost entirely to the fine work of the Spokane Labor Council's Beth Thew. Marilyn Golden and I met with Thew in Spokane. At that meeting, Thew accepted most of our arguments, but also felt strongly that this issue simply was not something organized labor should be involved with. In this view, she had another strong ally on the council's executive committee, the secretary-treasurer, Al Link, another friend of mine from my days with Kaiser.

Thew went to the annual State Labor Council meeting, and when several other representatives from other councils tried to introduce resolutions of support passed by their home councils, she forcefully blocked their adoption by the executive committee. Proponents tried to take the issue to the floor of the state convention, but since it requires a two-thirds majority vote to reverse the executive committee, they lost.

Another significant victory was getting Washington Women Vote, the PAC for Planned Parenthood, to reject a request from the proponents for an endorsement and access to the group's coveted mailing list. We owed this victory to CJ Gribble, the talented and shrewd registered nurse who had long lead the eastern Washington chapter of Planned Parenthood. When Golden and I met with Gribble, she intuitively understood the proponents' argument that this issue was a different form of choice was misleading. In her words:

"For years we have argued that the key issue underlying our cause is that government has no business involving itself in such a personal, private issue. For us to say to government to butt out of the decision between a woman and her right to decide actions pertaining to her body but butt in and encourage one to perhaps prematurely kill themselves because of a fatal disease is just totally inconsistent."

She spoke out at the PAC board meeting and her view carried the day, giving proponents another surprising setback. Trouble was, few voters knew about these victories, because despite press releases pointing out the rejections, virtually no news media carried any of these events to their audiences.

The difficulty in attracting early coverage of our side of the question was due in part to our violation of one of Andrus' political rules. After doing your research and then drawing up a game plan, Andrus believed in executing the plan by "staying on the offensive" and forcing the other side into a defensive posture wherein they are reacting to your initiatives.

Because Gardner and his cohorts had a four-year head start, a well-researched game plan, and a good strategy for implementing that plan, they remained on the offensive throughout the entire campaign, while we tried to catch up while on the defensive. Our victories in denying some endorsements in the scheme of things were minor and took us away from activities in which we could have been broadening our base of support.

Andrus would often be heard saying during a race that campaigns are games of both addition and subtraction. By this he meant one designs the activities to add to one's base of support, but also to take away an opponent's support. A good example is the formation of a group like *"Republicans for Andrus."* Those who joined such a group added to Andrus' totals while subtracting from his opponents. Andrus always called Republicans who supported him "two-fers" – one vote for him and one taken away from his opponent.

Andrus also knew that a critical part of any campaign, whether an election involving two individuals or an initiative, was putting forth an individual with whom voters would identify, posit trust and bestow confidence. In particular when an election involves a complicated matter or a controversial issue, some voters will defer to the spokesman with whom they identify and trust.

In Booth Gardner, the proponents of Initiative 1000 had a charismatic, articulate, witty former governor whom was greatly liked, still remembered fondly by many, and who was an object of sympathy because of the debilitating aspects of his Parkinson's disease. Our side had no one comparable. These factors ensured more favorable news media coverage for initiative supporters even before they began an extensive television and radio campaign.

Early in the campaign, several members of the steering committee met in Olympia on a Saturday to design a poll to benchmark where we stood with the voters and to test messages and arguments we hoped would resonate. We selected as the pollster Bob Moore of Moore Information in Portland, a veteran of northwest political wars with a reputation for sound work. Stan Shore and I had worked with Moore previously and had confidence in his work.

When we reviewed the results from our first major statewide poll there was keen disappointment. While the initiative did not win by the 2 to 1 margin Gardner had claimed in his initial fundraising appeal, it enjoyed clear majority support. Moore's polling showed the measure passing by a 58% to 42% margin. Eight months later, despite raising $1.8 million and disseminating thousands of brochures, primarily through hundreds of churches, despite numerous speeches, editorial board appearances and radio and TV appearances, despite debates, despite a respectable television advertising effort, and despite the Washington State Medical Association's opposition, we lost by the same 58% to 42% margin Moore's first poll had predicted. For all our efforts, we never moved the needle.

Virtually every argument we mustered and tested lost decisively. Most disturbing to me was that between a quarter and a third of the respondents, depending on the question, said they simply *did not believe* what we were saying, even when we were quoting directly from the initiative. Never in all my years of analyzing polling data had I seen such a high number of "we don't believes".

194

Equally disturbing was that half of those who called themselves pro-life Catholics supported the measure. Despite an outstanding effort to educate Catholics on this issue lead by Sister Park and Catholic Bishops William Skylstad of Spokane, Archbishop Alex Brunett of Seattle, and Carlos Sevilla of Yakima, these numbers never budged.

Compassion and Choices had clearly done its homework, prepared well and executed its campaign strategy almost flawlessly. That and outspending us by a three to one margin, plus a sympathetic media (Every major newspaper in the state except my hometown *Spokesman-Review* and the widely circulated *Inlander* weekly came out for the initiative), spelled doom for our effort.

Besides the seductive charm of the choice argument proponents had going for them, Washington had the least "church-going" population in the nation in 2008. And to all outward appearances, the PAS law in place in neighboring Oregon for more than a decade appeared to be working. (It isn't, in my opinion.) There were also doctors and hospice nurses who, despite being a distinct minority in their profession, nonetheless created a sense of medical community support for this dubious proposition. The proponents developed a very powerful emotional-appeal ad featuring the widow of a man who allegedly had died in pain and agony.

The only temporary dent we put in the juggernaut of this pro-death, pro-suicide machine was an ad we put together featuring actor Martin Sheen, well-known as President Jed Bartlett on the television series *The West Wing*. Knowing we had practically zero credibility with a significant portion of the voters, we had to find a credible spokesperson whose personal stature would give pause to many undecideds before they voted. Martin Sheen fit the bill perfectly. Known as a champion of liberal causes, particularly supportive of the poor, minorities and the disabled, as well as being pro-choice, his "face" on our first major flight of ads was a coup which, for a brief time, seriously confounded the proponents.

The campaign owed a deep debt of gratitude to Dr. Shane McCauley, a member of our steering committee and liaison to the Washington State Medical Association, who had the connections to obtain Sheen's services, which the actor donated.

Proponents of PAS soon settled on the rebuttal of denouncing "out of state actors" who tried to tell Washington voters how to vote. That the ad made them nervous was confirmed when one of the national consultants to the their campaign spoke to the National Press Club about their effort in 2009. Their side could afford weekly tracking polls and the consultant conceded the Sheen ad temporarily put them off message and on the defensive. Their polling showed a strong opposition surge and for a brief time he said our campaign was ahead.

Stan Shore also drafted an ad featuring my story. Some folks argued that talking about how I could have utilized the law had it been in effect when I first received my diagnosis of Stage IV neuroendocrine cancer, but displaying that I was obviously still around, would be an effective testimonial for keeping government out of encouraging people to exit life prematurely.

The ad was filmed on a clear, warm spring day in a Seattle cemetery. With my sport blazer slung over my shoulder I walked among the tombstones and made my point in less than 30 seconds. Though I had often been before cameras and hosted my own quarterly *Inside Kaiser* television program, and had written a number of television spots myself, my ad received mixed reviews from the steering committee and campaign staff.

We left the raw footage and the TV ads "in the can," as the expression goes. With 20/20 hindsight, I have generally accepted various reports from folks who believe this additional ad should have run because many found even my brief 30 second argument compelling. The ad had its own emotional impact and perhaps could have countered the proponents' ads, all of which made emotional appeals.

Fundraising was without a doubt the campaign's Achilles heel. It was a constant source of mystery to me how and why the proponents of premature death, PAS and euthanasia were able to attract so much funding so easily. Final Public Disclosure Commission reports showed that just *six* individuals gave the pro-1000 campaign more money than the entire amount we raised from thousands of contributors. Gardner led the contributors, giving $500,000 from his personal fortune. At least he could vote in Washington. How does one explain a contribution of $250,000 from a professor at the University of Sussex in England?

"Money is the mother's milk" of politics is an old truism. From my days with Andrus I knew the importance of finding a banker like Bob Montgomery, who took the lead in fundraising for several of Cece's campaigns. While we had help from various folks in fundraising, especially Michael Pauley, another shortcoming of our effort was the failure to find one fundraiser in chief to spend hours each day "dialing for dollars."

From the very beginning, proponents characterized the Catholic Church as the main opponent of the initiative, even running radio ads in the Seattle area urging voters not to let one powerful church dictate the outcome of the issue. They fed the news media a bill of goods that the Church would pour massive amounts of money into our campaign in the waning days, as they alleged had happened in other states. They even seized upon Pope Benedict XVI's visit to the United States in April as an occasion to remonstrate and castigate the church for its "interference" in American politics, as if the Church had no right to make its views known.

Even more insidiously, proponents threatened lawsuits challenging the Church's tax exempt status if it played a major role. While bishops did solicit funds for the campaign, the amount the church was able to raise constituted less than 40% of the total raised. Proponents need not have worried, but, of course, the Church was a convenient villian. As one writer put it, "Anti-Catholicism is the new form of legitimate bigotry for the intelligentsia and the cognoscenti!"

The truth is the Catholic Church has been substantially weakened by the sexual abuse scandal that plagued almost every diocese across the country with compensation payments totally more than a billion dollars. This had considerably constrained the ability of many bishops to raise and direct funds to a campaign like ours.

Secondly, most other protestant and evangelical churches, while paying lip service to our goals, contributed next to nothing. Or, like the Mormons, they were directing their resources to passing California's Proposition 8, an amendment to that state's constitution outlawing same-sex marriages. An effort I made to gain an audience to plead our case with a key Apostle of the LDS Church in Salt Lake City was politely rebuffed.

Third, our campaign was reportedly denounced by a prominent person in the anti-euthanasia movement to the leader of the national Knights of Columbus organization, Carl Anderson (a former Washington resident). The result was that despite personal pleas from Washington bishops and the state leadership of the Washington Knights, the one organization that could have poured millions into our campaign largely stayed on the sidelines and contributed only nominally to our effort. This weak response came despite incredibly strong support from the Knights' state organization and the numerous Washington state Knights who worked hard passing out brochures, soliciting funds and putting up signs, unaware that their efforts were being undermined at the national level.

That someone could stand in the way of the right course and deliberately sabotage a cause they allegedly supported still boggles my mind. I couldn't help remembering another political truism Andrus liked to recite: "Success has a thousand fathers. Failure is a bastard." There could have been plenty of credit to spread around had we won. It became clear to me after the campaign was over that I was the bastard.

Some readers may wonder what this lengthy chapter on assisted suicide and end-of-life issues has to do with reminiscence primarily about the rise of Cecil Andrus, my years working for him, and my subsequent business relationship with him. The simple fact is end-of-life issues are faced by all of us, whether it is dealing with the imminent passing of a parent or a loved one, or facing our own mortality.

When one has been in public life as long as Cecil Andrus, he develops a large extended family and he gets to know by first name literally thousands of people. As the years go by, more and more of these supporters and extended family members grow older and pass out of this life. News of death comes incessantly. Andrus could literally attend a funeral every day of the year.

Like many, he has buried his parents. Unlike many, he has had two of his three daughters face life-threatening illnesses, which, while proving manageable nonetheless, serve as constant reminders of life's fragility. Both of us are still scarred and will remain scarred by the inexplicable death of Larry Meierotto.

Like me, he has also had to face up to a life-threatening cancer diagnosis. In his case it was prostate cancer, which appears to have been caught early, treated properly and cured. All victims of any form of cancer live with the knowledge it could reoccur. I would argue that the only way to conclude a book of remembrances is by writing a chapter reflecting our attitudes towards death.

Most of us don't like to even think about the subject until forced to do so. And almost all of us are seduced by the false but noble-sounding notion that we "don't want to be a burden to our families." Few understand there is true grace in allowing others to minister to us through loving care at life's end. Most of us are further taken in by the insidious notion that we are the captains of our own destiny and masters of our own fate.

The more I campaigned and listened to proponents of assisted suicide, the more I realized how many people – even those professing to be practicing Christians and believers – really do not trust God. Not to over-simplify, but if one believes in God, one truly trusts God and recognizes the Almighty exerts mastery of our lives. From conception to natural death, we are in God's hands, not our own.

It is true of course that we can all take our own lives if we wish. We do have free will. But there is a reason why almost all societies and all the world's great religions have prohibitions against suicide. It is recognized for the ultimate act of selfishness that it is, a breach of faith with family and society, an act that visits lifelong pain on the surviving members of one's family. The desire to kill oneself has always been viewed as an unnatural act and a cry for help.

The challenge for society is to eliminate the root causes for such despair and answer the *cri de coeur*, the desire to kill oneself represents. Those of us on the steering committee recognized early on it was not enough for our campaign to be against PAS, we also had to be *for* better and improved end of life care. In response, our web site established a link to places where one thinking about PAS, or their family, could go to find assistance. We expressed support for hospice and for additional funding that could provide more and better trained caregivers who, could among other things, provide relief for the one or two family members who always seem to be burdened with providing a disproportionate share of the care in a family member's dying days.

This part of the campaign received virtually no media coverage. Who wants to read about good news and positive programs that help those in need? Who wants to read that there actually are truly compassionate alternatives to offering someone a quick fix pill to end it all? Some months after the campaign, Eileen Geller, who had become a part-time president of the surviving campaign organization, wisely renamed the committee "True Compassion Advocates" to underscore the importance of providing alternatives.

There is one member of the proponent's group I have come to grudgingly admire, though I have never met him. Derek Humphrey is a co-founder of the Hemlock Society, and is brutally candid and totally honest. He refuses to sugarcoat what PAS is all about. He has chastised his colleagues in an interview with Oregon's *Eugene Register-Guard* for utilizing euphemisms rather than acknowledging that what they were proposing was physician-assisted suicide, pure and simple. He forthrightly sees phrases such as "Aid in Dying" and "Compassion and Choices" as disingenuous at best and deceptively and deliberately misleading at worst.

In an attempt to get audiences to think, I would often end my remarks by quoting Humphrey and repeating one of his brutally candid statements: "Euthanasia and physician assisted suicide will inevitably prevail in our society because they make economic sense." Humphrey is a true economic determinist who sees the rising cost of health care as being in direct conflict with people living longer. And in "crunching the numbers," he tacitly acknowledges that insurance companies and the decisions they make will more and more determine who lives and who dies.

His view of the future, shared by many others, is one of rationed health care and more discrimination based on lifestyle choices people have made and making them accountable, fatally accountable, if you will, for their poor choices. For Humphrey it is completely logical to offer those deemed terminally ill with only a few months to live the option of saving their family's and estate's money by opting out early. It is a view that dresses despair in the gown of realism and says "abandon hope" to all who enter.

Later, proponents started acknowledging the damage Humphrey's candor was doing by dismissing his views as that of an extremist and not reflective of their movement.

As the campaign moved into September and October, it became clear voters were not moving from their initial inclinations. Especially disappointing was the campaign's failure to garner editorial support. Newspaper after newspaper came out for the initiative, with the exception, as I mentioned earlier, of my hometown newspapers, the *Spokesman-Review* and the *Northwest Inlander.* Especially galling to me was the loss of the *Tri-City Herald,* where in a debate before their editorial board I had truly clobbered the proponent's spokesperson. On several occasions she had readily conceded the validity of my points. Equally disappointing was the defection of Seattle's venerable *Post-Intelligencer* despite several insightful columns by Joel Connelly. The P-I had been against the earlier ballot measure in 1991.

During the final weeks of the campaign, the members of the steering committee made dozens of appearances before Rotary clubs, at Church Life committee meetings and at parishes and churches across the state. We did radio interviews locally and statewide, and some nationally. Most of us participated in memorable debates (where the proponents had obvious "plants" who asked emotional questions), wrote op-ed columns, gave speeches to any who would listen – all in what we knew was likely a losing effort.

All of us not only donated from our modest treasuries, we also gave generously of our time and talent. Andrus had drilled into me during his campaigns as well as his tenure in office, the importance of personal thank you notes. He seldom made use of automatic signature machines and often scribbled a brief personal p.s. to the recipient so they would know for sure he had seen and signed the note. Being a good student, I personally signed hundreds of thank you notes to donors, the envelopes of which were carefully hand-addressed by Marcia, who also donated considerable time and talent to the cause. For us, there was no other choice.

When the votes started to roll in, reporters called early. I minced few words, conceding we had been beaten badly. Once again, I cited Derek Humphrey as to the choice the voters had made, adding how sad and wrong it was for the voters of Washington State to start down the path of death and despair. Though the figurehead of the campaign against the initiative, there was no way I even considered calling Gardner to "congratulate" him on his "success."

I made one public appearance afterwards to do a post-mortem of the campaign, at Gonzaga President Robert Spitzer's annual "Healing the Culture" seminar in Bellevue. I went in large part because Camille and Michael Pauley, who assist Father Spitzer, had both worked hard to help the campaign. Michael had been one of our best fundraisers and Camille has an extensive network of pro-life contacts she worked diligently on behalf of our effort.

At the seminar I laid much of the blame at my feet for a variety of mistakes, big and small. The list started with my placing several people from out of state "outside the tent." I recognized also the campaign should have had a full-time, rather than a part-time chair. I did a mea culpa for trying to bring on a campaign coordinator to work with Stan Shore and the steering committee, but one who lived east of the Cascades. I belatedly recognized proximity made a difference. I left unspoken our failure to produce a strong emotional counter ad, the struggles encountered in raising money, and the number of Andrus' Rules for a Campaign that had been ignored because of circumstances or violated out of necessity.

I also opined on what was needed to go forward and defeat Compassion and Choices on other battlefields across the nation, making it clear that to help give the organization a fresh start and a new face I would resign before January 1, 2009, which I did.

On March 5, 2009, the initiative 1000 became law. Unable to let the sad date go by unobserved I submitted this rant to the *Spokesman-Review,* which they published:

BIG BROTHER CAN NOW ENCOURAGE YOU TO KILL YOURSELF

*The state of Washington this week started down the slippery slope of incentivizing its citizens to kill themselves prematurely, with the implicit support of health insurance companies, and the connivance of some physicians, and even some hospitals, despite their supposed adherence to the Hippocratic Oath of doing no harm to people.*

*Fortunately, here in Spokane, the Providence System Hospitals (Sacred Heart, Holy Family) exercised their right under the voter-passed initiative to "opt out" by invoking a conscience clause. We'll see how long that lasts as the relentless forces of doom and death predictably are already attacking that right also.*

*Unfortunately, the State Department of Health, charged with developing regulations for implementing the new physician-assisted suicide initiative, merely (and blindly) adopted Oregon's regulations which even a mini-*

202

*mal review by an objective observer show to be inade-
quate and rife with problems.*

*Quite simply the Department shirked its responsibil-
ity to protect our vulnerable populations (the aged, the
infirm, the disabled, minorities) whose lives, make no mistake about it, could be terminated without their consent.
Voters of this state bought into the false notions that the
initiative would somehow insure their right to choose to
end their life (a right already existing), but will soon dis-
cover they have empowered the state to appropriate to itself and others that power. This law would allow someone
with your power of attorney to have you killed under the
guise that you really wanted to kill yourself!*

*To state it bluntly, voters endorsed something intrinsi-
cally wrong. The state should not be incentivizing people
supposedly given six months or less to live, to prematurely
end their lives. The fundamental purpose of people band-
ing together, the first law of the social contract, is we come
together to protect life, especially the weak, the lame, the
disabled, those who might not be economic producers and
generators because as a society we in America have always held life to be of intrinsic and incalculable value.*

*Now, instead of trusting God to determine the natu-
ral course of one's life, and turning to focusing on better
compassionate care for those who have to deal with the
challenges of end-of-life issues, Washingtonians can now
play God and ask the state to assist them to die earlier
than their natural course of life. It is a Faustian bargain
I believe voters will come to regret, as folks soon realize
the state and insurance companies can and will more and
more determine who lives and who dies, with economic
issues over-riding ethical concerns.*

*And if you think the state will protect you, guess again.
Despite numerous concerns raised by physicians and others with the Department of Health regarding the shortcomings of Oregon's regulations, the department rubber-
stamped Oregon's rules for here.*

*Thus there is no adequate enforcement of the report-*
*ing requirements and no real transparency in this new*
*law. Nor are there any real penalties for failure to report.*
*Additionally, the informed consent form is grossly inad-*
*equate. It requires less information and has fewer safe-*
*guards than the forms the department requires for mun-*
*dane procedures like piercing one's ears. A physician is*
*not required to be in attendance; indeed, while the request*
*form requires two witnesses there is no requirement for*
*anyone let alone an impartial observer to witness the sui-*
*cide.*

*The definition of mental competency is sorely lacking*
*also with no real requirement for counseling with mental*
*health professionals even though we all know that almost*
*always a desire to commit suicide is a sign of a depressed*
*mind seeking to do what we once knew to be totally ir-*
*rational. But suddenly this intrinsic wrong can be con-*
*sidered rational. What kind of Orwellian world are we*
*sinking into my friends?*

*The list of shortcomings is much larger, but why both-*
*er? The people of this state sadly bought the classic pig in*
*a poke and few will care until they realize towards the end*
*of their own life that someone else is driving the decision*
*on when and how their life may end. So lift that cup of*
*hemlock, my friends, and drink deeply from the draught of*
*insanity redefined as sanity, of the irrational being called*
*rational, of your supposed new found right to play God!*

The newspaper received exactly one letter to the editor opposing my rant. On March 7, 2010, shortly after the anniversary of the law's implementation, I wrote another column (rant some might say) which appeared in the weekly *St. Maries Gazette Record,* published some 25 miles from where we now reside in retirement on Cave Lake in southern Kootenai County.

I suspect this will become an annual event for me though it will continue to fall on deaf ears. Folks appear to have concluded, at least in the state of Washington, that the issue was decided and have moved to other things.

Compassion and Choices, for its part, is not resting. It is using the success in Washington State to jump start campaigns in other states. Fortunately, others have picked up the banner and, to date, have successfully staved off any new state laws. When the proponents' attorney, Kathryn Tucker, signaled her introduction of the issue into Idaho through an op-ed in the local newspaper, I wrote a harsh, and sarcastic response. Working again with Eileen Geller, we identified doctors to object publicly to Tucker's appearance before the Idaho Medical Association. We also flagged to all of Idaho's heavily conservative legislators what the group was really all about. She will make little, if any, headway in Idaho. Part of their tact in Idaho, as well as elsewhere, is to bore-sight and attack the "conscience clause" in laws which allows hospitals and doctors to opt out of providing PAS services, looking towards the day when doctors will be required by law to offer the suicide option to any distressed patient, whether facing a terminal disease or not.

Chilling as the thought is, perhaps Derek Humphrey will be proven correct.

# Epilogue

As I finish writing this in the fall of 2010, I'm pretty much out to pasture, as the saying goes. At the behest of Andrus and several friends, who were justifiably concerned that my penchant for continuing to work was generating stress that inevitably would exacerbate my Parkinson's and, perhaps, rekindle my still dormant neuroendocrine cancer, I applied for a disability determination, which was approved and granted.

In May of 2009, Marcia and I signed with a northern Idaho contractor to build our new home on Cave Lake adjacent to her parents on seven acres we had purchased from them near the little burg of Medimont. Marcia designed the house and drew up the floor plan. The work went smoothly with few delays and we moved into our lake place retirement home in mid-December of 2009. The house has ramps in the front and the garage, extra wide doors and other ADA requirements in anticipation that someday I most likely will be wheelchair bound.

Our moving next door was fortuitous for Marcia's mother, Mary Lou Andersen, who also has Parkinson's disease, more advanced than mine. On Ash Wednesday 2010, just as we drove up to take her mother to evening Mass with us, her father, Ralph, died suddenly of a heart attack at age eighty-seven. That we were right there and able to take charge of emergency efforts to revive him, then deal with the EMT folks, the Sheriff's office and the County Coroner was truly a blessing for her.

Three weeks later the family received another devastating blow upon learning that the youngest sibling, Erik, aged forty, had been killed in an auto accident in North Dakota, leaving a devastated wife and four young children. Two funerals in less than one month were almost too much to bear, but having her oldest daughter right next door was great

*Carlson family file*

Chris standing on top of Mt. Borah, September of 1989, with a "message" for anyone tempted to challenge Governor Andrus in his 1990 re-election bid.

comfort to Mary Lou. The Lord does work in mysterious ways.

Once the boxes were unpacked and I had my study, I began finishing this project in earnest. I also returned to my journalistic roots by signing up with the nearby weekly newspaper, the *St. Maries Gazette Record,* to produce a weekly column on politics and commentary.

Those projects, a never-ending list of honey-do's, and an ability to get away most Wednesdays for a day of fly-fishing on the nearby St. Joe River or on the South or North Forks of the Coeur d'Alene River, serve to keep me busy. I walk, or ride my bike, admittedly rather slowly, a couple of miles a day – primarily the half mile out to the paper and mail boxes in the morning and at noon to get the mail. And I read the *New Yorker, Economist* and *Atlantic Monthly* religiously, besides answering a fair amount of e-mail.

While my Parkinson's is progressing ever so slowly (mercifully so) and my cancer continues to remain dormant (mercifully so), I recognize the challenges entailed in managing my health will grow inevitably more complex and demanding. For the time being, I'm managing well and have an incredible sense of being exceptionally blessed. I greet each day grateful to see the sun rise and to still be alive. I am among men, most richly blessed and I trust I'll be able to carry this sense of gratitude for having been granted "borrowed time" through to the end of my days, hopefully quite a ways down the road.

Cece turned 79 in August, 2010. His stated goal is to make it to one hundred. Given that his father, Hal, lived to ninety-nine, his prospects are good. Cece had his cancerous prostate removed in a robotic surgery procedure mid-summer of 2010. It appears all the cancer was contained within the prostate and had not spread, which is key to the excellent prognosis he has received. There also is a history of cancer in the Andrus family, with both Hal and Cece's older brother, Steve, having contracted it, and having also successfully beaten it.

A wise old internist doctor, Ev Coulter, once told me that if a man lives to be a hundred he has a 100% probability of contracting prostate cancer, the only critical question being whether it is symptomatic or not, with one form truly being life–threatening and the other more of a nuisance. He also said the probability rises in remarkable relation to one's age – when one is in his sixties, there's a 60% probability; when one is in his seventies, a 70% probability; and, from there upward to 100%. So there's no escaping either that form of cancer or the fact that we're all terminal. It is just matter of when, where and how.

A zest for living, proper diet, minimum use of alcohol and tobacco, moderate but regular exercise – we are all familiar with the formula that helps minimize the prospects of a premature demise, but the end comes to all and when it does what counts is whether one can face it with a clear conscience. Did we give our best effort? Flawed though we all are, did we also have a positive influence on our children? Did we make a difference in a positive way for our time in sojourning through this world?

Certainly, Cecil Andrus has made a huge difference in the lives of many Idahoans, and in the lives of others. I'd like to think too, that his redefining the notion of national parks and extending them into urban areas where so many people live, people who may never travel to Alaska or see the Redwoods, is part of his legacy. Obviously his role in preserving and protecting much of Alaska's scenic wonders will forever remain his environmental legacy.

His Idaho legacy ranges from protecting Hells Canyon, the Sawtooths, and the Birds of Prey. To keeping the state from becoming a nuclear dumping ground. From holding resource extraction companies to higher standards of environmental protection to obtaining ground-breaking land-use planning legislation. From providing state support for kindergartens, to laying the ground work for the growth and expansion of Boise State University. He provided the critical vote as a state senator that brought about the implementation of a state sales tax dedicated primarily to providing better support for public education, and reorganizing state government into its modern form.

Even more important than these definable accomplishments was his ability to inspire faith in the proper role of government. He burnished the notion that public service and holding elective office as a noble calling. Cecil Andrus said, "Governors are elected to solve problems," and solve problems he did. He will forever remain the standard by which other governors in Idaho will be measured, and few will measure up. Politicians like him are exceptional, and rare. Hell, people like him are exceptional and rare.

My privilege and the privilege of so many who had the opportunity to work with and for him was to know we had a small part in helping to achieve a fine legacy by one of America's gifted office holders. I'll always believe he would have made a superb president. His legacy is written in many hearts and many memories and won't be forgotten.

# A Day in the Life of a Cabinet Secretary

*A Cabinet member's day is filled with reminders of a dual role – as head of a department and the President's agent – as Interior's Cecil D. Andrus has learned.*

(editors note:  the following is reproduced as orginally published)

Reprinted with permission from *National Journal*
By Dom Bonafede
*National Journal*, May 12, 1979

It is 6:30 a.m. in suburban McLean, Va., when the Cabinet member emerges from his home to enter a chauffeured sedan waiting by the curb. But first, the Interior Secretary has to take out the garbage.

The irony isn't lost on Cecil D. Andrus' wife, Carol, who reminds him that as governor of Idaho he didn't have to perform such mundane chores. That is only a minor, yet symbolic, accommodation that Andrus has had to make with Washington: like the 11 other members of President Carter's Cabinet, he is endowed with prestige and perquisites but, in the final accounting, he is essentially one of the President's hired hands.

The day that begins by hauling garbage will be a typical one for Andrus: he'll spend some time with aides and some time on Capitol Hill, some time with his department's constituents and some time with his most important constituent, the President. And, if he's lucky, he'll get some time to devote to thinking quietly by himself.

A Cabinet Secretary's day, of course, varies with his or her department. Secretary of State Cyrus Vance, Treasury Secretary W. Michael Blumenthal and Commerce Secretary Juanita M. Kreps are likely to spend more time than the others on foreign trips. Energy Secretary James R. Schlesinger and Housing and Urban Development Secretary Patricia Roberts Harris are likely to spend more time on Capitol Hill, lobbying for Administration programs. And Attorney General Griffin B. Bell is likely to spend less time with interest groups. Since his department's constituency is not so well defined.

What they all have in common, however, is their dual role: program administrators and constituent hand-holders on the one hand and agents and troubleshooters for the President on the other; VIP's in their own right, but very much the President's men and women.

## CABINET PARADOX

Of all federal institutions, the Cabinet, paradoxically, is one of the best known but least understood.

Since its existence is based on custom and tradition rather than any statutory requirement, the President may use it as he wishes: he may seek its counsel as a whole or individually; he may call on it simply to signify unity within his Administration or to show that he is taking action; or, he may ignore it altogether. The influence and public exposure of each member frequently depends on the Secretary's own personality and political talent or merely on the accident of time – whether he or she happens to head a department dealing with a currently critical issue. And the President is free to rely on and confide in certain Cabinet members more than others.

While a president may use the Cabinet to gauge public opinion or obtain a sense of the esprit within his Administration, the notion of his using it as a collegial decision-making body is ill-founded.

The Constituion is vague on the legal basis for the Cabinet and does not mention it by name. Article II, Section 2 merely states that the President may seek "the opinion, in writing, of the principal officer in each of the executive departments..."

212

In The President's Cabinet (Harvard University Press, 1959), Richard F. Fenno Jr. wrote: "The simple fact that the President is not required by law to form a Cabinet or to keep one helps to explain its dependence upon him... The President's power to use or not use it is complete and final. The Cabinet is his to use when and if he wishes, and he cannot be forced into either alternative."

And Arthus M. Schlesinger Jr., in his book, The Coming of the New Deal (Houghton Mifflin Co., 1958), quotes Harold Ickes – one of the most famous of Andrus's predecessors – from a notation in his diary after a 1935 Cabinet session during the Administration of Franklin D. Roosevelt: "Only the barest routine matters were discussed... The cold fact is that on important matters, we are seldom called upon for advice. We never discuss exhaustively any policy of government or question of political strategy. The President makes all of his own decision."

In all probability, the same lament could be sung by several of Carter's Cabinet members. However, given the size of the federal bureaucracy, the complexities of contemporary issues that call for interagency cooperation, and the need for managerial techniques in government, it is unlikely that a President would completely abandon the Cabinet tradition in the foreseeable future. It is more likely that the departments would be reorganized and consolidated.

During the formative phase of his Administration, Carter went through an elaborate selection process in appointing his Cabinet. He maintained that his would be a "Cabinet Government" and that he would rely more heavily on its members for counsel and support than on the White House staff. It has not, however, worked out that way.

In the beginning, Carter's Cabinet Secretaries were allowed considerable autonomy in running their departments and appointing their staffs. With increasing intensity, however, the White House has tightened control over departmental patronage and personnel review. Theoretically, Cabinet members have liberal access to the President, but even there, almost all have to go through formal channels.

But in the massive Interior Department complex on C Street in northwest Washington, Cecil Andrus is in charge. And it is there that this day – on which a reporter was allowed to accompany him – begins.

## THE DAY BEGINS

Andrus's office reflects his western roots – a huge wood-paneled room, with photos and paintings of western and Alaskan mountain ranges, including a photograph of California's Yosemite by Ansel Adams. And there is a picture of Castle Peak in Idaho's White Clouds Mountains – which reminds Andrus of how he rode a campaign issue stressing environmental protection of the Peak to his first victory as governor in 1970.

It's 7:45 a.m. on a warm spring day, but a fire is already blazing in the office fireplace, one of the perks of his job. Andrus, in shirtsleeves, sits in an easy chair, discussing two policy reports – one on timber and the other on the proposed Department of Natural Resources (DNR). He is a winner on the latter; under the proposal, other Secretaries would have to give up parts of their departments to him. It's part of his award for dutifully giving up some of Interior's duties to the new Energy Department early in the Administration.

As it is, his department's responsibilities are already among the broadest in the federal government. Its 77,000 employees administer 500 million acres of federal land, promote mine safety, manage national parks and seashores, protect fish and wildlife, control mineral and oil reserves, help preserve scenic and hisotoric sites, operate irrigation projects and hydroelectric power systems, watch over American Indian affairs, and exercise jurisdiction over U.S. trust territories.

And weighing all those claims can bring frustration. "It's not just the oil companies and the coal operators," Andrus says. "There are the miners, ranchers, cattlemen, timbermen, save-the-wildlife-people, the protectionists, the environmentalists and any number of others. You can decide 80 per cent of the time in their favor, and it's still not enough."

Andrus discusses the policy reports with four aides, seated on couches on either side of him---Greg Ritchey, Steve Freudenthal, Gary Wickes and Dan Beard, as well as his press assistant, Chris Carlson. The Secretary confidently ticks off statistics, acreage estimates, budget figures and policy principles. He outlines options available to the President on timber policy, voices concern for the viewpoints of both industrialists and environmentalists and suggests that the language of one of the reports be refined.

214

The meeting over, Andrus's personal secretary, Billie Jeppesen, reminds him that he is due on Capitol Hill to testify at a confirmation hearing for June G. Brown, a project manager for the Bureau of Reclamation in Denver who has been nominated to serve as the department's new inspector general.

He rides a private elevator to the garage, where he climbs into the front seat to sit next to his driver. He reflects for a moment on the frustrations of dealing with the federal bureaucracy while trying to balance the competing claims of environmentalists and developers. "There's no way you can please everybody." But, as he notes later on, "Anytime I have industry and the environmentalists mad at me, I'm not in bad shape."

> *"It's like running into a large marshmallow. As Governor... I could make a decision, even if it was a poor one, and it would be implemented. Here, after four months, I find they are still not implementing it."*
> Cecil D. Andrus
> Secretary of the Interior

It's 9:05 and Brown's hearing begins, with freshman Sen Bill Bradley, D.N.J., presiding. Only one other Senator has bothered to show up.

It's obvious that Bradley isn't familiar with the procedure. But Andrus, an old hand by now, introduces the nominee, lists her background and qualifications and says that she is "superbly qualified."

Along with his Cabinet peers, Andrus has to refer nominees for department vacancies to the White House. But that, he said, is not particularly troubling. "I've never had them deny a prospective appointee to a job here. They have sent me names; that entitles them to a look, but it doesn't guarantee them a job."

Andrus is not required to be at the hearing, but attends as a matter of courtesy to Brown. Not all appearances on the Hill are so ceremonial, though, like other Cabinet officers, he must appear to testify on Administration programs or on his own department's budget. And from time to time, he is called on to lobby for the White House. "I got one Senate vote on the Panama Canal treaties that I doubt the boss (Carter) could have gotten," he said with a smile.

Back in his office by 9:30, Andrus takes about 20 minutes to attend to some paperwork. He is then briefed by his two chief aides, undersecretary James A. Joseph and Solicitor Leo M. Krulitz, before a meeting with a large contingent of environmentalists. Krulitz is an old friend from Boise who managed one of Andrus's political campaigns and served as an unofficial adviser when he was governor. Joseph, a former vice president of the Cummins Engine Co. of Columbus, Ind., on the other hand, had never met Andrus before he was recruited to become one of the Administration's top-ranking blacks.

The three comprise a troika that handles all major policy decisions and administrative actions. In a rough division of labor, Andrus takes the lead on natural resources issues and Joseph, the human resources issues such as Indian affairs, the trust territories and departmental personnel. Joseph sometimes gets involved in the natural resources area, on issues such as the federal coal management program and Alaska land policy.

Andrus said internal changes he instituted at the department have meant "a break with the past." Thus, to get a grip on what he calls the "fiefdoms" in the department, the Secretary established a strong line operation, in which all actions and decisions are supposed to flow up through regular channels. Bureau chiefs are prohibited from going around assistant secretaries having jurisdiction over them. Speeches and press releases have to be cleared by the department's public affairs section.

He also installed a "critical issues management system," designed to monitor more than 50 legislative and administrative items. "If you don't keep on top of things like that, they have a way of slipping," said Charles M. Parrish, former executive assistant to Andrus and now field director of the Carter-Mondale Campaign Committee.

THE CONSTITUENTS

At 11 a.m., about a dozen representatives of various environmental groups troop into Andrus's office. He has checked the list of those who are to attend, many of whom he knows. A number are young, all wear somber expressions.

As if to even things, there are an equal number of Interior officials attending. The room, as spacious as it is, is nearly filled. Andrus, perhaps in deference to the group, has put on his suitcoat.

216

The topic of the day is the Administration's coal leasing program. The discussion begins immediately with few amenities. A leader selected by the visitors speaks first but doesn't get far before Andrus suggests that time can be saved by not discussing the legal aspects of the issue since that is not the point of today's meeting.

Each visitor, in turn, is allowed to have his or her say. They are disturbed about certain parts of the program and think that there should be greater public participation and comprehensive planning.

Andrus listens patiently to the critique, which is forceful but not hyperbolic. Occasionally, he makes notes on a yellow legal pad on his lap. When the last speaker has finished, Andrus tries to assuage their concerns, to assure them that they have a friend in him, that final decisions have not been made, that "preferred alternatives" are being studied.

"We'll meet, consult and try to work out the problems," he tells them. They leave, looking about the same as when they arrived, satisfied that they got their points across but uncertain how much good it did.

Andrus acknowledges that he has heard almost all the arguments before, but recognizes that such meetings are an integral part of his job. More than 10 per cent of his time is spent meeting with constituent groups, he said.

Andrus already has lasted as Interior Secretary 27 months – the average of his predecessors. However, if Icke's 13 years and Stewart K. Udall's 8 years are excluded, the average tenure is only 11 months. "At first, I couldn't understand it," Andrus says. "But now I do. There is no way you can please everybody in this job."

It is now 11:35. The meeting with the environmentalists has taken longer than scheduled. Andrus sits behind his desk and begins returning telephone calls. If he needs it, he has a direct line to the White House. Often he dials the numbers himself instead of going through his secretary.

One call is to Agriculture Secretary Bob Bergland. During the conversation, Andrus suddenly laughs and says, "Do I know how to stand up in a boat? For Chrissakes, all you Minnesota people sail on are flat lakes."

Another call goes to an Administration official whose child has just undergone surgery. One of Andrus's three daughters has suffered from

Hodgkin's disease and he offers his sympathy and understanding to the official. "If I can help you, don't hesitate to call me," he says.

Lunchtime now, and Andrus has a bowl of soup at his desk. He laughs: "Can you imagine Joe Califano doing this?"

Early in his Administration, Carter handed down an edict that austerity would be the keynote of his term and that Cabinet officers would have to eliminate many of the frills of their offices. That presidential proclamations are sometimes disregarded – even by Cabinet Secretaries – is underscored by the fact that few of the luxuries of rank have been eliminated, including a $16,000-a-year steward for Health, Education and Welfare Secretary Joseph A. Califano Jr.

Andrus, however, was one Cabinet member who took Carter's directive seriously. He closed Interior's private dining room and eliminated two employees who used to prepare and serve meals. When he doesn't eat at his desk, the Secretary dines in the department's cafeteria. When he has important visitors for lunch, which is rare, a catered meal is ordered. His one concession is his chauffeured sedan, but when he rides, he sits up front with his driver.

He eats amid a pile of papers, documents and memos and recalls when he was governor of Idaho, he usually had a clean desk.

PRESIDENT'S MAN

A half hour for lunch and then, at 12:30, four aides arrive to discuss a White House meeting later in the afternoon with representatives of the National Oceans Industries Association on the proposed Natural Resources Department.

Andrus knew Carter better than most of the department heads when he was asked to join the Cabinet. They first met In November 1970 at the National Governor's Conference in Pinehurst, N.C., shortly after each was elected governor. "They hit it off right away," said Carlson.

The President has said of Andrus that they have been "close friends since we were elected governor." When Andrus was sworn in, Carter said, "I guess of all the Cabinet members, he has been the one closest to me in the past... I have to say he is the only Cabinet member I never had to hesitate at all about."

Yet Andrus makes no extravagant claims of friendship. "We have a good working relationship," he says. "I see him whenever necessary;

it varies a great deal." In running the department, Andrus reported, "the President has basically given me a free hand."

The Cabinet's "free hand" has been restrained some since the early days of the Administration. Cabinet meetings, held weekly at first, have been cut back to twice a month. Andrus, like all the Secretaries, sends Jack H. Watson Jr., the secretary to the Cabinet, a personal report on the Friday before each Monday Cabinet meeting. This was the President's idea, presumably because he thought it would keep him abreast of what was going on within the departments. The reports, however, tended to be self-serving, too wordy and of little value, and Carter asked the Secretaries to shorten them.

Andrus says he tries to keep his reports to one page, or two at the most. "I try to confine them to information about current issues, and maybe include some political intelligence," he says.

"The Cabinet meetings were important early on," he recalls. "They gave us a chance to get to know one another, so we wouldn't be dealing with each other as strangers. But later there was a lot of show-and-tell. Before, the President went around the table and asked for comments. Now, we discuss fewer topics and not everybody participates."

It has been clear to the Secretaries since then that presidential issues must receive first priority and that the resources of departments and agencies are to be placed at the White House's disposal ahead of any purely departmental issues.

While many of these steps were necessary in view of Carter's erratic relationship with Congress, they represent the increased centralization of White House authority and the retreat of "Cabinet Government."

And Andrus has played the loyal soldier.

Only three months after taking office, the President made waves by recommending that 18 water projects already under construction be terminated. Carter later was forced to trim his "hit list" substantially, but the reaction from Members of Congress whose districts were involved shook the Interior Department.

In the West, where neither Carter nor environmental measures are very popular, Andrus loomed as a convenient scapegoat. One Colorado newspaper, The Grand Junction Sentinel, called him "Bad News Andrus." A New York Times story, indulging in journalistic excess, carried a paragraph that said, "It is better than even money that Cecil D. Andrus is the most hated government figure in the West."

Andrus laughs now at that, but admits "I swam upstream in that mess for months."

Although the Interior Secretary took most of the heat, it is not clear whether he was deeply involved in the original decision on the water projects or whether he simply kept silent and defended the Administration's position. Andrus does not openly complain, but it is apparent that he resents the spot on which he was placed and that he has taken action to assure that it does not happen another time.

Andrus says he gets along well with senior White House aides, notably Stuart E. Eizenstat, assistant to the President for domestic affairs and policy, with whom he works closely. He says, however, that beneath the top layer, the White House "needs more depth."

He says he is satisfied with his ability to contribute on policy and to get his message across to the White House.

"On the Alaska (lands) bill, they came down on my side, and we have been in the lead on energy leasing and the nuclear waste issue. On the energy message, part of the words came from me through Eizenstat. If I feel strongly, I have the right to see or call the President."

Now, a half hour before the White House meeting, Andrus and his aides are deep into preparation. They go over "talking points" to stress. A detailed agenda has been provided and includes who should speak, at what time and for how long. One line reads: "Suggested approach: DNR will help achieve goals of President's Energy Message (see talking points)." Another line says: "Expect to hand out green book and speak from organization chart."

The meeting has been called to win industry support for the reorganization proposal. Obviously, little is left to chance. This is hardball.

The meeting is held at 1 p.m. in the Roosevelt Room of the White House. Despite a request by Andrus, White House officials refuse to let a reporter accompanying Andrus attend. Those who do attend include William Simpson, a deputy assistant to the President under Hamilton Jordan, and Richard A. Pettigrew, assistant to the President for reorganization.

The meeting lasts an hour and 40 minutes, and Chris Carlson, who sat in, fills in the reporter after it is over. The Administration spokesmen presented their arguments, the industry representatives gave their analysis and told what was necessary to win their support: appointment of a deputy secretary of development (a new post); a division in the department between renewable and non-renewable resources; a significant cut in the budget; a 30 per cent reduction in paperwork; and, an experienced professional to head each division.

Following standard operating procedures, no decisions or commitments were made. The two sides would keep in touch. Democracy in action.

OFFICE BUSINESS

3:00. Back in the office, back to the department's business. Carlson makes some changes in a press release the department is putting out. "I think I already signed off on it," Carlson says. "If you did, you may have collected your last paycheck here," Andrus replies. Then he smiles. Carlson has served as his press assistant for about seven years.

Andrus begins to tackle some of the paperwork that has accumulated on his desk. Looking up, he says, "Bureaucrats have two ways of exerting control over you – get you to travel and deluge you with paperwork."

He says of the federal bureaucracy: "It's like running into a large marshmallow. As governor, I could call the National Guard and it would be out in a half-hour. Or I could make a decision, even if it was a poor one, and it would be implemented. Here, after four months, I find they are still not implementing it."

At 3:20, Steve Freudenthal comes in to discuss the Secretary's regular 5:00 meeting with Joseph and Krulitz. There is a reference to a letter from a member of Congress. Their discussion is interrupted by an unscheduled visit from some Idaho friends. Andrus seems genuinely glad to see them and stops what he is doing to show them his office.

The guests leave and, without missing a beat, Andrus and his executive assistant talk about a coal study for the White House. Freudenthal says it could be done in one of two ways. "Let's do it both ways and see what way they want it," Andrus says. His experience as a politician shows.

Another aide enters and she and Andrus go over a business trip she is scheduled to make. Alone again, Andrus studies some papers on his desk. Five minutes later, he leaves, saying he is going down the hall to talk to Krulitz. Five minutes after that, he returns to his office.

He puts through a call to Harrison Wellford, executive associate director of the Office of Management and Budget for reorganization. They discuss a forthcoming meeting with a group of lumberjacks, presumably to drum up more support for the Natural Resources Department. It should be familiar turf for the Secretary; he once worked as a lumberjack, hauling and skidding logs.

He makes another phone call, this time to Governor Thomas L. Judge of Montana. The two of them discuss a court case involving Indian water claims. Andrus appears to urge Judge to try to have the case heard in a federal court instead of a state court. "I used to appoint some of those guys and I know," Andrus tells the governor.

The Secretary then devotes nearly an hour to a reporter's questions before his top aides return for the senior staff's daily evening meeting. Andrus reports on his conversation with Judge. Freudenthal, who has an agenda before him, says that a 10 per cent cut in fuel by the department vehicles would save 2.2 million gallons of gasoline a year. He recommends that the department's cars be used only by officials at the assistant secretary level or higher, except on government business.

The other three seem taken aback by the suggestion, a somewhat bold gesture by bureaucratic standards. Freudenthal insists he is serious. He is also new to his job. "That's a death wish," Andrus comments. "I applaud your courage," he says to Freudenthal.

They discuss a wide range of matters: the possibility of bringing ia detailee for a particular assignment; the appointment of a commissioner for Indian affairs and prospective appointments to an Indian Arts and Crafts Board. Andrus suggests that Joan Mondale, the Vice President's wife, be consulted about the arts board names – "She helped us before," he says.

Next, the discussion turns to whether Interior or the Comptroller of the Currency should investigate possible abuses at the American Indian Bank. The issue is left unresolved. Personnel problems are taken up by the group, as are some problems that involve an Arizona water claims dispute.

Freudenthal begins reading a long report filled with figures. Andrus abruptly stops him and points out that he made a $10 million error. Freudenthal goes over the figures and agrees. It's an amazing performance by Andrus, considering that it's the end of the day and every body is exhausted and wants to get home. The meeting soon breaks up.

It's 5:55. Andrus tightens his tie once again, puts on his coat and announces that he is ready to close up shop for the day, return to his home and have a drink.

"Some of the glitter has worn off – oh yes!" he says of his Cabinet tenure. "If I was home, I'd say, 'I rode hard and came up wet.'"

But he adds, "Every once in a while, you'll win one, and that helps."

*Appendix B*

# Andrus Gubernatorial
# Election Results

## 1966 Primary Election Results

| Counties | Andrus | Herndon | Dee |
|---|---|---|---|
| Ada | 3,415 | 2,905 | 1,436 |
| Adams | 105 | 152 | 190 |
| Bannock | 4,494 | 3,131 | 1,148 |
| Bear Lake | 298 | 209 | 119 |
| Benewah | 186 | 292 | 400 |
| Bingham | 1,384 | 1,203 | 301 |
| Blaine | 153 | 314 | 161 |
| Boise | 66 | 113 | 46 |
| Bonner | 651 | 730 | 366 |
| Bonneville | 1,329 | 2,091 | 625 |
| Boundary | 229 | 355 | 162 |
| Butte | 190 | 172 | 35 |
| Camas | 15 | 26 | 106 |
| Canyon | 1,379 | 1,555 | 656 |
| Caribou | 131 | 203 | 67 |
| Cassia | 361 | 506 | 143 |
| Clark | 19 | 46 | 23 |
| Clearwater | 1,187 | 317 | 275 |
| Custer | 71 | 240 | 153 |
| Elmore | 722 | 612 | 261 |
| Franklin | 104 | 101 | 40 |
| Fremont | 364 | 550 | 143 |
| Gem | 237 | 437 | 245 |
| Gooding | 229 | 260 | 469 |
| Idaho | 384 | 520 | 1,523 |
| Jefferson | 309 | 618 | 370 |
| Jerome | 218 | 297 | 172 |
| Kootenai | 646 | 2,219 | 842 |
| Latah | 954 | 699 | 290 |
| Lemhi | 163 | 775 | 152 |
| Lewis | 253 | 396 | 234 |
| Lincoln | 81 | 60 | 117 |
| Madison | 824 | 372 | 123 |
| Minidoka | 440 | 584 | 186 |
| Nez Perce | 2,032 | 1,441 | 588 |
| Oneida | 254 | 174 | 144 |
| Owyhee | 160 | 207 | 124 |
| Payette | 245 | 439 | 184 |
| Power | 176 | 173 | 108 |
| Shoshone | 1,125 | 1,411 | 606 |
| Teton | 82 | 125 | 84 |
| Twin Falls | 1,120 | 1,327 | 544 |
| Valley | 133 | 265 | 224 |
| Washington | 231 | 304 | 224 |
| Totals | 27,649 | 28,926 | 14,409 |

## 1966 General Election Results

| Counties | Andrus | Samuelson | Swisher | Jungert |
|---|---|---|---|---|
| Ada | 13,527 | 17,761 | 6,030 | 3,653 |
| Adams | 456 | 524 | 83 | 263 |
| Bannock | 7,443 | 3,166 | 7,029 | 862 |
| Bear Lake | 1,159 | 1,188 | 312 | 54 |
| Benewah | 759 | 865 | 110 | 540 |
| Bingham | 3,434 | 3,790 | 1,486 | 637 |
| Blaine | 796 | 756 | 261 | 425 |
| Boise | 235 | 294 | 63 | 139 |
| Bonner | 1,991 | 4,043 | 92 | 304 |
| Bonneville | 5,550 | 8,115 | 2,360 | 1,678 |
| Boundary | 642 | 1,122 | 66 | 143 |
| Butte | 657 | 445 | 92 | 126 |
| Camas | 115 | 28 | 816 | 62 |
| Canyon | 7,060 | 10,094 | 1,793 | 1,721 |
| Caribou | 946 | 1,074 | 256 | 41 |
| Cassia | 1,894 | 2,748 | 650 | 380 |
| Clark | 93 | 229 | 9 | 15 |
| Clearwater | 1,833 | 574 | 264 | 275 |
| Custer | 293 | 448 | 112 | 346 |
| Elmore | 1,523 | 1,034 | 238 | 432 |
| Franklin | 1,191 | 1,875 | 196 | 60 |
| Fremont | 1,392 | 1,765 | 187 | 188 |
| Gem | 1,431 | 1,600 | 241 | 444 |
| Gooding | 1,052 | 1,973 | 222 | 590 |
| Idaho | 1,872 | 1,710 | 324 | 554 |
| Jefferson | 1,297 | 2,401 | 269 | 369 |
| Jerome | 1,212 | 2,333 | 250 | 431 |
| Kootenai | 5,093 | 4,923 | 526 | 1,470 |
| Latah | 3,555 | 2,207 | 956 | 446 |
| Lemhi | 705 | 1,034 | 240 | 325 |
| Lewis | 834 | 432 | 196 | 104 |
| Lincoln | 382 | 757 | 69 | 196 |
| Madison | 1,593 | 1,701 | 441 | 109 |
| Minidoka | 2,142 | 2,062 | 428 | 447 |
| Nez Perce | 5,361 | 2,165 | 1,862 | 1,435 |
| Oneida | 62 | 174 | 965 | 44 |
| Owyhee | 675 | 931 | 196 | 247 |
| Payette | 1,575 | 2,189 | 292 | 495 |
| Power | 647 | 661 | 320 | 157 |
| Shoshone | 3,594 | 2,231 | 270 | 532 |
| Teton | 442 | 588 | 44 | 42 |
| Twin Falls | 5,098 | 7,631 | 1,661 | 1,403 |
| Valley | 540 | 659 | 191 | 400 |
| Washington | 1,034 | 1,451 | 143 | 555 |
| Totals | 93,744 | 104,586 | 30,913 | 23,139 |
| Plurality | | 10,842 | | |
| Percentage | 37.1% | 41.4% | 12.2% | 9.2% |

226

## 1970 Primary Election Results

| Counties | Andrus | Ravenscroft | Walker |
|---|---|---|---|
| Ada | 4,515 | 2,747 | 1,573 |
| Adams | 55 | 191 | 47 |
| Bannock | 4,470 | 2,178 | 1,593 |
| Bear Lake | 258 | 220 | 168 |
| Benewah | 299 | 538 | 50 |
| Bingham | 1,104 | 766 | 392 |
| Blaine | 207 | 401 | 280 |
| Boise | 57 | 56 | 40 |
| Bonner | 876 | 455 | 171 |
| Bonneville | 1,751 | 1,058 | 621 |
| Boundary | 387 | 362 | 71 |
| Butte | 143 | 85 | 42 |
| Camas | 5 | 116 | 17 |
| Canyon | 1,930 | 865 | 453 |
| Caribou | 204 | 208 | 104 |
| Cassia | 161 | 393 | 111 |
| Clark | 25 | 50 | 15 |
| Clearwater | 1,130 | 471 | 112 |
| Custer | 34 | 92 | 16 |
| Elmore | 443 | 610 | 311 |
| Franklin | 122 | 193 | 42 |
| Fremont | 207 | 372 | 89 |
| Gem | 284 | 414 | 101 |
| Gooding | 98 | 1,274 | 68 |
| Idaho | 644 | 549 | 161 |
| Jefferson | 327 | 411 | 160 |
| Jerome | 75 | 649 | 134 |
| Kootenai | 1,639 | 1,042 | 555 |
| Latah | 1,049 | 413 | 115 |
| Lemhi | 77 | 140 | 52 |
| Lewis | 226 | 298 | 63 |
| Lincoln | 38 | 360 | 30 |
| Madison | 178 | 319 | 77 |
| Minidoka | 163 | 901 | 176 |
| Nez Perce | 3,198 | 1,089 | 445 |
| Oneida | 91 | 114 | 47 |
| Owyhee | 150 | 154 | 90 |
| Payette | 275 | 196 | 206 |
| Power | 109 | 138 | 39 |
| Shoshone | 1,240 | 427 | 487 |
| Teton | 43 | 122 | 22 |
| Twin Falls | 453 | 1,488 | 1,038 |
| Valley | 120 | 207 | 58 |
| Washington | 176 | 237 | 223 |
| Totals | 29,036 | 23,369 | 10,664 |
| Plurality | 5,667 | | |

227

## 1970 General Election Results

| Counties | Andrus | Samuelson |
|---|---|---|
| Ada | 21,705 | 1,456 |
| Adams | 434 | 777 |
| Bannock | 11,625 | 5,690 |
| Bear Lake | 1,457 | 1,049 |
| Benewah | 1,656 | 594 |
| Bingham | 4,516 | 4,339 |
| Blaine | 1,093 | 1,163 |
| Boise | 295 | 537 |
| Bonner | 3,099 | 3,181 |
| Bonneville | 7,751 | 9,478 |
| Boundary | 984 | 1,079 |
| Butte | 541 | 607 |
| Camas | 139 | 262 |
| Canyon | 9,443 | 10,877 |
| Caribou | 1,202 | 1,220 |
| Cassia | 2,402 | 2,835 |
| Clark | 125 | 245 |
| Clearwater | 2,299 | 636 |
| Custer | 135 | 1,164 |
| Elmore | 1,789 | 1,546 |
| Franklin | 1,542 | 1,585 |
| Fremont | 1,580 | 1,883 |
| Gem | 1,531 | 2,057 |
| ˙ooding | 1,727 | 1,956 |
| Idaho | 2,292 | 2,056 |
| Jefferson | 1,492 | 2,581 |
| Jerome | 1,703 | 2,080 |
| Kootenai | 6,531 | 4,592 |
| Latah | 5,889 | 2,209 |
| Lemhi | 550 | 1,498 |
| Lewis | 935 | 545 |
| Lincoln | 527 | 784 |
| Madison | 1,765 | 2,171 |
| Minidoka | 2,638 | 1,965 |
| Nez Perce | 7,775 | 2,927 |
| Oneida | 673 | 819 |
| Owyhee | 836 | 1,107 |
| Payette | 1,772 | 2,313 |
| Power | 1,004 | 768 |
| Shoshone | 3,817 | 1,968 |
| Teton | 428 | 621 |
| Twin Falls | 6,187 | 7,102 |
| Valley | 831 | 967 |
| Washington | 1,289 | 1,819 |
| Totals | 128,004 | 117,108 |
| Plurality | 10,896 | |

228

## 1974 General Election Results

| Counties | Andrus | Murphy | Victor |
|---|---|---|---|
| Ada | 34,214 | 12,321 | 1,169 |
| Adams | 878 | 336 | 19 |
| Bannock | 14,387 | 3,443 | 491 |
| Bear Lake | 1,585 | 887 | 135 |
| Benewah | 1,909 | 481 | 14 |
| Bingham | 6,480 | 2,284 | 369 |
| Blaine | 1,881 | 533 | 55 |
| Boise | 902 | 356 | 34 |
| Bonner | 4,961 | 1,636 | 163 |
| Bonneville | 11,559 | 5,122 | 428 |
| Boundary | 1,902 | 430 | 34 |
| Butte | 857 | 311 | 19 |
| Camas | 296 | 102 | 10 |
| Canyon | 15,127 | 6,834 | 413 |
| Caribou | 1,470 | 802 | 107 |
| Cassia | 3,066 | 1,831 | 420 |
| Clark | 199 | 164 | 7 |
| Clearwater | 2,348 | 294 | 43 |
| Custer | 576 | 534 | 45 |
| Elmore | 2,712 | 774 | 53 |
| Franklin | 2,105 | 1,059 | 173 |
| Fremont | 2,283 | 1,169 | 91 |
| Gem | 2,628 | 1,139 | 69 |
| Gooding | 2,461 | 1,192 | 91 |
| Idaho | 3,150 | 1,066 | 84 |
| Jefferson | 2,460 | 1,801 | 122 |
| Jerome | 2,655 | 1,237 | 135 |
| Kootenai | 9,512 | 3,272 | 112 |
| Latah | 7,301 | 1,307 | 112 |
| Lemhi | 1,017 | 1,148 | 111 |
| Lewis | 1,147 | 240 | 6 |
| Lincoln | 832 | 492 | 48 |
| Madison | 2,964 | 1,634 | 138 |
| Minidoka | 3,215 | 1,338 | 259 |
| Nez Perce | 8,280 | 1,249 | 120 |
| Oneida | 967 | 440 | 46 |
| Owyhee | 1,228 | 695 | 27 |
| Payette | 2,759 | 1,239 | 63 |
| Power | 1,476 | 404 | 44 |
| Shoshone | 4,056 | 1,186 | 52 |
| Teton | 722 | 424 | 18 |
| Twin Falls | 9,898 | 4,170 | 737 |
| Valley | 1,404 | 463 | 19 |
| Washington | 2,313 | 892 | 54 |
| Totals | 184,182 | 68,731 | 6,759 |
| Plurality | 115,451 | | |

## 1986 General Election Results

| Counties | Andrus | Leroy |
|---|---|---|
| Ada | 42,361 | 38,418 |
| Adams | 596 | 1,177 |
| Bannock | 17,520 | 10,435 |
| Bear Lake | 990 | 1,726 |
| Benewah | 1,706 | 1,173 |
| Bingham | 7,050 | 7,448 |
| Blaine | 2,908 | 1,976 |
| Boise | 723 | 891 |
| Bonner | 5,993 | 3,384 |
| Bonneville | 12,290 | 15,762 |
| Boundary | 1,579 | 1,397 |
| Butte | 768 | 793 |
| Camas | 157 | 287 |
| Canyon | 13,589 | 18,464 |
| Caribou | 1,158 | 1,791 |
| Cassia | 2,682 | 4,587 |
| Clark | 131 | 272 |
| Clearwater | 2,514 | 980 |
| Custer | 584 | 1,296 |
| Elmore | 2,428 | 2,775 |
| Franklin | 1,142 | 2,024 |
| Fremont | 1,644 | 2,832 |
| Gem | 2,599 | 2,675 |
| Gooding | 2,122 | 2,672 |
| Idaho | 2,665 | 2,892 |
| Jefferson | 2,047 | 4,296 |
| Jerome | 2,361 | 3,276 |
| Kootenai | 12,742 | 10,241 |
| Latah | 8,018 | 3,340 |
| Lemhi | 997 | 2,093 |
| Lewis | 1,054 | 484 |
| Lincoln | 660 | 821 |
| Madison | 1,912 | 4,528 |
| Minidoka | 3,376 | 3,738 |
| Nez Perce | 10,418 | 3,964 |
| Oneida | 817 | 920 |
| Owyhee | 820 | 1,718 |
| Payette | 2,448 | 3,284 |
| Power | 1,610 | 1,327 |
| Shoshone | 4,075 | 1,510 |
| Teton | 530 | 918 |
| Twin Falls | 8,861 | 11,211 |
| Valley | 1,190 | 1,748 |
| Washington | 1,586 | 2,250 |
| Totals | 193,429 | 189,794 |
| Plurality | 3,635 | |
| %age | 50.5% | |

230

## 1990 General Election Results

| Counties | Andrus | Fairchild |
|---|---|---|
| Ada | 55,177 | 18,012 |
| Adams | 794 | 617 |
| Bannock | 16,556 | 4,631 |
| Bear Lake | 1,152 | 1,031 |
| Benewah | 1,584 | 767 |
| Bingham | 7,507 | 4,054 |
| Blaine | 3,936 | 824 |
| Boise | 906 | 513 |
| Bonner | 5,942 | 2,755 |
| Bonneville | 14,330 | 9,276 |
| Boundary | 1,616 | 1,169 |
| Butte | 665 | 448 |
| Camas | 284 | 145 |
| Canyon | 16,246 | 8,919 |
| Caribou | 1,428 | 977 |
| Cassia | 2,947 | 2,537 |
| Clark | 195 | 190 |
| Clearwater | 2,175 | 726 |
| Custer | 653 | 635 |
| Elmore | 2,984 | 1,365 |
| Franklin | 1,401 | 1,348 |
| Fremont | 2,027 | 1,668 |
| Gem | 2,945 | 1,328 |
| Gooding | 2,668 | 1,276 |
| Idaho | 2,711 | 2,166 |
| Jefferson | 2,324 | 2,636 |
| Jerome | 2,852 | 1,622 |
| Kootenai | 14,364 | 6,637 |
| Latah | 7,559 | 2,351 |
| Lemhi | 1,107 | 1,322 |
| Lewis | 902 | 352 |
| Lincoln | 829 | 385 |
| Madison | 2,766 | 2,467 |
| Minidoka | 3,362 | 1,882 |
| Nez Perce | 8,255 | 2,747 |
| Oneida | 886 | 587 |
| Owyhee | 1,135 | 924 |
| Payette | 3,181 | 1,391 |
| Power | 1,574 | 539 |
| Shoshone | 3,772 | 946 |
| Teton | 659 | 583 |
| Twin Falls | 10,410 | 5,264 |
| Valley | 1,835 | 813 |
| Washington | 2,072 | 1,112 |
| Totals | 218,673 | 101,937 |
| Plurality | 116,736 | |

*Appendix C*

# The Carlson Chronicle

*Editor's Note: Appendix C contains a few columns the author wrote for his weekly column carried by the St. Maries Gazette Record, called "The Carlson Chronicle". The columns contain anecdotes or insights regarding Governor Andrus not previously published. They are reproduced as they originally appeared in the Gazette Record.*

March 17, 2010

# It's All About Relationships

A couple weeks back, following Mass at Harrison's Our Lady of Perpetual Help, Father Tim Ritchey told a story about doing the Saturday morning cleaning of the parish house only half dressed when the doorbell rang. Hurriedly pulling on his jeans he hustled to the door, opened it, and there stood the familiar smiling face of Idaho's 32nd Governor, C.L. "Butch" Otter and his wife, Lori. Not exactly who one expects to come calling on Saturday morning.

For the next half hour the three friends regaled each other with stories and kidded around with each other. Father Ritchey, you see, was the priest that performed Butch's marriage to Lori a few years back and also the one who designated at the wedding from that day forth Lori to be in charge of Butch's security.

The fact that Butch would take the time to visit with an old friend in St. Maries says much about why, despite the challenges facing him as Governor, and according to some his less than stellar performance in the job, he is nonetheless an odds on favorite to be returned to the Governor's chair.

The story Father Ritchey tells can be repeated in countless communities across Idaho. Everybody knows Butch. More importantly, everyone, even his critics, can't help liking him. It's more than just the fact he has basically been around Idaho's political scene since his first election to the Legislature in 1972, and it is more than the fact he served longer than any Idahoan as Lieutenant Governor or served three terms in the Congress.

Rather, it is all about understanding the importance of building and maintaining personal relationships all across the state. Butch has that ability, despite his wealth and his former marriage to J.R. Simplot's daughter, to come across to his constituents as "one of us," as someone who knows about people's struggles and someone who knows the state like the back of his hand

That he has a great sense of humor and can laugh at himself tells the voters he's not too full of himself. I used to wince, for example, when

Butch was my former boss' Lieutenant Governor, when he would tell an audience that his initials, C. L., stood for "Cecil's Lackey!" It always brought a chuckle from the audience though, as everyone understood working with Idaho's most successful Governor ever was not always easy.

The initials stand for Clement Leroy, but when Butch enrolled at St. Teresa's Academy (the predecessor to Bishop Kelly) the Nun in charge said there was not going to be anyone named "Clem" attending her academy and she dubbed him Butch.

The bottom line is there is no substitute for longevity in office and the building of countless relationships across the state. There is no substitute for likeability for it engenders trust. Nor is there any substitute for knowing thousands of Idahoans and being able to call them by their first name.

Idaho is still a small enough state population-wise that people expect to know and see their Governor in person, or to know someone who has.

The edge this gives Butch over the presumptive independent-turned-Democrat, Keith Allred, cannot be underestimated. Nor can Butch's style of speaking to Idahoans as if they are his immediate neighbors, and keeping his speeches short, sweet and well-laced with humor.

Allred better learn this quickly for reports out of Boise about his 40-minute lecture on government at the annual Frank Church dinner have to be music to the Governor's ears. Likeability, personality, self-deprecating humor, and maintaining personal relationships will beat Harvard lectures on the philosophy of government and policy-wonkish knowledge of the issues every time.

March 31, 2010

# Butch Could Still Lose...

Despite his considerable personal charm, and his long string of electoral successes, Governor C. L. "Butch" Otter, improbable as it seems, could still lose his race for re-election in November. Several red flags loom on the horizon. How he and his campaign, led by the talented veteran, Debbie Fields, handle the items will dictate the outcome.

First, Otter's own polling I suspect shows his automatic re-elect number to be well below the 50% or above threshold most incumbents like to have. Additionally, I'd wager his polls also show over half the voters are willing to look at another candidate. This alone should be cause for pause.

Secondly, no less an authority on winning and holding onto the governorship than Cecil D. Andrus, Idaho's only four-term elected Governor, has often said, "it's always your friends, not your enemies that do you in." And in Governor Otter's case this may prove to be true. The threatening friend is Butch's director of administration, Mike Gwartney, who is at the center of a controversy regarding playing favorites in the administration of a contract to bring broad-band internet services to schools across the state. He is alleged to have also threatened the principal of a company ostensibly awarded a piece of the joint bid, but whose services have then never been utilized. The matter is now in court but it has all the hallmarks of an item which could easily mushroom into catastrophe.

Having Gwartney's conduct also blasted by long-time Rupert Republican State Senator Dean Cameron, chair of the Joint Finance and Appropriation Committee, signals too there's lots of troublesome undercurrents below seemingly still waters. One can easily portray Cameron's stinging rebuttal of Gwartney as the act of a loyal friend sending to Butch a public warning that there's a real problem looming.

Given the relationship Butch has with Gwartney, arguably his longest and best friend, there's little prospect for credible plausible deniability. Butch could be subject to numerous what-did-he-know and when-did-he-know-it questions. These questions could erode one of his most valuable assets – his image of personal integrity and candor, depending on how he and his campaign handle them.

Third, there's the real danger of Butch becoming the reincarnation of former three-term Republican Governor Bob Smylie who served as Idaho's governor from 1954 to 1966. Smylie was cruising he thought towards election to a fourth term when he suffered a stunning primary loss to conservative Sandpoint State Senator Don Samuelson largely because he alienated the rising conservative Goldwater wing of the party due to his support for the newly enacted 3% state sales tax. Sound familiar?

It is this latter item that presents the most risk to Butch. The hard-core right wing ideologues, the Ron Paul crowd and the tea-baggers, haven't forgotten nor will they forgive Butch for supporting an increase in the gas tax to underwrite his road improvement program. Such heresy has to be punished in the minds of these types. One suspects this will dampen considerably Butch's conservative support and it could manifest itself on Election Day by many simply not voting.

Keep in mind also that Butch supported Kirk Sullivan for Republican State chairman but was rolled by the hard right types who favored Norm Semanko. In the terms of political junkies this is known as a hard fault-line.

One final thought: there are now ten announced candidates for Governor, five Republicans including Butch and three independents. In every Idaho election going back to 1986 a third party candidate, no matter how weird or unknown, has received at least 3% of the vote. For example, former flaming Kootenai County Commissioner Ron Rankin, received nearly 16,000 votes when he ran in 1994 for Governor.

If the three independents stay on the ballot and together get 5% of the vote with all the anti-government, anti-incumbent sentiment around, it could get interesting. If one assumes Butch is weaker this time than last time, and because of the weak economy, alleged lack of leadership, and a possible Gwartney scandal factor, runs behind his slim 52.7% winning margin in 2006 over a lackluster campaign by Jerry Brady, it all could add up to a stunning loss.

Butch could beat Butch if he mishandles matters that could erode his personal qualities or further exacerbate the fault line between moderation and extremism. Never underestimate the ability of a supposedly solid lock for re-election incumbent to blow it.

236

April 21, 2010

# Politicians and Guns

If there is one issue in Idaho that generates more emotion and heat than that of guns, gun ownership, and whether there should be any regulation whatsoever of what many view as an untrammeled constitutional right, I don't know what it might be. It is the so-called third rail of Idaho politics---one doesn't touch it and one swears allegiance and fidelity to gun owner rights. And if one doesn't, they pay the price at election time.

Even avowed liberals like the late Democrat Idaho Senator Frank Church (1957-1981), and former House Speaker Tom Foley (1965-1995) from the neighboring Fifth Congressional District were strong defenders of gun owner rights. Consequently, if there is one endorsement from an interest group that most Idaho office seekers like to have it is that of the National Rifle Association. An endorsement usually means not only dollars but also a mailing to the association members in one's district, or state, making it clear where the office-seeker stands.

(Full disclosure: I belonged to the NRA for a couple of years in the early 1980's. I also own rifles, a shotgun, several pistols and a semi-automatic Glock 21 even though I'm much more of a fisherman than a hunter. I enjoy shooting clays and target practice. I'm very proud of my Marine Captain son who scored expert in both pistol and rifle during his attendance at the Basic School at Quantico and our youngest daughter is a better marksman than either my son or me and is the best hunter in our family. And I'm glad the U.S. Supreme Court has finally made it unequivocally clear that with or without my concealed weapons permit I have a right to have weapons in the home and a right to defend my family without having to belong to a "militia.").

As a professional communicator I greatly admire the NRA's ability to get its key messages across to a public increasingly suspect of gun owners as we move ever more away from a rural, hunting friendly society and towards a growing urban and suburban gun-fearing society. In particular their hunter training and gun safety courses are beyond reproach and I applaud their efforts to attract more women into the fold.

All that aside, I left the Association because to me it was becoming more and more an organization dominated by purists who insisted on absolute fidelity to all positions and would brook no dissent, and, at the national level a thinly-disguised arm of the Republican Party. An example illustrates my point.

When my old boss, Governor Andrus, mounted his comeback campaign in 1986 he wanted the NRA endorsement in part because its mailing would reinforce the mailing he always did to the list of those holding Idaho hunting and fishing licenses. Andrus is a true sportsman who has gone on an annual elk hunt for years, loves to hunt geese and pheasants, and has bagged even a mountain goat when he won a permit. His opponent, David Leroy, was the antithesis of all that.

Yet the field rep for the NRA gave their endorsement to Leroy because he endorsed all their positions on their litmus test questionnaire while Andrus did not. Andrus' sensible support for waiting periods, his opposition to the sale of so-called cop-killer bullets and his support for restrictions on the sale of fully automatic machine guns were positions deemed inappropriate. His quip that he'd never met a deer hunter armed with a fully automatic rifle used to drive the zealots nuts.

I thought about all of this when I read the other day that Jeff Knox, the son of Neal Knox (a former NRA honcho who lost out in the leadership contest to the late Charlton Heston for the association presidency) was opposing the re-election of former Idaho Senator Larry Craig to the NRA board of directors. Knox cited the Senator's personal issues as the reason, but don't believe that smoke-screen. (See The Knox Update, 2/18/10)

Senator Craig's real sin is that he has been one of the voices of reason and moderation within the NRA board. To his credit the Senator has always been wary of the real right-wing zealots who bring discredit to the responsible and reasonable members of the NRA. One should recall that it was the Idaho Senator who guided the last major gun reform bill through the Congress, but that of course required making compromises, and for the zealots of the world compromise is a dirty word.

Suffice it to say the Senator does enjoy the NRA management's support and has the endorsement of the nominating committee as well. A member of the board since 1983, here's hoping the Senator is re-elected to another three-year term and serves as long as he wants. We'll know by early May.

Frankly, the NRA needs people like Senator Craig a lot more than folks like Jeff Knox.

# The Pilgrimage to Kirkwood Bar

For the 20th spring in a row some members of my family and I made our annual trek into Hells Canyon to visit the old sheep ranch run in the 1930's by Len and Grace Jordan at Kirkwood Bar on the Snake River. Most years we've backpacked the six miles from Upper Pittsburg Landing to camp out for a few days in the old alfalfa field adjacent to the ranch.

Other years we've had a jet boat come down from Hells Canyon Dam, pick us up and run us back up to Granite Creek, some 36 miles upstream from Pittsburg Landing and then have taken three to four days to backpack back down the trail. Always we've stopped and spent the night camping out on Kirkwood Bar. This year we chartered a jet boat and went all the way from Lewiston upstream to the ranch.

Kirkwood Bar, and the Jordan Ranch, is one of Idaho's special places that every Idahoan should visit and see not just because it is far from the madding crowds but because it helps to provide insight into one of Idaho's more talented, but not well known political figures: former Governor and U.S. Senator Len B. Jordan. Whether standing in the old bunkhouse that is now a museum, or in the old work shed or where the sheep shearing sheds once were, as one looks around at the splendid isolation of that place deep in the canyon, miles from any settlements, one begins to appreciate the tenacity of the Jordan's to make a living, survive and even thrive during the heights of the depression in that lovely but inhospitable place.

Len Jordan was the real deal, a genuine rancher, a man's man, well educated (both he and Grace graduated from the University of Oregon) but taciturn with no pretensions. His word was his bond and he, of course, was a conservative by nature, what I call a rock-ribbed, black hearted Republican, but he was someone you couldn't help but admire.

He emerged from the Canyon with Grace and their three children in the early 1940's, after spending nine years in their ranch below Hells Canyon, settled in Grangeville and started a car dealership and

240

in 1948, at the age of 49, was elected to the Idaho House of Representatives. In 1950 he looked at the field of Republican wanna be Governors and decided he was better than them all, and proceeded to win the GOP nomination and then the general election.

A previous session of the Idaho Legislature had changed the term for a Governor from unlimited two year terms to one four year term. During his term the Legislature again changed the gubernatorial term back to unlimited four year terms. Jordan, though, would not seek re-election, saying the people had voted for him expecting him to serve one four year term and a deal was a deal. His abdication made way for the rise of Attorney General Robert Smylie, who won the governor's chair in 1954 for the first of his three consecutive terms.

Though not particularly close, when Senator Henry Dworshak died in office in 1962, Governor Smylie realized there was really only one person to replace Dworshak, and after an absence of eight years from elected politics, on August 6, 1962, Jordan returned by virtue of Smylie naming him to the vacant seat. Jordan easily won an election that November to fill out the remaining years of Dworshak's term and then won a full six year term in 1966. He chose not to run again in 1972.

Always a defender of water rights and an expert of sorts on water law, Jordan often would characterize the Snake River as the living artery that united Idaho, a working river whose primary purpose was to assist Idahoans in making a better livelihood. He also was a champion of private power in its long fight against public power and his support for dams even extended to supporting the construction of High Mountain Sheep Dam that would have flooded the Snake with another reservoir from its proposed site just above the confluence of the Salmon with the Snake all the way to Hells Canyon Dam.

Of course this would have placed the Jordan Ranch itself underwater, which, as one stands in the yard of their former home, is hard to imagine anyone having lived in that place could have supported demolishing it. Needless to say, though, the Hells Canyon National Recreation Area was not created until sponsors swore there would be no adverse impact nor diminishment of upstream water rights.

The senator's other claim to notoriety while serving in DC came on the occasion when he entered an elevator only to have the elevator's other occupant pull a knife on him and demand his billfold. Jordan hauled off and cold-cocked the guy with one punch to the assailant's jaw. One just doesn't mess with an old rancher from Idaho.

During those ten years he enjoyed an excellent working relationship with Democratic Senator Frank Church. Though Church was decidedly more liberal they always could find common ground on issues of importance to Idaho and they personified a now hard to find bipartisan cooperation. Each, for example, would tacitly endorse their party's nominee when the other was up for election, but neither would campaign against the other.

My old boss, Governor Andrus, also deeply admired and respected the iconic senator and in his 1973 State of the State proposed that the "Hall of Mirrors" State Office Building be renamed in honor of the Senator and his service to Idaho. The Legislature promptly agreed and today one enters the Len B. Jordan Office Building.

For me, though, his legacy and persona will always best be recalled and preserved at the ranch on Kirkwood Bar.

May 12, 2010

# Hickel's Rendezvous with History in Hell

Walter J. Hickel, the former twice-elected Governor of Alaska and for a brief period of time, Richard Nixon's Secretary of the Interior, passed away at the age of 90 in Anchorage on May 6th. Few Idahoans realize the man had a significant impact on Idaho history and was a catalyst in bringing to the attention of the nation through the media, the beauty of and the importance to protecting the Hells Canyon area.

Largely at the instigation of Lewiston jet-boat operator Floyd Harvey, Hickel, in the late spring of 1969, agreed to jet-boat up the river to Harvey's fishing and hunting cabin at Willow Creek. He brought along with him, one of the then best-known television and radio personalities of the day, Arthur Godfrey, and Godfrey brought along his good friend, the singer and stand-up comedian Burl Ives..

Plans were to spend two nights at Harvey's place while fishing during the day and jet-boating up and down the canyon to view its scenic wonders, its historical sites, and to enjoy the peace and tranquility. Legend has it that the group sat around the camp fire at night listening to Ive's playing and singing songs that got progressively more ribald as the evening went along and the Bourbon was downed.

Accompanying the group from the local media was a reporter for the Lewiston Morning Tribune as well as the news director for KLEW-TV, John Hough (to whom I owe much for reminding me of this story's details.). Hough went on to serve Governor Andrus as a talented and adept campaign press secretary, his first press secretary (I followed John as the Governor's press secretary in December of 1972), a staff assistant for natural resources, deputy chief of staff and eventually chief of staff.

To many the outspoken Alaska Governor was a political paradox. His rags-to-riches story of arriving in Alaska as a young man with five cents in his pocket but through hard work eventually prospering in construction and as the developer of Anchorage's largest hotel, was the stuff of legends and appealed to many Alaskans. His success in business led to a long political career with his being mentioned once Alaska achieved statehood in 1958 as a candidate for all the major offices from Governor to U.S. Senator. His first statewide success came in 1966 when he defeated Alaska's first governor, Bill Egan, who was seeking a third term.

In 1968 Nixon plucked him from relative obscurity to be his Secretary of the Interior. In Alaska Hickel had been know as a boomer, a man who sought the development of Alaska's abundant natural resources with thoughts of environmental protection a very secondary consideration. As Interior Secretary, though, he started to carve out an image of an early Republican environmentalist.

According to Hough, Hickel definitely felt the Canyon deserved federal protection and he definitely thought it was crazy for Idaho Power to proceed with the construction of the High Mountain Sheep Dam being proposed just above the Snake River's confluence with the Salmon as well as Oregon's Imnaha River. Constructing High Mountain Sheep to paraphrase the Sierra Club's David Brower would have been akin to flooding the Sistine Chapel.

Hickel also knew how to relax and have a good time, in particular the catching of a large sturgeon in front of Harvey's place in a deep hole in the Snake, which had been caught numerous times to which its scar-studded snout attested. Hickel also had a less than amicable run-in with a Canyon sheep rancher who wanted to shoot any eagles he saw. He claimed to Hickel that eagles had carried off and killed 60 of his lambs that spring.

The dubious Interior Secretary basically told the sheep rancher he was full of it, that he must not be a very good sheep rancher and that he sure as hell shouldn't be shooting or even asking to shoot birds increasingly in need of protection themselves. Of such stuff are new legends born.

Hickel was sacked later that year by the President after he criticized him in a letter correctly saying that Nixon was losing the support of young people for his handling of the Vietnam conflict and the aftermath of Kent State.

Governor Andrus and I met the iconoclastic Alaskan some eight years later when the newly appointed Interior Secretary journeyed to Alaska to attend the summer meeting of the Western Governors Con-

244

ference. Invoking gubernatorial courtesy for a former governor as well as a former Interior secretary, Hickel asked the Governor to see him. Andrus took me along and the three of us met at the top of Hickel's Captain Cook Hotel.

Hickel politely discussed with the new interior secretary his views on the critical issues surrounding the needed passage of the Alaska Native Land Claims Act in order to satisfy section 17-d-2 of the bill that had made possible the Trans-Alaska Pipeline being constructed. Section 17-d-2 was the quid pro quo that mandated at least 110 million acres be set aside in the four preservation systems of national parks, wilderness areas, wildlife refuges and wild and scenic rivers for the enjoyment of future generations. Many Alaskans including Hickel were concerned that such large set asides would constrict the future development of Alaska's economy.

Hickel made one appeal that evening that I've never forgotten. He said to Secretary Andrus, "Mr. Secretary do yourself and Alaskans a favor. Most people from the lower 48 only come to Alaska during the two months of summer and almost 24 hour daylight when it looks and is so beautiful. Come visit us sometime during the almost ten months of winter and almost perpetual darkness. Only then can you really understand this land and its people." He was of course correct and somehow we never did make it up there in the wintertime.

He was an Alaskan original. May he rest in peace.

 June 9, 2010

# Political "Handles"

Heard a funny story a while back that is probably apocryphal, but funny nonetheless. It seems during the latter days of former Governor Dirk Kempthorne's time in office he was complaining to then Congressman and now Governor C.L. "Butch" Otter about his name and the easy target it was.

"How would you like to be known as "Dirk the Jerk," he allegedly asked Congressman Otter? The current governor reportedly replied "I have no sympathy for you. How would you like to be known as "Butch," to have been married to a "Gay" (as in Gaye Simplot), and your best friend is "Dyke" (as in Dyke Nally, the recently retired head of the State Liquor Dispensary)?

True or not, the story points to an important political fact of life: politicians who are known by one-word "handles," or nicknames, are almost always successful officeholders with the one-word handle demonstrating a high degree of acceptability by the electorate. Think of it not as a status symbol, but a success symbol.

Idaho political history is rife with examples validating this observation. Conversely, it also has its fair share of other long-term officeholders who were seldom called by a nickname or a one-word handle, and thus one could legitimately consider their hold on office to be a bit tenuous.

A good example of this latter category would be former Democratic Senator Frank Church, who served four terms in the U.S. Senate, and even though he was the only Democrat ever re-elected to the Senate in Idaho political history, never was viewed as a shoo-in for re-election. Not surprisingly one seldom heard him referred to as Frank, or his nickname of "Frosty" (except by his accomplished spouse-in-arms, Bethine). It was always "Senator Church."

Arguably the most successful Governor in Idaho history, Cecil D. Andrus, is still known to and referred to as "Cece" by most Idahoans. At first it used to put me off a bit when I heard so many different folks refer to him as Cece while I always (and still do) call him Governor.

Then I realized how indicative it was of his acceptance by so many voters, Republicans and Independents as well as Democrats.

And a few years back when Cece was serving as Secretary of the Interior in the Administration of Jimmy Carter, during the so-called Sagebrush Rebellion, his critics took great delight in putting out a bumper sticker punning on his nickname. It read: "Cease Logging/Cease Mining/Cece Andrus!"

Cece, who has always had a great sense of self-deprecating humor, simply commented "At least they spelled my name correctly and I've sure been called worse!"

The next longest serving governors of Idaho, Robert E. Smylie (12 consecutive years), and John V. Evans (10 years), conversely, did not have nicknames or handles and despite their length in office never achieved the degree of popularity Andrus achieved.

Worst of all, though, is for a politician to have bestowed upon him or her a less than flattering nickname, the best, most recent example being former Governor Don Samuelson, who served one term from 1967 to 1971. The media dubbed him "Dazzling Don" because he was anything but dazzling. Less kind pundits simply referred to him as "Big Dumb Don."

Perhaps the best of all handles for one to have though is to be called "Doc," which St. Maries own and only gift to Idaho's governors, C.A. Robins, who served one term from 1947 to 1951, was known as. By most accounts "Doc" Robins was a wonderful person with a very winning bedside manner.

Think about it. Everyone posits trust in their doctor, especially a long-time family doctor. And if a person can parlay his legitimate role as a medical doctor into his public persona as a politician, they've got it made.

Thus, I'm always surprised by politicians who are medical doctors who don't take advantage of their profession and deliberately cultivate their status as an M.D. To me it's as good as gold for political capital.

I can't help thinking that former Coeur d'Alene Senator and Lieutenant Governor Jack Riggs, had he campaigned as "Doc" Riggs, would be Idaho's governor today instead of "Butch" Otter.

Those that know Jack know of his extraordinary success when, still a practicing doctor, he founded a series of emergency clinics and hospitals that reflected his commitment to quality care and his attention to details. Like "Doc" Robins, patients reported a very winning bedside manner that for whatever reason he chose not to utilize in his runs for office.

No longer practicing medicine today, Jack has continued to show a flair for entrepreneurial business development with his founding and developing the successful Pita Pit franchises adjacent to so many college campuses.

I just happen to think that had he sought office as "Doc" Riggs, he would today be the very successful governor of a state that would have responded well to his form of medicine. It's all in the "handle."

June 16, 2010

# The Politics of Medical Education in Idaho

Former Lewiston Tribune reporter Bill Loftus has an excellent article in the spring edition of the University of Idaho's alumni magazine, HERE WE HAVE IDAHO, on how Idaho provides medical education for the state's aspiring doctors without having invested in a medical school.

The article faithfully recounts how in 1971 the state entered into an alliance with Alaska and Montana to purchase seats at the University of Washington's renowned medical school in Seattle. Each year since Idaho has purchased seats for 20 pre-med students to obtain their first four years with part of the understanding being that students in the so-called WAMI (Washington, Alaska, Montana, Idaho) program would, following their residency, return to their home state to practice medicine.

In this way places such as Salmon, Orofino and St. Maries would hopefully be able to attract and keep doctors in their community without losing everyone to the larger hospital complexes that have grown up in places like Boise (St. Al's and St. Luke's) or Spokane (Sacred Heart and Deaconess). Loftus points out that currently the Idaho Legislature appropriates $3.5 million annually to support the 80 Idahoans in the WWAMI (Wyoming joined in 1996, thus the second W) program.

Indeed, St. Maries own Dr. Rick Thurston, the son of long-time St. Maries Dr. Walter Thurston, is a sterling example of the program. Dr. Thurston, a former president of the Idaho State Medical Association, entered the WAMI program in 1982 and returned to St. Maries in 1992 to practice family medicine.

In focusing on the future of the WWAMI program Loftus quotes Dr. Rick Thurston's very on-target comment: "I think it's a program that's proven itself; if you have something that works, don't break it!"

Yet that is what some supposedly well-meaning folks are trying to do.

First, one has to understand that like everything else in life, there are politics involved. WAMI got its start in part because one very astute governor of Montana, the late Forrest Anderson, could look over the horizon and see in the not too distant future there would be a looming conflict in the Legislature over whether and where Montana should locate and build a medical school.

The rivalry between the University of Montana at Missoula and Montana State at Bozeman would have been a bloody, divisive, take no prisoners conflict. He recognized the same sort of conflict was not too far off in Idaho where the University of Idaho would be drawn into a consuming competition with Idaho State (Boise State was barely beyond its community college role at that point), and could also be predicted for Alaska, where the cities of Fairbanks and Anchorage would compete.

So Forrest called the then Governor of Washington, Daniel J. Evans, and broached the idea of a regional alliance with states like Idaho, Montana and Alaska, which didn't have medical schools and realistically could never afford the hundreds of millions of dollars to build one, to see if the non-med school states in the northwest could purchase seats at the U of W's med school. Evans bought the idea and advanced it with the med school folks at the University including Dr. Jack Lien who became one of the real champions of the idea.

Forrest then got on the phone and sold newly elected Idaho Governor Cecil Andrus on the idea and Andrus put the initial appropriation into his very first budget. Likewise, Forrest sold Alaska Governor Bill Egan on the concept, so the critical element of high level political support was in place.

Today, advocates of the program are seeking a doubling of the number of seats Idaho would purchase, meaning of course that the appropriation would have to be doubled at a time when budgets are declining because of declining tax revenues. WWAMI is still the best option, and the best buy with the best return on the investment.

Proponents should move quickly, however, because there is an internal threat and an external threat. The internal threat is the not so subtle campaign by Idaho State University's president, Arthur Vailas, to capitalize on ISU's pharmacy and nursing programs and get the

Legislature to shift its support to the idea of ISU being designated as Idaho's primary publicly funded leader of medical education. Some say the term "medical school" is misleading because much of the course offerings would be via the internet, thus more of a "virtual" medical school than one with new bricks and mortar. Nonetheless it would signal a shift away from WWAMI.

The external threat is posed by Greater Spokane Incorporated, the area's chamber and economic development group, to have Spokane build its own medical school. This group of Spokane business leaders is canny enough to capture WWAMI supporters by promising more seats at their future medical school than the UW could conceivably offer.

Both options should be dropped. Idaho will never be able to fund adequately a med school at Pocatello or anywhere else, nor will Washington state be able to afford a med school in Spokane. The killer is the all-critical factor of med schools today being able to advance medicine through ever more costly research. The infrastructure is simply not there, nor will it ever be.

Dr. Thurston hit the bull's eye when he said "if you have something that works, don't break it!" Here's hoping Idaho legislators as well as Washington legislators listen. Long live WWAMI.

# Senator Heyburn Revisited:
# Mount Heyburn or Mount McClure?

Thinking I might have been unduly influenced by others' characterization of Senator Weldon B. Heyburn, the early Idaho senator who fought most of President Theodore Roosevelt's progressive programs, including the creation of the U.S. Forest Service, I spent an afternoon reviewing the Congressional Record account of the Memorial statements spoken by Members of Congress in a special ceremony some six months after the Senator's passing in mid-October of 1912.

It was fascinating reading as Senators like his junior partner, William E. Borah, and his successor, James H. Brady, rose to speak sweet things about their gruff, opinionated, stubborn, iconoclastic companion. On the House side, Idaho Congressman Burton L. French spoke at length about the senator from Wallace. Several themes emerged: he was praised for his courage for essentially working himself to death, ignoring his doctor's advice to pare it back, and even continuing to speak to some issue while experiencing on the floor a mild brain hemorrhage that left him blind in his left eye for awhile.

Despite all the lofty rhetoric the members of Congress could cite only one major legislative accomplishment, surprisingly, the passage of the Pure Food Act. One suspects given his record for taking on clients who had business before his committees or before the Senate, that food manufacturers had decided some sort of sham law that created the appearance of trying to disclose food ingredients was the best way to stall real reform.

He also was praised for insisting Arizona and New Mexico be admitted as separate states, as they were in 1912, and for a hand in rewriting part of the Federal Code. His conservatism and his animosity to any public ownership of public resources on the public lands came through loud and clear. And it was very apparent he had an opinion, sometimes informed and sometimes not, on everything that came before the Senate. While some cited his Quaker upbringing and called him a devoted family man, few speakers really had any idea who he was or what of significance he accomplished.

Yet he is immortalized in Idaho not just by his name adorning the State's first state park, but also one of the beautiful peaks that make up Idaho's incredibly scenic Sawtooths: 10,229 foot high Mount Heyburn.

This has to change. A much more worthy designee would be a Republican Senator who served Idaho with distinction, intelligence, integrity and truly laudable ability for three terms in the House and then three terms in the U.S. Senate: James A. McClure. Folks should call on the current members of the Idaho Congressional delegation (Rep. Mike Simpson, R-2nd; Rep. Walt Minnick, D-1st; Senator Jim Risch; Senator Mike Crapo) to draft a special bill changing the mountain's name. Congress, after all, can pretty much do anything it wants.

As some folks know, Senator McClure was a long-time member and former chair of the Senate Energy and Natural Resources Committee. What many don't know but if they bothered to check into the Senator's background might be surprised to learn that in his younger years he was an avid backpacker and had a particular fondness for the Seven Devils Mountains above Hells Canyon. While not exactly a posey-sniffin', tree-huggin' greenie, he nonetheless has always appreciated Idaho's great out of doors.

Having covered McClure as a rookie reporter in D.C. in 1971 and 1972, and then having watched him work in mostly constructive ways with my former boss, Cecil D. Andrus, both when Andrus was governor and Secretary of the Interior, I can testify to McClure's legislative skills and his fine sense of humor. While he and Andrus would often disagree on aspects of public land policy, they rarely were disagreeable with each other. Both recognized the importance of compromise in trying to achieve the greatest good for the greatest number.

I will forever carry in my mind's eye the two of them on their hands and knees in the Governor's office in 1975 poring over maps and identifying hydrological divides as they drew the lines of what would become the Idaho side of the Hells Canyon Recreation area.

Today, the former Senator is recovering from a series of debilitating strokes in his Boise home. While he has received deservedly many accolades over his career, I can't help thinking his wife Louise, and the many fine staffers who served him over the years, including my former Gallatin colleague and Jim's former state chief of staff, the late Jim Goller, wouldn't all feel renaming Mount Heyburn would indeed be a most fitting tribute.

Some legislative purists will point out the U.S. Geographical Place Names Act requires a person to have been with his Maker for five years before such an honor can be bestowed, but Congress can and has made exceptions. One of the more recent was the naming of Idaho's Frank Church River of No Return Wilderness while the late senator was still alive but dying of cancer. That bill was carried by Senator McClure, by the way.

Mount Heyburn should be renamed Mount McClure, for James A. McClure, unlike Weldon B. Heyburn, truly deserves to be so immortalized as a part of Idaho lore and place names forever.

July 28, 2010

# Second and Third Acts
# in Political Lives

It never ceases to amaze me how some politicians reinvent them-selves, walk away from their often dubious records and present a new face to the public unrelated to prior public faces.

I was reminded of this when I saw a recent item on former Alaska Sen. Mike Gravel (pronounced gruh-vel), who is offering an internet comedy in which he plays the president of the United States. Thank the Lord it is fiction for Gravel is one of those shamelessly ambitious folks who from the time he was 15 saw a future president when he looked in the mirror.

He is now 80. When last seen he was on the stage with seven or eight other Democrats, vying for primary voters' attention in the 2008 race for his party's presidential nomination.

He played the cranky uncle, who tells every one the way things are without fear of the consequences, the one truth-teller in the room, the one passionate advocate for bringing the troops home from Iraq. If only the man had spoken out of conviction instead of poll-tested ambition, but for most Alaskans who recall his two terms in the U.S. Senate (1968-1980) and for reporters who covered him, like I did for the Anchorage Daily News out of Washington, D.C., only his phoni-ness and dishonesty will always be remembered .

During my first reporting stint in our nation's capital reporting for some 20 Pacific Northwest newspapers, I was assigned the Alaska beat. Thus, almost every day during my rounds, I was in the offices of Gravel and fellow senator, Ted Stevens, as well as the late congress-man, Nick Begich ( father of today's Alaska Senator Mark Begich).

At the age of 38, Gravel, with a slick, Hollywood-produced televi-sion feature film about his rags-to-riches story that inundated Alaska television and other venues, upset veteran incumbent Ernest Gruening in the 1968 Democratic primary. Stevens also came to the Senate in

1968, but as the appointed replacement for the sainted Bob Barlett, Alaska's other original Senator.

It rapidly became clear that Stevens was the work horse and Gravel the show horse. One cared about Alaska and improving the lives of Alaskans. The other was constantly thinking up new ways to make a splash on the national stage. And splash Gravel did, but they were in the form of belly-flops. Never have I been so embarrassed for a state and its people as the night in Miami Beach during the summer 1972 Democratic National Convention when Gravel tried to force himself onto the presidential ticket of South Dakota Senator George McGovern. Gravel conned an Alaska Native speaker, who was seconding the nomination, into introducing him and he seized the podium.

To everyone's astonishment, he launched into a speech about why the convention should support him and, without the candidate's say, place him on the ticket as the running mate. Delegates, reporters and, of course, the McGovern people (lead by his campaign manager, future Colorado Senator Gary Hart) were mortified. Some were apoplectic. It was the major reason McGovern's acceptance speech did not begin until well after prime time had ended across the nation.

Five years later, when I returned to D.C. for a second stint, this time as Interior Secretary Cecil D. Andrus' director of public affairs, I remember telling Idaho's former governor that when it came to Alaskan affairs he would end up working with the Republican Senator Ted Stevens and not the Democrat Mike Gravel.

Andrus asked why? "Because Mike Gravel is going to look you in the eye and lie to you," I responded. "Ted Stevens will fight you tooth and nail, but he will keep his word."

Andrus replied that in his 20 years in the political arena, he had never had another person look him straight in the eye and lie.

"Get ready because he will," I warned.

We had not been on the job two months when the phone rang in my office with Andrus on the other end.

"You were right," he said. "That son of a bitch Gravel lied to me."

From then on, difficult as it was in trying to meet the requirements of section 17-d-2 of the Alaska Native Land Claims Settlement Act that at least 110 million acres of federal land in Alaska be placed in the four federal protection systems (wilderness, national parks, national wildlife refuges and wild and scenic rivers), we dealt exclusively with the cantankerous, obstreperous but honest Stevens.

Some folks may laugh at Gravel in his new internet comedian role, but those of us with memories will not. Dishonesty, duplicity and rank ambition are things few find amusing.

# Why I like Mike!

The stranger was chasing our two young daughters in the pool at the Lodge at Sun Valley. They were squealing with delight as he, playing the shark role, pursued. What made it especially noticeable was he was holding his prosthetic leg in front of him.

They frolicked for a good half hour and then he got out of the pool, reattached his leg, waved at us and walked away. Tall, tanned, balding though curly hair, he had one of those instantly infectious smiles.

That evening, as my wife and I had dinner with those attending the summer meeting of the Western Governors Conference, we were able to put a name to the Shark: Donal Neil "Mike" O'Callaghan, governor of Nevada.

One of the most beloved governors in Nevada history, he was one of those people who instill pride and restore belief in our democratic system's ability to produce extraordinary leaders from humble origins. In O'Callaghan's case, it was a hardscrabble farm from which he ran away at age 16 when the family enterprise went broke.

In a letter to the editor last week, Merle Craner reminded me that besides Vernon Baker there were other heroes associated with St. Maries rightly worthy of mention. Craner was privileged to have the future governor of the Silver State as a roommate when they were attending the University of Idaho. He briefly recounted O'Callaghan's heroics during the Korean War. They won him a Silver Star, Bronze Star and two Purple Hearts, but they also cost him a leg.

He began work on his college degree and teaching certificate at the then Boise Junior College. He paid his way by boxing and teaching the sport. He enrolled in the University of Idaho following his discharge and secured his undergraduate and master's degree in education in 1956.

One of O'Callaghan's first jobs after graduation brought him to St. Maries. He married his college sweetheart, Carolyn Randall, from Twin Falls, and subsequently moved to Henderson, Nev., to take up a teaching position there.

Besides being a gregarious Irishman, O'Callaghan was one of the most disciplined people I ever met. He attended Mass daily, even when he traveled. He believed firmly in starting one's day with a prayer of thanksgiving as well as seeking forgiveness for one's shortcomings. He also was a teetotaler.

On one occasion, I had spent the night as a guest in the governor's home in Carson City, having been sent by my boss, Idaho Governor Cecil D. Andrus, to discuss the two governors adopting the same position with regard to a proposal, being circulated by the Atomic Energy Commission, to store the nation's commercial nuclear waste in barren states like Idaho or Nevada.

I attended morning Mass with him at the Catholic cathedral. As we exited, we encountered on the steps an individual obviously mentally challenged.

"Hi, Jimmie," the governor said as he warmly greeted the man, shaking his hand.

"Governor," Jimmie asked. "Are you headed for Reno today? If you are, can I hitch a ride?"

The governor, about to take me back to the Reno airport for my return flight, said "Sure, Jimmie. Hop in." And the man did, riding "shotgun" up front while we sat in back still talking politics with O'Callaghan occasionally quizzing Jimmie on how he was doing.

It was vintage Mike O'Callaghan. He loved people, treated every one with respect and was equally comfortable with princes and paupers.

He inspired uncommon loyalty among those with whom he worked because he was intensely loyal in return. As he was leaving office, he worked diligently to see that his personal staff landed jobs.

One day in 1978, sitting at my desk in the Public Affairs office of the Interior Department, I picked up the phone. O'Callaghan was on other end.

"Chris, you remember my press secretary?" he asked.

"I sure do, Governor," I replied.

"Well, I'm pretty sure he's one of three finalists to be the public affairs officer for the Nevada BLM office." he stated.

"Say no more, Governor," I replied. "I know what to do." And I did. The governor knew that as the assistant to the Interior secretary and director of the department's public affairs office, I had to sign off on all public affairs hires.

Politics really is all about relationships, maintaining and nurturing them. After leaving the governorship, O'Callaghan became the editor of the Las Vegas Sun, a position from which, in H. L. Mencken's words, he could continue "to afflict the comfortable and comfort the afflicted." He later bought and ran the newspapers in Henderson.

He was a larger than life figure and upon his death, thousands attended his services, including my old boss, Governor Andrus, with whom he bore so many similarities.

Fittingly, Mike O'Callaghan died of a heart attack at the age of 75 on March 5, 2004, while kneeling in prayer at morning Mass.

August 18, 2010

# Rest in Peace, Uncle Ted

As a member of the famous "Flying Tigers," he survived Japanese attacks on the P-40 he was flying "over the hump" between India and China, escorting shipments of arms and goods to Nationalist Chinese forces, our allies during World War II.

As a United States senator from Alaska, Ted Stevens survived the crash of a Lear jet at the Anchorage Airport in December 1978 that killed four others and his wife, Anne. As the jet was landing a freak gust of wind literally flipped the jet over. Anne died of a broken neck.

Rather than let her father know by phone, he literally left the hospital in bandages, with slings holding his broken arm and shoulder, boarded a commercial flight to Denver where he delivered the heartbreaking news to his father-in-law.

But on August 9, 2010, fate caught up to the 86-year-old former Republican Senator known affectionately to thousands of Alaskans as "Uncle Ted." He died when the plane carrying him and eight others to a remote fishing lodge near Dillingham, Alaska, crashed in rugged terrain.

The longest serving Republican Senator in history, Stevens entered the Senate in 1968 and served until upset in 2008. He leaves a rich legacy of having delivered, as only a master of the congressional appropriations process can, literally billions of taxpayer dollars to modernize Alaska and improve the lives of his constituents. He traveled extensively, often by small plane, as one must in Alaska, to every village, town and city. He flew home almost every weekend.

He indeed was every Alaskan's Uncle Ted.

This sterling legacy was besmirched somewhat by a government investigation into alleged favors he accepted from a contractor working on his modest summer retreat. Federal prosecutors, though, in their zeal to nail a big dog, engaged in unethical behavior. The conviction was invalidated and the charges dropped.

Not before, however, the questions raised caused enough doubt in the minds of Alaskan voters who by the narrowest of margins chose to replace Stevens with the talented young mayor of Anchorage, Mark Begich, who, ironically, knows only too well the pain of losing a loved one in an Alaskan air crash.

The senator's father, Alaskan congressman Nick Begich, disappeared in a small plane carrying him and House Majority Leader Hale Boggs of Louisiana from a fund-raiser in Juneau to one in Anchorage in 1972. The plane was never found, in part because, as I reported at the time in my capacity as Washington correspondent for the Anchorage Daily News, the locater beacon had been left in the hanger at the Juneau.

My reporting duties took me to the offices of all three members of Alaska's Congressional delegation almost daily. Of the three, Stevens easily was the hardest working – and the best.

In spite of Stevens's pugnacious, acerbic style, it was clear he cared deeply and respected the Senate and his colleagues. He was smart as a whip and did his homework. Beneath the gruff exterior, lay a heart of gold and, on occasion, a keen sense of humor. He also had a terrific temper and was demanding of his staff. Consequently, he went through staff and chiefs of staff quickly.

I also knew Stevens to be an honest man of his word. I had a hard time giving any credence to government charges that he accepted corporate favors and could easily see him paying bills for work on his modest summer retreat, not realizing they had been heavily discounted by the contractor. Stevens loved the Senate and his work too much to risk losing it over nickel and dime greed.

If he was guilty of anything, it was the insidious arrogance of power that few can stymie. Even "Uncle Ted" started to believe his own press clippings. He must have thought he was bullet proof and certainly believed he was indispensable in the voters' minds.

He was a realist, though, and when President Carter, following the suggestion of his Interior Secretary, my old boss, used the Antiquities Act in November of 1978 to put much of Alaska into National Monuments, he knew he would have to negotiate and get passed decent and fair legislation. He knew, too, that Carter had acted largely because his "show horse" colleague, Senator Mike Gravel, in typical grandstanding fashion, had blown up the previous negotiations in October.

Thus, he blamed Gravel, and forever held him accountable for the December 1978, accident that killed Ann. Because of Gravel's actions, he and Anne were on that jet with Tony Motley, the director of the coalition representing Alaska business interests in the effort to get the Alaska lands legislation.

To many he seemed to become angrier, even mean, after her death. To me, though, he had good reason to be angry, and time did work its healing ways. From then on though, he did all he could to see that Gravel would be defeated in his bid for re-election in 1980.

He took great satisfaction when his friend, banker Frank Murkowski, took out Gravel in 1980. It was vintage Uncle Ted. He got over being mad; instead, he got even.

September 8, 2010

# Trying to Circumscribe
# Presidential Power

In late July, Idaho's U.S. senators, Mike Crapo and Jim Risch, jointly introduced the latest in a long list of historic efforts to legislatively constrain the power of a president with the stroke of a pen to set aside for future protection areas of the public domain by declaring them to be National Monuments.

In 1906, apparently without much thought to the "unintended consequences," Congress granted the president this extraordinary authority. Like clockwork every ten years or so Congress tries to take it back because activist presidents from Teddy Roosevelt to Bill Clinton, and yes, even George W. Bush, have used this power, judiciously and some claim injudiciously, to protect public lands when Congress seems unable to step up to the plate and provide the needed protection.

Even though they found a few, mostly western co-sponsors, the Crapo/Risch effort is doomed to fail. Though laudable in its goals requiring a public hearing in the area to be set aside as well as prior notification to a state's governor and its congressional delegation, and mandating an active positive approval of the land withdrawal within two years by Congress, it is still not going to happen.

As Yogi Berra, the great Yankee catcher once said: "It's déjà vu all over again!"

The simple fact is it is ridiculously easy for even one senator, threatening a filibuster, to slow down and stop legislation. As Governor Andrus likes to say, it is easier to chuck a spear than to hold a shield. And so the two senators are chucking spears, but they belong to the minority party in a very partisan Senate. They will be lucky if a hearing is ever even scheduled by the committee chairman, New Mexico Senator Jeff Bingaman.

If the bill were to pass both houses by some miracle, it would be vetoed instantly. No president, regardless of party, willingly agrees to a curbing of their power. There is virtually no chance such a veto would be over-ridden.

Besides, invoking the Antiquities Act, or threatening to use it, can be a useful device when jousting with a Congress reluctant to move, as Governor Andrus, when Secretary of the Interior, demonstrated to President Carter. The specific event was the stalled Alaska lands legislation.

In 1978, President Carter, with a stroke of a pen declared 56 million acres of Alaska to be new national monuments, doubling the size of the National Park Service overnight.

He acted because Andrus had tired of the Alaska delegation's continuing failure to bargain in good faith and fulfill the promise contained in the 1971 Alaska Native Claims Settlement Act that upwards of 80 million acres of Alaska would be protected under the four protection systems (parks. wilderness, wildlife refuges, wild and scenic rivers). It was a key concession to the nation's growing environmental community in order for the Trans-Alaska Pipeline to be constructed.

Prior to building the line, the aboriginal claims of Alaska's natives had to be settled, but the Congress was given five years (Congress extended the deadline twice) to address the environmental community's demand that many of Alaska's stunningly beautiful and untouched areas be permanently protected. All parties agreed to this deal, including Alaska's two senators, the late Ted Stevens and Mike Gravel.

Then the foot-dragging began. It became clear that Alaska's delegation was engaging in delay, obstruction and obfuscation in the hope that missing the deadline would mean few if any additions to the National Park system or the federal wildernesses.

In early November 1978, Andrus met with the President Carter to outline his ability to use the Antiquities Act. Carter quickly agreed. On Nov. 16, 1978, Andrus used his authority under the recently passed Federal Land Management Policy Act to withdraw temporarily from the public domain in Alaska (and block selection of some of those lands by the state) 110 million federal acres for three years.

On Dec. 1, Carter signed the Antiquities Act monument designations. I played a small role, as an aide to Andrus, in sending a memo to the president's press office on Nov. 28 reassuring them that we should still prefer legislation to resolve the issue, that use of the Act was a major tactic to force parties to stay at the table because candidly, there was less flexibility for agency management under a national monument regimen.

The rest is history. Sen. Stevens had to stay at the table to get legislation that would be less stringent but still protective.

There is a lesson here for Idaho's senators. They appear to be acting pre-emptively, and, in my view, compounding their duplicity regarding their now obvious nominal support for their Republican colleague, Rep. Mike Simpson's carefully crafted Boulder-White Clouds wilderness bill.

They are signaling the White House not to mess with them by threatening, as President Carter actually did do, to invoke a National Monument declaration in the Boulder-White Clouds area should Rep. Simpson's ten year effort to come up with protection for the incredibly scenic high country fail to pass this session.

My guess is such a move isn't even on the White House's radar screen, and one can rest assured, despite his patient ten-year effort to secure passage of a protective bill, Rep. Mike Simpson is not about to ask the Obama Administration for that kind of help. It's a shame because that is precisely what it may take to keep every one at the table continuing to bargain in good faith.

September 15, 2010

# Alaska and Idaho
# Share a Sad Legacy

Alaska and Idaho share many things in common besides Sarah Palin. Both states are home to people who largely eschew big government, pride themselves in their independence, vote heavily Republican but tend to be closet libertarians, support the NRA, and love hunting, fishing, backpacking, snowmobiling, skiing, hiking, boating, running their ATVs or dirt bikes, or just simple camping.

Both states also have rugged mountains and extensive wilderness areas, which, when campaigning, have to be crossed often using small aircraft. All too often, this has led to tragedy and the sad legacy of politics being shaped by fatal plane accidents.

Alaska consistently ranks first in the nation in the number of small aircraft accidents, many of which do not include fatalities, with Idaho usually in the top ten. Over the last five years, according to data compiled by the National Transportation Safety Board, there were 596 small aircraft accidents reported in Alaska, and 204 in Idaho.

Some older political observers believe the state likely would never have been served by Jim McClure in either the House or the Senate had Kellogg's John Mattmiller lived. Mattmiller, a devil-may-care Republican businessman who used to race at blinding speeds in a Studebaker Avanti, had come out of nowhere to nearly upset First District Democratic Congressman Compton White, Jr., in 1964.

Mattmiller lost that general election by approximately 3,000 votes in the year of the "Johnson landslide" presidential election (the last time a Democrat carried Idaho). Energetic, charming, charismatic, dynamic and a talent for winning friends instantly, he was the presumed nominee for the 1966 Republican nomination.

Unfortunately, he carried his dare-devil approach to his flying and on February 2, 1966, while trying to land in a light early morning fog at the Kellogg airport he struck the power line stretching across the canyon at Big Creek, flipping the plane which then crashed and killed him instantly.

Mattmiller was a testimonial to the saying "there are old pilots and there are bold pilots. There are no old, bold pilots." Exit John Mattmiller, enter James McClure.

The year 1966 was a bad one for Idaho office seekers. The most famous air crash with an equally famous impact on Gem State politics occurred in mid-September. State Senator Charles Herndon of Salmon, who had narrowly defeated my old boss, State Senator Cecil D. Andrus, by a thousand votes in the August gubernatorial primary, died when his small plane crashed in central Idaho's Sawtooth Mountains.

A week later the Democratic party, by a two-vote margin, selected Andrus to pick up its banner, but by then it was a worthless nomination with little prospect for success. Having been the nominee though in 1966 gave Andrus front-runner status in 1970 and helped him to secure the nomination and win the job that year.

Andrus held a single-engine rating pilot's license for years and would sometimes charter a plane to fly to events in distant parts of this vast state. He also tells a wonderful story of his early day campaigning when he over flew the Jaypee Potlatch-run logging camp in northern Idaho and dropped a bunch of his campaign cards after circling but not being able to land on the runway.

Two other air accidents merit mentioning because of their impact. In 1986, young and upcoming State Senator Terry Reilly from Caldwell was running for lieutenant governor, expected to get the nomination and many thought had a shot at taking out the GOP nominee, then state representative and now governor C.L. "Butch" Otter.

He and Pete Busch, a candidate on the Democratic ticket for the First Congressional District, also died in a plane crash. My, oh my, how Idaho history might have changed if Otter had never been elected lieutenant governor. It is doubtful he would be governor today.

Another rising star in the ranks of Idaho Democrats whose life was cut short prematurely was that of State Senator Jerry Blackbird from Cataldo. He died in a helicopter accident in May of 1979 near Clarkia.

One of America's most famous air crashes, though, happened in Alaska in 1972, when a plane carrying House Majority Leader Hale Boggs of Louisiana from Anchorage to Juneau, with freshman Alaskan congressman Nick Begich on board (Boggs was making fundraising appearances for Begich) disappeared. Not a trace was found despite one of the most massive air, ground and sea hunts in history.

A few weeks later, though deceased, Begich defeated Don Young on Election Day. In a rematch special election, however, Young defeated Pegge Begich, Nick's widow.

In one of those ironical historical footnotes, one of Begich's sons, Mark, went on to be elected mayor of Anchorage and, in 2008, with the help of an overzealous federal prosecutor, Begich was able to upset the late Ted Stevens in the race for an Alaskan Senate seat held by Stevens since 1968.

Boggs' widow, Lindy, fared better than Pegge. She did win and held her husband's seat in the House for many years. While neither of their children went on to elected careers in politics, they nonetheless carved out distinguished political affairs careers. Son Tommy is one of the truly powerful super lobbyists in Washington, D.C., today, and daughter, Cokie, is the prize-winning Washington correspondent for National Public Television and Radio.